Also by the Author
GERMAN SWORDS OF WORLD WAR II: A PHOTOGRAPHIC REFERENCE (*three volumes*)
GERMAN DAGGERS OF WORLD WAR II: A PHOTOGRAPHIC REFERENCE (*four volumes*)
GERMAN DAGGERS OF WORLD WAR II: A PHOTOGRAPHIC REFERENCE (*four volume boxed set*)
GERMAN WAR BOOTY: A STUDY IN PHOTOGRAPHS

Imperial German Edged Weaponry

Volume One
Army and Cavalry

Thomas M. Johnson, LTC (*Ret.*)
with Victor Diehl & Thomas Wittmann

Schiffer Military History
Atglen, PA

Acknowledgements

These new reference books on Imperial edged weapons would not have been possible without the kind contributions of the following friends, collectors, and historians – Jack Arnold, the late James P. Atwood, William Bish, Jacques Bliard (France), Roscoe "Rockie" Blunt, Paul Boland, Jan Börgesson (Sweden), Dr. Michael Boucher, Kevin Bourgeois, John Boutell, the late Robert J. Boward, Wilfrid Uhlmann Bradach, Larry Braun, Homer M. Brett, Barry Brown (England), Douglas Brown, James A. Brown, the late Tom Buckley, J. Burden, Jason P. Burmeister, Jack Buske, the late Anthony Carter, Mike and Mark Chenault, Alan Clark (Scotland), Peter Coccoluto, Brian Conkle, Thomas L. Conner, SSGT (Ret) T. Wayne Cunningham, (USAF), Rudy A. D'Angelo, Gailen David, Cleo Diehl, Rurik Diehl, Stacey M. Diehl, Victor Diehl, David Delich, Thomas R. Duflo, Carl Eberl (Germany), Gentry R. P. Ferrell, the late W. E. Fitzgerald, Johannes Floch (Austria), Mark A. Flors, Andrew Gates (England), the late Peter Gauf (Germany), Dr. Clarence Geier, Robert Gilmore, Kurt Glemser (Canada), Dr. Douglas Gorman, Doug Gow (New Zealand), Jill Halcomb, Bonnie Hameister, Cliff Hamill, Hermann Hampe (Germany), Richard Hansen, Neil Hardin, Mark Harper, Major (Ret) John L. Harrell, Robert Heiduk, Herman R. Heytmeiser, John Holt, Jean-Marie Irlande (France), Charles H. Jenkins, III, Sonny Johnson, Robert A. Johnston, Terry Jones (Canada), Jerry Jukich, SSGT William L. Junipher, (USAF), the late Ed Kaelin, Ralph E. Kaschai, Steve Kirby, the late Ron Klug, Jan K. Kube Auction (Germany), Bavin J. Lane (England), Terry Leaf, Jean-Marie Leclerq (Belgium), Edmund F. Leland, John W. Lingo, LTC (Ret) Michael E. Little, (US Army), Robert Long, Klaus Lorenzen (Germany), Stephen Luczkowski, Heinrich Lutjens, John E. Mack, the late Herman A. Maeurer, Capt. (Ret.) Dennis Majerski, Ed Malesky, Nick McCully, Robert E. McDivitt, Max McGrath (Australia), Edward McGuire, Mark McKibben, Robert Meistrell, CAPT Anthony C. Meldahl, , Arthur Meyer (Germany), the late Firmin F. Michel, the late Dr. Julian Milestone, Richard L. Miller, Brian Molloy (England), Jim Moore, Andy Mraz, R. L. Mundschenk, Jeff Naser, Earl Ohlgren, Karl Ortmann, Ken Ossian, Edward M. Owen, Jr., Major General Theodore W. Paulson, John P. Pearson, Ronald P. Pickart, Larry Pistole, Adam J. Portugal, Larry Price, Jan Piet Puype (The Netherlands), Mark Ready, J. Rex Reddick, Ian Reynolds (New Zealand), Ren Reynolds, Richard Ricca, Brian Rich, the late George A. Richardson, Carl W. Righter, Henning Ritter (Germany), Michael Roe (Saudi Arabia), David Rome, SGM (Ret) Kenneth Rouse (Germany), Karl Sauer (Germany), Frederick L. Schaefer, Eberhard Schmidt (Germany), Dr. Jeffrey V. Schmitt, John W. Schrader, Edwin Schulz (Germany), Joseph G. Sciascia, William Shea, Andy Shoredits (South Africa), Joel M. Smith, Andy Southard, Jr., Frank Southard, John J. Staehle, Claus P. Stefanski, (Germany), Dirk Stefanski (Germany), Frederick J. Stephens (England), David Stone, Joseph Stone, Robert C. Strodel, Joseph T.N. Suarex, John Swartele, Ronald W. Tait, Marty Taylor, The "Old Brigade Collection" (England), Dr. Virgil Thomason, Brian D. Thorogood, Eric Trosko, Dr. John J. Trosko, the late Jack Ulrich (Germany), Dr. Nicholas Vallado, Dr. David L. Valuska, Richard Van Heuvelen, Kurt Van Laere (Belgium), Joseph Viotto, Warren Vitellaro, LTC (Ret) John Wahl, the late Robert Waitts, Brian Ward, A. (Bram) Wasmus (Netherlands), Mike Welser, Ole Wildt, Richard R. Williams, Brett Wilson, Lindsey S. Wilson, Stewart Wilson (England), Gerhardt Windbiehl, Dr. William Windrum, Thomas Winter, Thomas T. Wittmann, Stephen D. Wolfe, William Young, Captain Thomas P. Ziemba, Robert P. Zill, and John Zweng. Major portions of the text in this comprehensive series were written by well-qualified fellow collectors, Victor Diehl, Hermann Hampe (Germany), Andy Mraz, Carl Righter, Andy Shoredits (South Africa), and Thomas Wittmann. Two of these individuals are listed as co-authors. Without any one of the aforementioned persons, this reference would not have been as complete or accurate. The importance of each of their contributions to this work is greater than I can adequately express. To those whose contributions I have neglected to note here from sheer failure of memory, please accept my sincere apology. Victor Diehl of Harrisonburg, Virginia greatly assisted the author by writing many of the several hundred detailed "in wear" photo captions for this reference. One final note, I would like to especially thank my wife Tink and my personal secretaries, Donna Kines, Sherry Burton, and Margarette Liljekvist for their continued and unwavering support in the preparation of this extensive Imperial German Edged Weapon Series for Schiffer Publishing.

Book design by Robert Biondi.

Copyright © 2008 by Thomas M. Johnson.
Library of Congress Catalog Number: 2007943631.

All rights reserved. No part of this work may be reproduced or used in any forms or by any means – graphic, electronic or mechanical, including photocopying or information storage and retrieval systems – without written permission from the publisher.

The scanning, uploading and distribution of this book or any part thereof via the Internet or via any other means without the permission of the publisher is illegal and punishable by law. Please purchase only authorized editions and do not participate in or encourage the electronic piracy of copyrighted materials.

"Schiffer," "Schiffer Publishing Ltd. & Design," and the "Design of pen and ink well" are registered trademarks of Schiffer Publishing, Ltd.

Printed in China.
ISBN: 978-0-7643-2934-0

We are always looking for people to write books on new and related subjects. If you have an idea for a book, please contact us at the address below.

Published by Schiffer Publishing Ltd.	In Europe, Schiffer books are distributed by:
4880 Lower Valley Road	Bushwood Books
Atglen, PA 19310	6 Marksbury Ave.
Phone: (610) 593-1777	Kew Gardens, Surrey TW9 4JF
FAX: (610) 593-2002	England
E-mail: Info@schifferbooks.com.	Phone: 44 (0)20 8392-8585
Visit our web site at: www.schifferbooks.com	FAX: 44 (0)20 8392-9876
Please write for a free catalog.	E-mail: info@bushwoodbooks.co.uk
This book may be purchased from the publisher.	www.bushwoodbooks.co.uk
Please include $3.95 postage.	Free postage in the UK. Europe: air mail at cost.
Try your bookstore first.	Try your bookstore first.

PREFACE

For the collector of today, it is practically impossible to comprehend the enormous production capabilities of the edged weapon industry in and about the German blade city of Solingen during the *Kaiserzeit* or "Emperor's Era" from 1871-1918. This period included the reigns of the Prussian Kings Wilhelm I from 1871-1888, the dying Friedrich III for a hundred days in 1888, and Wilhelm II from 1888-1918. Due to the fact that the reign of Wilhelm II lasted for thirty years, it can be said with justification that the *Kaiserzeit* was really the era of Kaiser Wilhelm II.

The impression one gets when looking through the manufacturers' edged weapons catalogs of that period is of the existence of a great number of official models or patterns and an infinite number of variations. Next to Prussia, which itself had about thirty different patterns of edged weapons, there were the German states of Saxonia, Bavaria, Württemberg, Baden, Hesse, Mecklenburg, and Brunswick. Each of these states had its own particular sword patterns, and all taken together would add another forty-odd different models to the total. These were all Army and civil servants' swords; the edged weapons of many other German institutions, societies, and groups are not included in this number. It should be pointed out there existed no Imperial German Army; each German state provided its own forces and supplied clothing and equipment according to its own patterns. In fact, the only common item on all German Army uniforms prior to 1918 was the small cockade in the nation's colors of black, white, and red worn on the front center of the soldier's cap. Only in wartime did these Armies become united under an Imperial General Staff, and Kaiser Wilhelm II himself was Commander-in-Chief of all German forces, including the Armies. The only exceptions were the Navy (Marine) and the so-called protection force (*Schütztruppe*) used overseas. These latter two were the only true *Deutsche*, or national German forces.

Some of the most ornate daggers of the Imperial period belong to the group known as Hunting and Forestry *Hirschfängers*. Countless numbers and variations of these daggers can be found. The *Hirschfänger* remains as one of the oldest surviving daggers in German history. It was carried during the time of Charlemagne and is still being worn today. Unquestionably, the workmanship, quality, and unsurpassed beauty of the *Hirschfänger* sidearm reached its zenith during the Imperial period.

While the numbers of edged weapon patterns existing simultaneously were already quite impressive for any nation of the period, the amount of varieties per pattern was practically infinite. Indeed, the catalogs clearly bear evidence of the many variations which were even extended by local outfitters and tailors all over Germany, many of whom had their own workshops and were able to exchange certain parts of an edged weapon for a higher quality or more decorated specimen. A good example is the *Kaiserliche Marinedolch* or Imperial Naval *Dirk*.

In 1901/2 a new *Dirk* was introduced for officers in the *Kaiserliche* Marine. In its scabbard, this weapon measured about 48 cm (approximately nineteen inches) overall. However, almost simultaneously, a short version of this *Dirk* was supplied by the Solingen blade manufacturers. That weapon measured on the average about 41 cm (approximately sixteen inches) and became immediately popular. Although entirely unofficial, it was widely carried as many period Navy photographs in this reference series will show. No doubt the authorities must have at least tolerated these short *Dirks*. In fact, they were a continuation of a likewise popular short version of the predecessor of the 1901 Officer's *Dirk*, the Prussian Naval *Dirk* of the 1848 Pattern which was worn until 1872. All such Prussian *Dirks* remaining in known collections today – several scores of them – are all short versions of the officially recognized *Dirk* of 1848 measuring about 48 cm (approximately nineteen inches). Not one Prussian Naval *Dirk* of the prescribed length is known by the undersigned.

Be that as it may, Carl Eickhorn, in his 1908 Jubilee Issue of his *Blankwaffenkatalog* (edged weapons catalog) already offered fourteen short Naval Officer *Dirks* of the new pattern, all with scabbards featuring decorations entirely different from each other. These fourteen short *Dirks* were in addition to the standard long *Dirk* and three more decorated versions also illustrated in the same Eickhorn catalog. From existing Eickhorn Naval *Dirks* in collectors' hands, we know that there existed even additional patterns.

Additionally, one of the best-known Naval outfitters in the city of Kiel of that day, the firm of August Lüneburg, in a sales catalog brochure probably datable to 1902, offered twelve more scabbard variations. The firm of August Lüneburg was founded in 1881. It sold swords, *Dirks*, and military accouterments until the end of the

Second World War. It continued to exist as a cutlery shop in Kiel until the 1980s when the firm was dissolved. A large, black granite name sign still adorns the gable of the former premises at *No. 24, Danische Strasse*.

The interesting observation (besides that of the forced tolerance of the authorities) about the existence of all these variations is (a) the apparently strong influence of the manufacturers and retailers, and (b) the whims of fashion. Solingen, of course, had for ages a reputation for a massive output of high-quality swords, and it supplied virtually the whole world with sidearms from early Medieval times onward. However, the heyday of the city came in the 19th Century when swords increasingly became ordered to exact patterns and specifications. Production ran literally into the tens of thousands, with many factories turning out hundreds of swords and other sidearms each year for long periods. It is a well-known fact that it was, and to some extent still is, the blade manufacturers and not the several German states and/or forces who designed new patterns for their swords and daggers in most cases. Designing and casting new dies and molds was an expensive business, and in many cases, they were reused with minor alterations. So, in order to keep the cost of production down, it was in the interest of the manufacturer to have a big hand in the design of any new edged weapon model.

The other constant factor responsible for the large number of deviations from the pattern was the demand, indeed the whims, of fashion. As a retired officer, formerly serving in the *Kaiserliche Marine*, wrote in his memoirs:"…Clothing plays an important role in life, and 'fine feathers make fine birds.' "Later,…" in the year 1902, Naval Officers got the *Dirk* as a sidearm, which had already been introduced in 1891 for the Naval Cadets. Changes in the cut of coats, shape of caps, ties and shirt-collars, in the lengths and widths of swords and *Dirks*, came about, more or less capriciously and bravely, by 'Lady Fashion.' Younger gentlemen, of course, had a more intimate relationship with her than the older officers who as superiors regarded her whims with disapproval, yes, even chased her with reprimand and punishment." (U. Hopman, *Das Logbuch eines deutschen Seeofficiers* Berlin, 1924, p. 79-80.)

We know that all this must have been to no avail, for the number of variations in German edged weapons of the *Kaiserzeit* is really enormous. There are pros and cons to this. The advantage for the collector is that he is able to specialize in all kinds of edged weapon variations of pattern, decoration, quality, etc., and that he may have a fair chance of encountering even unknown variations. The disadvantage connected with the collecting of these weapons is more apparent to the serious student and arms historian – it is sometimes very difficult to judge to what pattern a certain variation belongs or when the certain detail that caused the variation was introduced. Moreover, many of the variations are so minute or indiscernible (for instance, because the blade is often concealed in the scabbard), that scrutinizing period photographs is of little help.

The single fascinating factor in collecting and studying the edged weapons of Imperial Germany is that it concerns an era which is completely historical. The fascinating fact of the *Kaiserzeit*, in my personal view, is that it is fairly recent history – many people having consciously experienced it are still among us – but that at the same time, it is completely gone and has left few apparent traces in either German society, or in today's German forces. In fact, the German Navy may be one of the few institutions whose tradition and *esprit de corps* are still partly based on the prowess, glory and esteem that the *Kaiserliche* Marine once had in the world.

It is to be hoped that his new series of books from Schiffer Publishing, Ltd. by LTC (Ret.) Thomas M. Johnson will follow in the wake of his successful eight-volume series entitled, *Collecting the Edged Weapons of the Third Reich*, and that these new volumes on the edged sidearms of an earlier period will evoke so much interest and encourage so much further research that a number of additional volumes with even more information on this fascinating and inexhaustible collecting field will appear.

Jan Piet Puype, Librarian
Nederlands Scheepvaart Museum
(Netherlands Maritime Museum)
Amsterdam, Holland

Contents

Preface 5

Chapter 1   Swords of the German Army During the Imperial Era 8
Chapter 2   The Edged Weapons of the German Cavalry 256

CHAPTER ONE

SWORDS OF THE GERMAN ARMY DURING THE IMPERIAL ERA

"We Germans Fear God and Nothing Else in the World"
— 19th Century Sword Inscription

BACKGROUND

When Bismarck stunned the world by declaring, "The great questions of our day cannot be solved by speeches and majority votes, but by blood and iron!", he was summing up much of German history since the Thirty Years War. Germany stood at the crossroads of Europe. Its castles and vineyards, cities and forests had been ravaged from every direction.

In such a "crucible of conflict," the development of the professional soldier and his trappings was a real necessity. The sword was an important aspect of this weapon development. German sword production and style reflected both political and military fashions of the day. Army sword types were quite numerous and were influenced not only by the particular culture of the sovereign German states, but also by styles of nations surrounding Germany, such as France and Austria.

The moment King Wilhelm I of Prussia was proclaimed "*Deutscher Kaiser*" in the Palace of Versailles at the conclusion of the Franco-Prussian War, the coronation politically allied the German states under the Prussian *Hohenzollerns*. Most of the smaller Grand Duchies, Duchies, City States and kingdoms adopted the Prussian military system. Their troops were absorbed in the German line under the command of the German General Staff. The Kings of Bavaria, Saxony, and Württemberg retained sovereignty, even though they owed fealty to the Kaiser. Saxony and Württemberg kept their own War Department and Headquarters staffs. The Armies of both states maintained the characteristics of their old uniforms. The Bavarian Army remained autonomous under command of its king, and maintained its own staff. The traditional Bavarian uniforms were retained with some Prussian characteristics incorporated into their design.

When the *Allerhöchste Kabinett Orden* (A.K.O.) which was composed of heads of most of the Army groups, adopted new sword patterns in 1889, a high degree of tolerance was allowed for individual German states. These sword directives served only as guidelines rather than imposing a generalized national model. Great variance was permitted in hilt form, dimension and style, as well as blade length and decoration. A.K.O. directives regarding scabbards were more comprehensive and uniform. Scabbards before 1906 were generally nickel-plated and had two hanger rings. Between 1906 and 1910, it was decreed that all scabbards be chemically blued or painted black. On 14 December 1910, the lower hanger band and ring were eliminated.

To the Imperial German sword collector, these changing regulations seem to provide an endless diversity of patterns. There were, despite these variations, a number of distinct models in use during the period 1850 to 1918 that contain an easily identified state coat-of-arms, a royal cypher, or a distinctive hilt or other features prescribed by specific regulations. The purpose of this overview will be to examine these well-defined models in terms of historical adoption, distinctive features, and private purchase options.

SWORD PATTERNS

Prussian Lionhead Saber
PREUSSISCHER LOWENKOPF KAVALLERIE UND ARTILLERIE OFFIZIER SÄBEL

The gleaming lionhead sword with ruby eyes has been a favorite among German Officers since the early 16th Century. The variations of this pattern are vast, as each officer could have the weapons personalized to meet his own wishes.

The pommel may be a complete lionhead or the jawless "*Wachmeister*" variety. The head may be with or without ruby eyes. The hilts were cast brass and single, double, or fire gilted. A nickeled version could also be purchased. During the war period, many hilts were produced of iron. The fittings may be chiseled to the degree specified by the purchaser. The hilt fittings were available in light, medium, or heavy grade, and were produced in either standard or "*Grosser*" (larger) size.

The "D" or "P" shaped knuckle-bow may be solid or pierced. The backstrap may contain any of a variety of military motifs, and may include a panel for the engraving of the purchaser's monogram. The knuckle-bow extended to a quillon end that may be in the shape of a pantherhead, scrolled, plain, or one of numerous custom designs available.

The formed grip had either a wooden base with fishskin or black celluloid covering, or was produced entirely of ebony wood or black horn. The grip wire was gold or silver, or a combination in either double or triple wrap. A decorative ferrule completed the grip.

The obverse langet may contain cast swords, cannons, coats-of-arms, or an applied Guard Star. The ornamentation may be silver or gold and pinned to the langet. The reverse langet contained an escutcheon for monograms, but this was seldom used.

The curved saber blade may be single-fullered or the English rod-back (pipe/quillback) variety. The rod-back blade is based on the British model 1822 Infantry Officer sword. The blade may be plain or etched, nickeled or gilded. Damascus steel was available in over twenty-five different patterns. The typical Damascus pattern was "*Damastahl*," usually called "maiden hair." The "maiden hair" pattern was so named because it resembled the long, flowing hair of a young maiden swirling around the blade. The more complicated patterns were designed as "ribbon," "large rose," "small rose," "ladder," and "Turkish" Damascus. The Solingen firm of Hugo Weyers and *Sohn* lists seventeen different Damascus patterns, which include such varieties as "ultra," "nonpariel," and special patterns named after Friedrich II and Joseph II. The blade width ranged from 18 mm to 50 mm at the ricasso.

The scabbard was usually metal with color, and the number of hanger rings was determined by the period regulations. A black leather scabbard with brass or nickel fittings could also be purchased. Collectors should note that black leather scabbards were required for *Fusiliers*, Police, Navy, and certain Government officials.

Prussian Infantry Officer Sword Model 1889
PREUSSISCHE INFANTERIE OFFIZIERDEGEN

The gilted, bent hilt, folding guards, and straight, double-fullered *Degen* blade make the Infantry Officer *Degen* (*I.O.D.89*) one of the most recognized of the new sword patterns adopted by the A.K.O. in 1889. The pattern is generally based on the Prussian *Cuirassier* broadsword, but with a distinct, pierced, semi-basket brass guard.

The hilts are cast brass in a variety of gilt treatments. Wartime iron versions also exist. The hilt was offered in two sizes – regulation and "*Grosser*."

The pommel cap screwed off and may be plain, engraved, or personalized. The regulation pattern had a smooth, polished hilt, and a non-folding guard containing a Prussian Eagle. Private purchase swords had obverse and/or reverse rounded folding guards; both guards may contain the specified emblem of state. The reverse guard was occasionally engraved with presentations. The semi-basket guard may be cast, and/or chiseled, or pierced.

The grip had a wooden base covered in either fishskin or leather. Black horn and ebony wood grips could be purchased. The grip may contain a royal cypher, Guard Star, or a number of other applied devices. A *Fingerschlauf*, which was a leather strap for the insertion of the fingers, was usually included. The grip was wrapped with double or triple silver or brass wire, depending on the uniform buttons. The grip incorporated a ferrule.

The nickeled blade was straight, single-or double-fullered with a false edge. A few special-order models have been observed with a curved saber blade, but these are non-standard. The blade may be etched or plain. Damascus blades were also available. A 110 mm presentation style ricasso was from 18 mm to 30 mm.

The scabbard finish and rings depended on the date of manufacture.

Prussian Cavalry Saber Model 1889
PREUSSISCHE KAVALERIE-EXTRASÄBEL MIT VERNICKELTEN MONTUREN

Among the new sword models adopted by the A.K.O. was a special nickeled Mounted Cavalry *Degen*. The *Kavalerie Degen* (KD-89) regulation model featured a hilt with a horizontally-grooved black horn or celluloid grip with *Fingerschlauf*. The grip had no backstrap. The pommel was flat, topped with a rounded tang nut protruding from the top. The half-basket guard contained a D-shaped knuckle-bow and three sheetmetal sidebars which extended to a pointed, downward-sloped quillon end. The guards were folding or nonfolding, and the obverse guard contained the state coat-of-arms. The hilts were offered in standard or light weight. All mounts were polished, except for the addition of decorative grooves around their perimeters.

A straight, single-fullered blade with false edge completed the sword. The blades were plain or etched. The blades of many KD-89's contained regimental inscriptions recognizing "Honorary Colonies" of the regiment. The engraving may be blued or gilted.

A metal scabbard was produced with one hanger ring.

Prussian "Dove Head" Officer Saber
PREUSSISCHE OFFIZIER EXTRA-SÄBEL

The "Dove Head" Pattern saber is certainly one of the most utilitarian of all German sabers. Its use extends through many ranks and nearly all branches of the service. The saber's original form was identified as the Hussar and *Uhlan* saber model 1808, and was based on the British Light Cavalry Pattern of 1796. Early patterns of this saber were iron mounted and had a wide, curved, slashing blade. As the 19th Century progressed, the blade became straighter and narrower, and variations in mounts and scabbards were produced. The lighter pattern was identified as the *Uhlan* model 1873.

The typical hilt was steel with high polish nickel plate. The mounted *Reitsäbel* or riding saber may have an additional hanger ring adorning the pommel top.

The knuckle-bow was shaped like a reverse "P", "B", or "D", and extended to a straight crossguard ending in a flat, rounded quillon end. The knuckle-bow may be slotted near the top to facilitate the tying of the portepee. The crossguards of many NCO combat sabers were regimentally marked. The backstrap was either straight or contained the lobe needed to pin the grip. The grip was either fishskin, celluloid, or horn, in black or brown. The grip may or may not be steel wire-wrapped. A langet may be present and contain affixed devices such as a Guard Star.

The curved or straight, nickeled blades were usually single-fullered and/or pipe backed. The blades may be etched or plain. Damascus blades are rarely found. Blade widths ranged from 18 mm to 30 mm.

The scabbards were of the usual variations in color and hanger rings.

A variation of the "Dove Head" saber was the brass mounted *Fusilier's Degen*. The hilt on this *Degen* may be plain or chiseled, depending upon request. A dominant characteristic of many *Fusilier* swords was their scabbards, which were black leather with brass fittings. The scabbards may contain hanger rings on the top and center fitting, or a single hanger hook on the top fitting. The scabbard chape may be rounded or contain the usual violin-shaped end. One manufacturer offered *Fusilier* scabbards with hammered fittings. The NCO hilt patterns of these sabers are usually very plain and were ordnance issued. These swords carried inspector stamps on the blade, grip, and pommel. There are private purchase examples that contain exquisite etched blades.

Prussian Cuirassier Officer Broadsword
PREUSSISCHER KÜRASSIER-OFFIZIER PALLASCH

The *Cuirassier Pallasch* (broadsword), with its heavy hilt and long, straight blade, became the standard edged weapon of the heavy cavalry in 1817. These early broadswords were war booty from the Napoleonic Wars, and they trace their ancestry to the French *Pallasch* model 1802/3. A new *Cuirassier* model based on the French model 1854 was put into use at the close of the Franco-Prussian War.

The configuration of the hilt and guard are ample evidence of its patrimonial lineage with the *I.O.D. 89*. The standard *Pallasch* had polished brass fittings, a fishskin grip with double silver wire wrap, and a "D" shaped knuckle-bow with three oval sidebars ending in a downward-sloped quillon end. Private purchase options were generally the same as the *I.O.D. 89*. Folding guards were offered with the obverse guard containing two sidebars. National emblems are not found on the hilt; however, officers of the Guard had the Guard Star affixed to the grip.

The plain, nickeled blade was double-fullered, *Pallasch* blades were generally 8 mm to 10 mm longer than the typical Infantry officer's blade. The blade originally was 97.5 cm long and 35 mm wide, but this length was reduced to 82.5 cm in 1896. The scabbard was originally manufactured in one- or two-ring configuration which changed according to regulations.

The slightly different designs were identified as the "Russian" model and the "Extra" pattern. The "Russian" model had a lighter hilt with a narrow-waisted pommel and a "D" shaped knuckle-bow with three sidebars. The "Extra" model had a ridged and domed pommel and could be ordered with a single-fullered blade. This model usually had a leather grip with brass wire wrap.

Prussian Officer Double Clamshell Smallsword
PREUSSISCHER OFFIZIER STICHDEGEN

The double clamshell smallsword traces its ancestry to the "town" or "small" swords that replaced the short rapier in the late 17th Century.

The hilt of this typical smallsword had a large, round pommel, with a baluster-shaped extension protruding from the top. The knuckle-bow met the straight, rod-shaped quillon which extended on both sides of the quillon block. The double clamshells located below the quillon were either folding or stationary. The grip was generally completely wrapped with twisted silver wire. The entire hilt was fire gilted, and ornamentation ranged from heavily chiseled to high polish.

The single- or double-edged blades mounted on these dress swords were either flat, single-, or double-fullered. The blades were polished and usually etched on both sides. Early models may be lightly engraved.

Army leather scabbards were usually constructed with a brass throat and chape. The top scabbard fitting contained the single carrying hook. Metal scabbards were also available.

Prussian Basket Hilt Saber Model 1852
PREUSSISCHER OFFIZIER-KORBSÄBEL M-52

The gilt or nickeled "Dove Head" style pommel and massive knuckle-bow with three flat, metal sidebars are the dominant characteristics of this historic saber. The pattern was in service from 1852 until 1879, when a rod-back blade was adopted. This M-52/79 was used until 1889. From 1889 until 1914 the pattern was not issued. After the outbreak of World War I, the pattern was reissued to rear units. Around the turn of the century, Train Battalions adopted a smaller pattern M-52 for their use.

The standard wooden grip was fishskin, covered with double silver wire wrap and *Fingerschlauf*. An optional horn grip was available with or without the silver wire wrap.

The basket guard ended in a single, downward-sloped quillon end. The sidebars were generally plain; however, at least one regiment wore the M-52 with a large, silver eagle on the obverse of the basket guard. One manufacturer offered a signal whistle built into the quillon end.

The blades of earlier models (M-52) were single-fullered with a false edge, while those of later models (M-52/79) were of the "quillback" variety. The blades were polished and etched with various military motifs. Damascus blades were also available.

The scabbards had either one or two hanger rings.

Prussian "French Pattern" Eagle Head Saber
PREUSSISCHER OFFIZIER SÄBEL

The "Eagle Head" saber generally offered the same options as those of the lionhead saber. The gilt or nickel hilt configuration was either a single "D" shaped knuckle-bow or a knuckle-bow and two oval sidebars ending in a single, downward-turned quillon end. The crossguard contained either the standard langet over the ricasso, or a pointed, extended oval which reached over the ricasso and grip ferrule. The standard langet may contain a variety of affixed insignia, while the oval langet was usually unadorned.

The backstrap may be either straight, or contain the central lobe extension for pinning the grip to the backstrap. The entire hilt may be highly polished, or chiseled to conform to the wishes of the purchaser.

The grip was the standard formed type, but a straight, cylindrical style was available. The grip was usually fishskin covered, but leather was an option. The grip was wrapped with either double or triple silver or brass wire.

The straight or curved blade with false edge was single-fullered. Blades could be purchased plain, etched, or of genuine Damascus.

One manufacturer of this model offered a scabbard for Baden which contained large, flat, round hanger bands rather than the traditional narrow bands. This configuration is the only way to identify Baden swords that are without unit marks or Ducal initials.

Bavarian Infantry and Cavalry Officer *Pallasch*
BAYERISCHER INFANTERIE UND KAVALLERIE OFFIZIER PALLASCH

The indomitable spirit of Bavaria was also reflected in its edged weapons. Bavarian swords were developed independently from those of other German states until the 1880's.

The basic Bavarian *Pallasch* contained a gently rounded *I.O.D. 89* style gilt or nickeled hilt with a "D" shaped knuckle-bow ending in a scrolled quillon end.

The screw-off pommel secured a fishskin, horn, or celluloid grip. The grip was double or triple silver, brass or copper, wire-wrapped. The grip backstrap was straight without the medial lobes. The hilt fittings ranged from hand chiseled to high polish.

A basket hilt accessory with a "D" shaped knuckle-bow and two sidebars could be purchased for Artillery, *Schwere Reiter*, or Train Regiments. This accessory was interchangeable with the standard hilt and may be gold, silver, or blued. The basket hilt was without langet, while the standard hilt contained a langet which was plain or cast with the national emblem.

The *Pallasch* blades were straight, but the same hilt may be purchased with an extremely curved saber blade for cavalry wear. The nickeled blades were either single- or double-fullered. A large number of Bavarian edged weapons contained a blued panel with an etched national motto, "*In Treue Fest*", which translates, "Steadfast with Loyalty."

The scabbards of many Bavarian swords are distinctive, in that they contain no hanger bands. The hanger rings and holders were attached directly to the scabbard edge. A black leather scabbard with nickel fittings and two hanger rings was another option.

A highly detailed lionhead with "D" shaped knuckle-bow was also available as an optional Cavalry Officer *Pallasch*. The blade and scabbard configuration remained standard.

Bavarian Cavalry Officer Saber
BAYERISCHER KAVALLERIE OFFIZIER SÄBEL

The Bavarian Cavalry Officer could purchase a distinctive gilted lionhead version of the Prussian KD-89. The lionhead hilt featured a straight backstrap and polished "D" shaped knuckle-bow with three flat, sheetmetal sidebars. The basket guards were either folding or non-folding. The obverse guard contained a high relief Bavarian lion and shield. The grip was either horn or celluloid, and triple silver wire-wrapped.

The regulation blade pattern for this saber was the English rod-back, with the Bavarian motto usually etched on both sides of the blade. A standard scabbard completed the weapon.

Hessian Infantry Officer Saber
HESSISCHER INFANTERIE OFFIZIER SÄBEL

The edged weapons of Hesse generally followed the prescribed Prussian models after 1871. However, the infantry and cavalry saber were distinctly different. Their hilt design is attributed to an Austrian pattern of the mid-19th Century.

The gilt or nickeled "Dove Head" like hilt contained a graduated three- or four-tiered flattened pommel. The medium width half basket knuckle-bow was pierced with decorative scroll, "Honeysuckle" pattern, and concluded in a scroll-like quillon end. Many times the pierced knuckle-bow contained a crowned "L" for Grand Duke Ludwig.

The straight backstrap contained the cylindrical fishskin, horn, or leather-covered grip. The grip was silver or brass triple wire-wrapped.

The curved blade with false edge was generally single-fullered and may be etched.

The usual metal scabbard variations apply.

Saxon Infantry Officer Sword
SACHSISCHER INFANTERIE OFFIZIER DEGEN

The hilt of the Saxon Infantry Officer sword, like the United States Naval Officer Saber model 1852 was based on the French Artillery Pattern of 1845. This hilt is characterized by the helmet-like or *Phrygian*-style pommel.

The gilted hilt with "D" shaped knuckle-bow was without backstrap. The knuckle-bow extended through single or double, folding or non-folding guards as in the Prussian *I.O.D.89*. The obverse guard contained the Saxon coat-of-arms. The variations in hilt embellishment are as extensive as the officer desired.

The polished, straight blade with false edge may be single- or double-fullered, plain or etched. The ricasso of some blades may contain an etched royal cypher.

The usual metal scabbard variations are found.

Brunswick Infantry Officer Saber
BRAUNSCHWEIGER INFANTERIE OFFIZIER SÄBEL

The Duchy of Brunswick had a long association with Prussia, extending as far back as 1735. Due to this association, most edged weapons showed Prussian influence. However, Brunswick did maintain a distinctive saber for private purchase.

The nickel "Dove Head" hilt contained a domed, four-tiered graduated pommel. The half basket guard contained a "D" shaped knuckle-bow and three flat, sheetmetal sidebars based on the British Infantry Officer Model 1822, the so-called "Gothic" pattern. The three sidebars produced a pierced basket containing the crowned "W" of Duke Wilhelm. The sidebars extended into a decorative, scrolled quillon end. A gilt variation of this saber was used by the Brunswick Hussars.

The sword was available with either a straight or curved blade. The usual metal scabbard variations apply, except for a variation of the above saber prescribed for Hussars. The Hussar variation had large, flat, round hanger bands.

This concludes the description of the easily identified Imperial sword patterns. The reader is reminded that the subject of the Imperial German sword is, indeed, vast, and only a small portion of the total study is included here. For example, a separate study could be made of the small *Kinder Säbel* or child's sword, which generally copied each adult sword pattern offered for sale, but was usually sold with a rounded point.

SWORD KNOTS

Imperial sword knots also can help with sword identification, but the collector must remember that sword knots are easily changed. The following is a brief description of the sword knots of the major German states.

PRUSSIA – The strap is black leather with three silver stripes and a black plaited side interwoven with silver cord. The acorn is silver with a silver and black stem. The acorn core is black.

BAVARIA – The strap is crimson leather, faced with silver lace with two light-blue stripes and a silver and blue plaited slide. The acorn is silver with a silver and blue stem. The acorn core is blue.

SAXONY – The strap is black leather, edged with silver cord. The strap contains three stripes; the center one is green and the outer two are silver. The slide is plaited silver and green. The acorn and stem are silver and green. The acorn core is green.

BADEN AND OLDENBURG – The strap is black leather with three stripes, the center stripe is red and the other two are silver. The slide is plaited silver and red. The stem and acorn are silver, containing a red core.

HESSE – The strap is black leather, edged with a silver cord and a central red stripe. The slide is plaited silver and red. The acorn is silver with a red and silver stem. The acorn core is red.

WÜRTTEMBERG – The strap is black leather, edged with silver cord and a central red stripe with a red and silver slide. The acorn and stem are silver with a red and black core.

MECKLENBURG – The strap, slide and acorn are gold. The acorn has a red, yellow, and blue core.

As a further aid to the reader, a listing of Armed Forces and their preferred edged weapons completes this overview.

ORGANIZATIONAL LISTING OF SWORD TYPES

INFANTRY – Foot Regiments, *Fusiliers*, Grenadiers, and Infantry

OFFICER PATTERNS
1. Lionhead Saber
2. Infantry Officer *Degen M-89*
3. Dove Head Saber
4. Double Clamshell Smallsword
5. Eagle Head Saber
6. *Fusilier* Saber

NON-COMMISSIONED OFFICER PATTERNS
1. *I.O.D. 89*
2. Officer Saber

OTHER RANKS
1. Nickel "D" or "P" Guard Dove Head Saber
2. Brass "D" or "P" Guard Dove Head Saber

CUIRASSIER
OFFICER PATTERNS
1. *Pallasch*
2. *Pallasch* "Russian Form"
3. Lionhead Saber
4. Double Clamshell Smallsword

OTHER RANKS
1. "Extra" *Pallasch*

DRAGOON
OFFICER PATTERNS
1. Basket Hilt Saber M-52/79
2. Lionhead Saber
3. Eagle Head Saber

OTHER RANKS
1. *K.D.* Model 89 Saber
2. "D" or "P" Guard Ordnance Saber

UHLAN
OFFICER PATTERNS
1. Nickel Basket Hilt Saber M-52, 52/79
2. *K.D. 89*
3. M-1873 "P" Guard Saber

OTHER RANKS
1. *K.D. 89*
2. "P" Guard Ordnance Saber

HUSSAR
OFFICER PATTERNS
1. *K.D. 89*
2. Lionhead Saber
3. "*Wachmeister*" Lionhead with Cast Death's Head on the Knuckle-bow
4. Nickel Basket Hilt Saber M-52

OTHER RANKS
1. *K.D. 89*
2. "D" or "P" Guard Ordnance Saber

ARTILLERY – FOOT AND FIELD
OFFICER PATTERNS
1. Lionhead Saber
2. "D" or "P" Guard Dove Head Saber

NCO PATTERNS
1. Officer Saber

OTHER RANKS
1. "D" or "P" Guard Ordnance Saber

RAILWAY
OFFICER PATTERNS
1. Double Clamshell *Degen*
2. Officer Saber

NCO PATTERN
1. Officer Saber

OTHER RANKS
1. "D" or "P" Ordnance Saber

TRAIN
OFFICER PATTERNS
1. Nickel Basket Hilt Saber M-52
2. Lionhead Saber
3. Infantry Officer *Degen M-89*
4. Nickel Basket Hilt Saber M-52/79

NCO PATTERNS
1. Officer Saber
2. M-52 Saber
3. M-52/79 Saber

OTHER RANKS
1. M-52 Saber

BAVARIAN *CHEVAL LÉGERS*
OFFICER PATTERNS
1. Bavarian *Pallasch*
2. Lionhead Saber

OTHER RANKS
1. K.D. 89/91
2. "D". "P", or "B" Guard Ordnance Saber

JÄGER ZU PFERDE
OFFICER PATTERNS
1. *Pallasch*
2. Lionhead Saber
3. *K.D. 89*

OTHER RANKS
1. K.D. 89
2. "D" or "P" Guard Ordnance Saber

PIONEER
OFFICER PATTERNS
1. Infantry Officer *Degen M-89*
2. Officer Saber

NCO PATTERNS
1. *I.O.D. 89*
2. Officer Saber

OTHER RANKS
1. "D" or "P" Guard Ordnance Saber

MACHINE GUN UNITS
OFFICER PATTERNS
1. Infantry Officer *Degen M-89*
2. Officer Saber

NCO PATTERNS
1. *I.O.D. M-89*
2. Officer Saber

TELEGRAPH
OFFICER PATTERNS
1. Infantry Officer *Degen M-89*
2. Officer Saber

NCO PATTERNS
1. *I.O.D. 89*
2. Officer Saber

AIRSHIP (ARMY)
OFFICER PATTERNS
1. Infantry Officer *Degen M-89*
2. Officer Saber

OTHER RANKS
1. "D" or "P" Guard Ordnance Saber

AIRSHIP (NAVY)
OFFICER PATTERNS
1. Naval Lionhead Sword
2. Naval Officer Dagger

NCO PATTERNS
1. Officer Saber
2. *M-1898 Kurzes* Sawback Bayonet

OPPOSITE
Close-up color view of the *"Grosser"* obverse hilt of the Cavalry sword presented from Walter Durre to Kurt Bontheim. The obverse ricasso of the "large Rosebud" Damascus steel blade contains a short gold ribbon inscribed *"Echt-Damast"* (Genuine Damascus). The Lion head hilt is complete with red glass "ruby" eyes. *Richard R. Williams Collection. Photo by Dick Scott Fine Photography, Houston.*

BELOW
Close-up view of the raised gold dedication on the obverse blade of the "Bontheim" Cavalry Sword which reads (translated), "Walter Dürre to my good friend Kurt Bontheim, Lüneburg 1900". *Richard R. Williams Collection. Photo by Dick Scott Fine Photography, Houston.*

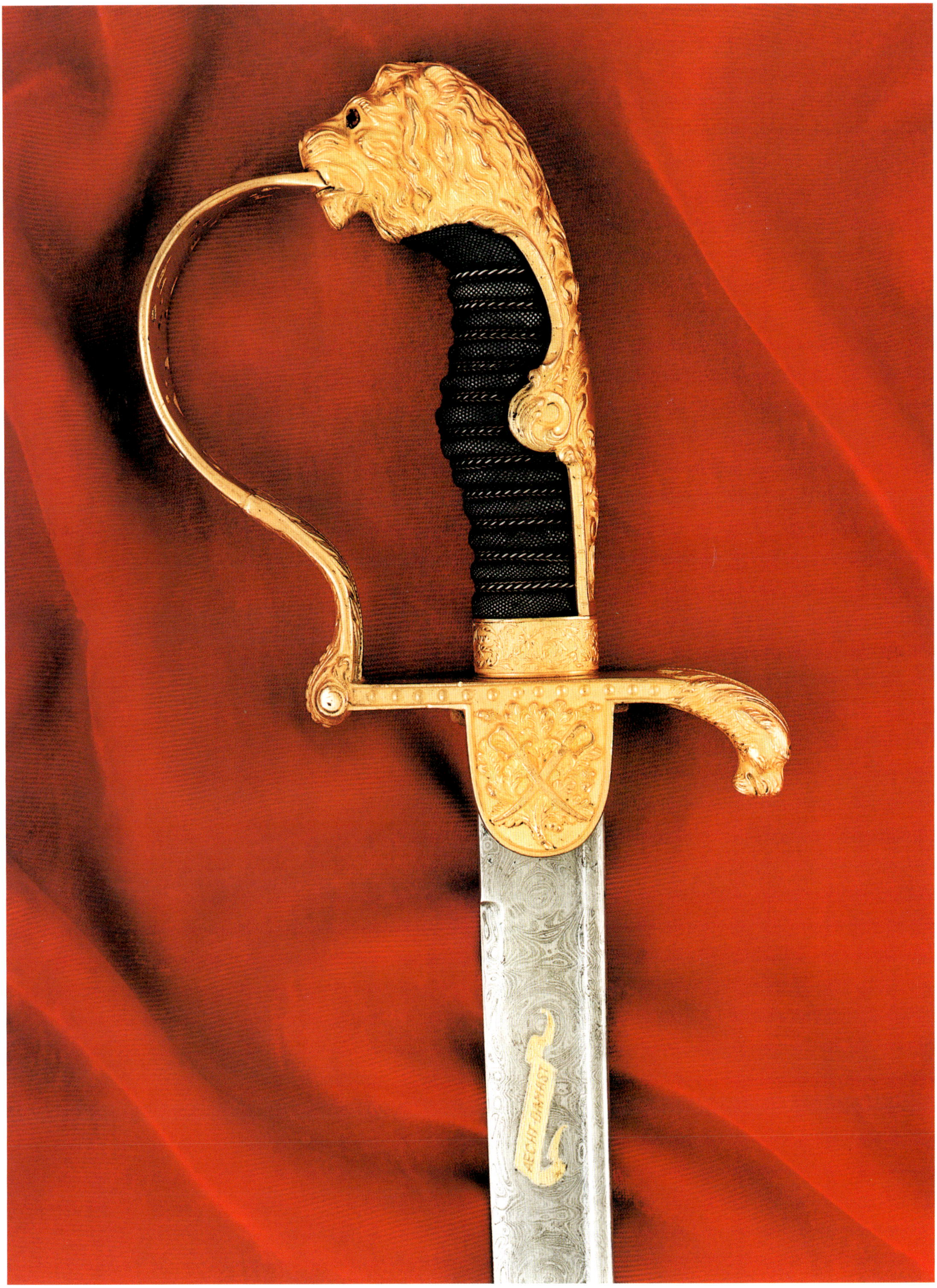

Imperial German Edged Weaponry

Deluxe pattern Lion head cavalry saber. This outstanding saber features a deeply cast gilt Lion head pommel with red ruby eyes. The fishskin grip is triple wire-wrapped. Fishskin-wrapped grips began appearing on European and New World swords about 1850. The use of this material is attributed to Japan. Before 1850, sword grips were usually leather-wrapped. The use of fishskin on German swords was discontinued circa 1925. The P-shaped knucklebow is cast with oak leaves and is filigreed, which is a rarely seen option. The quillon ends in a panther head, and the quillon bottom is stamped "*Ges. Gesch*". The obverse langet features cast Cavalry sabers. The scabbard is blued and contains a single hanger ring. *Jerry Jukich Collection. Photo by LTC (Ret.) Thomas M. Johnson.*

Reverse view of the deluxe pattern Lion head cavalry saber. The reverse langet features a chiseled escutcheon without an owner's monogram. Note the beautiful pattern of the "maiden hair" Damascus steel blade. *Jerry Jukich Collection. Photo by LTC (Ret.) Thomas M. Johnson.*

Imperial German Edged Weaponry

Extreme close-up of the deluxe pattern cavalry saber. The wide "Quill back" blade is "maiden hair" Damascus steel with a gold Imperial eagle and crown on the obverse. Note the detailed workmanship evident on the langet and quillon, including the small panther head. *Jerry Jukich Collection. Photo by LTC (Ret.) Thomas M. Johnson.*

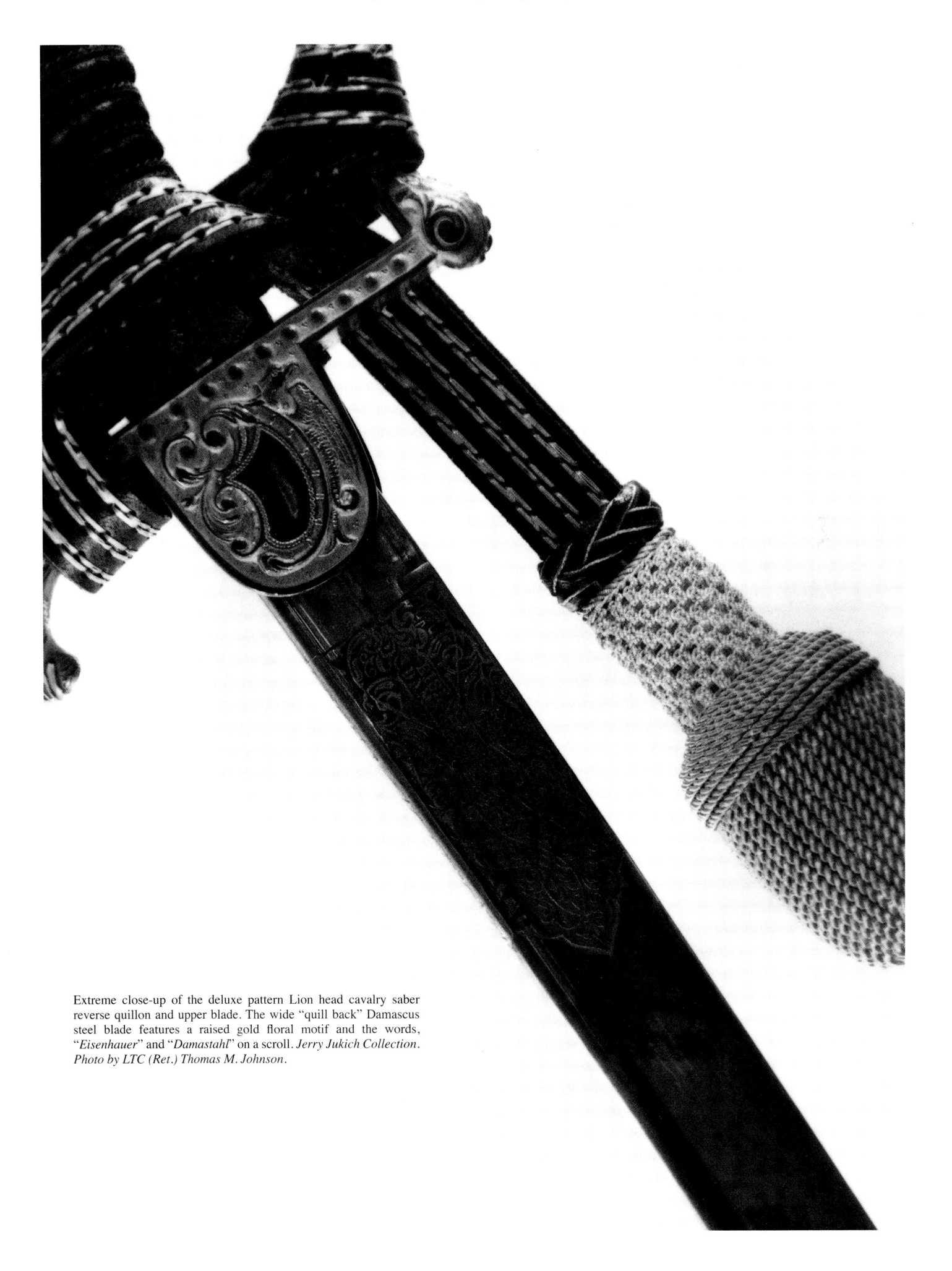

Extreme close-up of the deluxe pattern Lion head cavalry saber reverse quillon and upper blade. The wide "quill back" Damascus steel blade features a raised gold floral motif and the words, "*Eisenhauer*" and "*Damastahl*" on a scroll. *Jerry Jukich Collection. Photo by LTC (Ret.) Thomas M. Johnson.*

Extreme close-up of the beautiful filigreed knucklebow of the deluxe pattern Lion head cavalry saber. This angle photograph also provides a study of the massive Lion head pommel complete with "ruby" glass eyes. *Jerry Jukich Collection. Photo by LTC (Ret.) Thomas M. Johnson.*

Two outstanding Imperial *"Grosser"* Damascus swords are compared side-by-side. On the left is a presentation cavalry sword from Walter Durre to Kurt Bontheim followed by *"Lüneburg 1900"*. The blade is "large rose bud" Damascus. On the right is a magnificent *"Grosser"* pattern sword with "maiden hair" Damascus blade and a Guard Star affixed to the langet. Interesting comparison of the two knucklebows showing the intricate handwork done on the lions' faces and hand guards. *Richard R. Williams Collection. Photo by Dick Scott Fine Photography, Houston.*

Imperial German Edged Weaponry

This dramatic color photograph clearly demonstrates the difference in a filigree and a solid hilt knucklebow. Both Imperial swords are similar patterns with the exception of the finished knucklebows. This camera angle also vividly shows the intricate handwork executed by the swordsmith on the lions' faces and handguards. *Richard R. Williams Collection. Photo by Dick Scott Fine Photography, Houston.*

Swords of the German Army during the Imperial Era

April 1905 dated photo of an Imperial Army Officer named *Zechel* in the *Braunschweg Infantry Regiment No.92*. He is holding a *"Grosser"* pattern Lion head saber with properly tied sword knot. *LTC (Ret.) Thomas M. Johnson Photo Collection. Photo by Jos. Raab, Braunschweg.*

Two Imperial Army NCO friends photographed together in Metz. The *Vizefeldwebel* on the left is carrying an Infantry officer *Degen M89* with *Wilhelm II* cypher on the grip and non-folding clamshell. The NCO on the right prefers his "interim" Lion head saber. Note that the leather sword hanger on the left is black, while the leather hanger on the right is white. *LTC (Ret.) Thomas M. Johnson Photo Collection. Photo by Heinz Bensemann, Metz.*

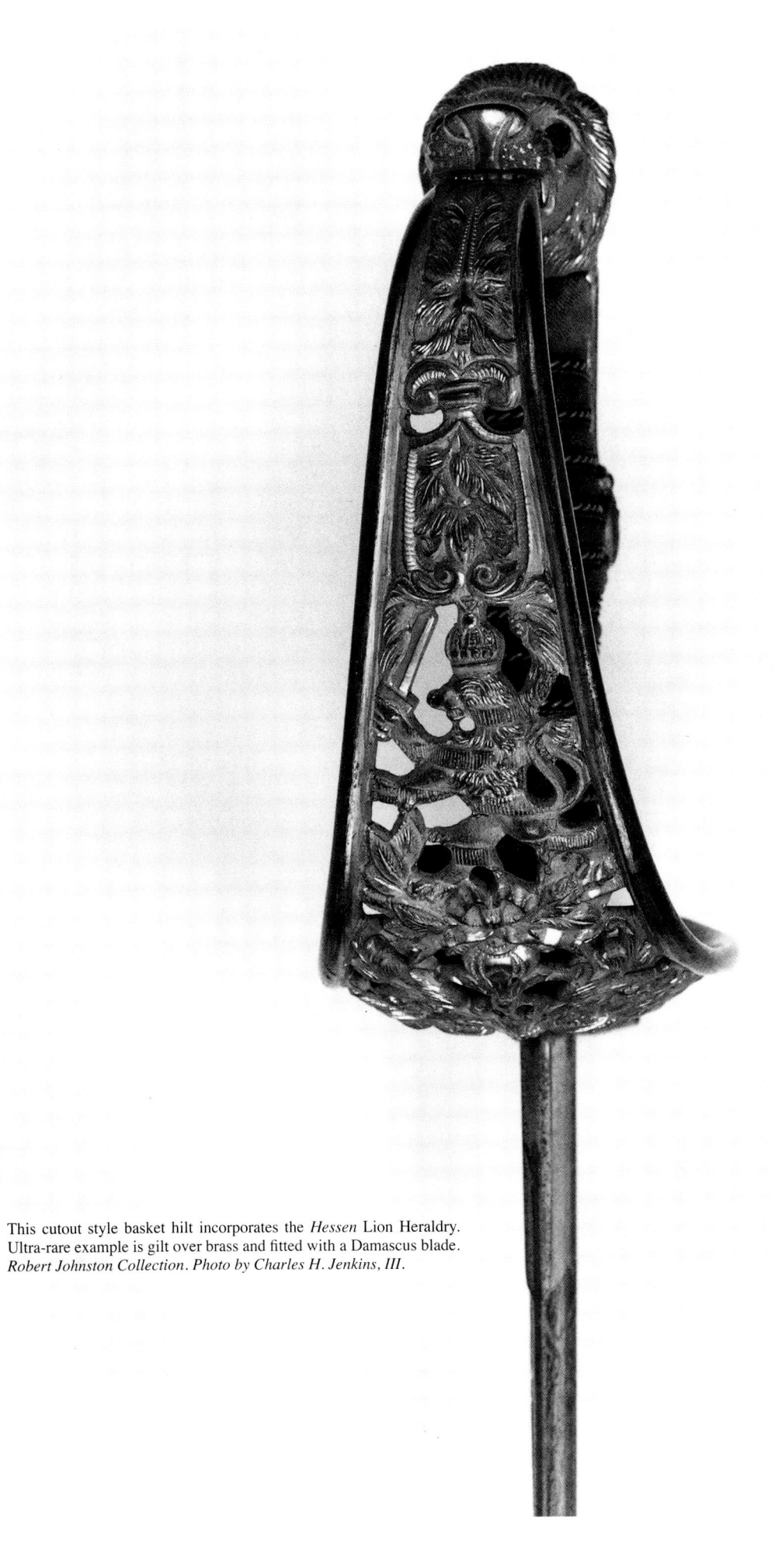

This cutout style basket hilt incorporates the *Hessen* Lion Heraldry.
Ultra-rare example is gilt over brass and fitted with a Damascus blade.
Robert Johnston Collection. Photo by Charles H. Jenkins, III.

A decorated Imperial veteran is wearing his Lion head saber with Guard Star on the obverse langet. The attached officer portepee shows extreme "battle" wear. *LTC (Ret.) Thomas M. Johnson Photo Collection.*

Swords of the German Army during the Imperial Era

A *Feldwebel* as signified by the sword knot, sergeant's color buttons, color lace, and a double row of lace on the cuff is pictured with his Lion head saber. The beautiful Lion head saber is secured in a pre-war nickel plated double ring scabbard – a much sought after combination. *Photo courtesy of Adam J. Portugal. Photo by R. Wunderlich, Hagen.*

The Carl Eickhorn factory Imperial Edged Weaponry sales catalog depicts the company's Model #977 in actual size. The accompanying caption reads, *Preussischer Kavallerie-und Artillerie-Offizier-Säbel mit Parderkopf und Augen, hochfein ziseliert."* (Prussian Cavalry and Artillery Officer Saber with Lion head and eyes, finely chiseled.) *Johnson Reference Books & Militaria Archives.*

This Imperial Infantry officer poses for a Christmas 1892 studio portrait for his family. He is wearing his *Pickelhaube* helmet and grasping his nickeled Lion head officer's saber. *LTC (Ret.) Thomas M. Johnson Photo Collection. Photo by Arnold Overbeck, Düsseldorf.*

In this early 1900s wedding photograph, the groom wears a very distinctive *Fusilier* saber with Lion head hilt. The officer portepee is tied around the grip and triple wrapped around the crossguard. *LTC (Ret.) Thomas M. Johnson Photo Collection. Photo by Georg Müller, Cöpenick.*

Swords of the German Army during the Imperial Era

Bavarian Lion head *Pallasch* for "interim" wear by the Bavarian heavy cavalry. The distinctive Bavarian coat-of-arms appears on the langet. The blade of this *Pallasch* is straight and double fullered, and the Bavarian motto is etched on the blade. *LTC (Ret.) Thomas M. Johnson Collection. Photo by LTC (Ret.) Thomas M. Johnson.*

Imperial German Edged Weaponry

Captain Max Wehrig's Christmas sword. Captain Wehrig served in the elite Guard Foot Artillery at Spandau Fortress, Berlin. Wehrig served the Regiment as *Rittmeister* (Captain of Cavalry) from 1914-1919. This sword was presented to Captain Wehrig by his parents on Christmas Day 1917. The sword is a deluxe Lion head model with presentation "band" pattern Damascus blade. The Guard Star with the motto, *"SUUM CUIQUE"* (to each his own) appears on the obverse langet. The backstrap is engraved with the initials "M" over "W". *Victor Diehl Collection. Photo by Victor Diehl.*

Swords of the German Army during the Imperial Era

Presentation inscription on the obverse blade of the Wehrig Imperial sword. The translated inscription reads, "To my son Max Wehrig – Christmas 1917 – Guard Foot Artillery Regiment – Spandau". *Victor Diehl Collection. Photo by Victor Diehl.*

Reverse inscription of the *Wehrig* Sword contains the ancient warrior's pledge: "For honor and duty until heart and sword break." *Victor Diehl Collection. Photo by Victor Diehl.*

A wooden scabbard liner of the *Wehrig* Sword. The name "Wehrig" is written in pencil on the liner, enabling the assembler to match the scabbard, which is marked with a "W", with the correct liners. *Victor Diehl Collection. Photo by Victor Diehl.*

Pictured in color is an exceptional Presentation "Jawless" Guard Officer's Sword distributed by *Joh. Friedr. Bock, Hoflieferant, Berlin*. No maker's trademark appears on the blade. A typical Guard Star is featured on the obverse langet. *Major General (Ret.) Theodore W. Paulson Collection. Photo by Major General (Ret.) Theodore W. Paulson.*

Reverse view of the hilt on the Presentation Jawless Guard Officer's Sword distributed by *Joh. Friedr. Bock*. Note that the Lion head pommel is void of glass eyes. The scabbard is the black, single fixed-ring version. *Major General (Ret.) Theodore W. Paulson Collection. Photo by Major General (Ret.) Theodore W. Paulson.*

Pictured is a close-up view of the obverse blade dedication on the Presentation Jawless Guard Officer's Sword, which reads, "*Fritz Scharf s./l. Walter Luttich*" and, in English this commonly seen presentation format translates as, "Fritz Scharf to his dear friend Walter Luttich". *Major General (Ret.) Theodore W. Paulson Collection. Photo by Major General (Ret.) Theodore W. Paulson.*

The reverse blade panel of the Presentation Jawless Guard Officer's Sword bears the inscription, "*Anklam* (town in Northern Germany) *1912*". The obverse blade is etched with a personal presentation panel. *Major General (Ret.) Theodore W. Paulson Collection. Photo by Major General (Ret.) Theodore W. Paulson.*

Splendid Lion head artillery saber given in friendship. The fire gilded hilt features ruby eyes and deluxe engraving. The langet is adorned with chiseled crossed cannons. The quill-back Damascus blade contains gilded and blued presentations on both sides. The obverse panel reads, *"Lubner s./l. Baum"*. This commonly seen presentation format translates as, *"Lubner Seinem lieben Baum"* or, "Lubner to his dear friend Baum". *Stephen Wolfe Collection. Photograph Courtesy of Stephen Wolfe.*

The reverse panel exclaims the universal axiom, "One for All, All for One". The saber is attributed to the firm of Weyersberg, Kirschbaum and Company (WK&C). WK&C was Solingen's most famous Imperial edged weapon producing concern. The company was founded in 1883 by the joining of *Gebrüder Weyersberg* and *W.R. Kirschbaum & Cie*. *Stephen Wolfe Collection. Photograph Courtesy of Stephen Wolfe.*

Pictured in color is a silver-hilt Bavarian Lion head saber. The Bavarian crest decorates the obverse langet. The sword is complete with the correct original silver bullion sword knot with four thin blue (Bavarian) stripes. *Private Collection*.

Pictured in color is the reverse view of the silver hilt Bavarian Lion head saber. The original Bavarian silver and blue sword knot is wrapped around the knucklebow. An unidentified crest decorates the reverse langet. *Private Collection*.

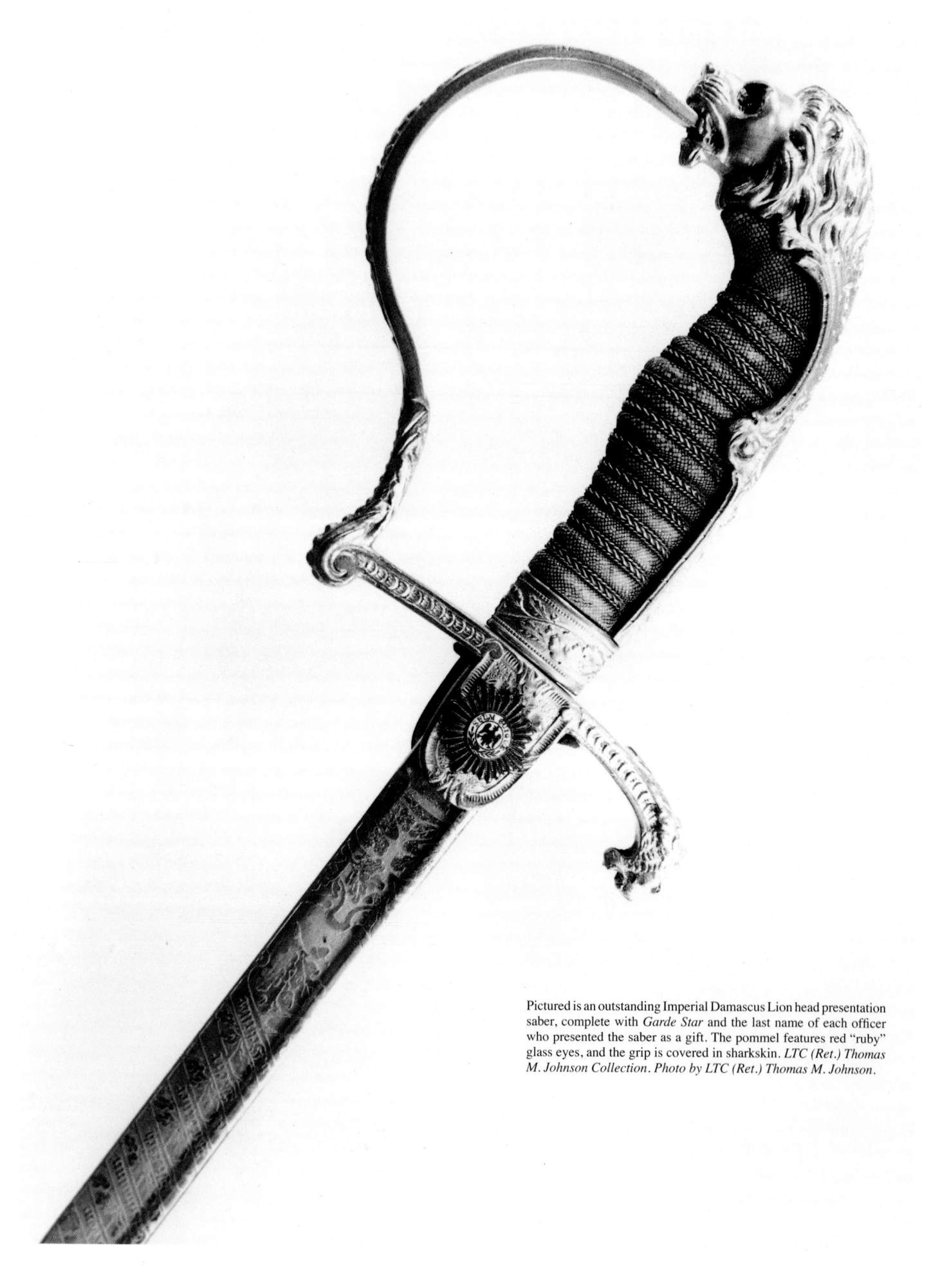

Pictured is an outstanding Imperial Damascus Lion head presentation saber, complete with *Garde Star* and the last name of each officer who presented the saber as a gift. The pommel features red "ruby" glass eyes, and the grip is covered in sharkskin. *LTC (Ret.) Thomas M. Johnson Collection. Photo by LTC (Ret.) Thomas M. Johnson.*

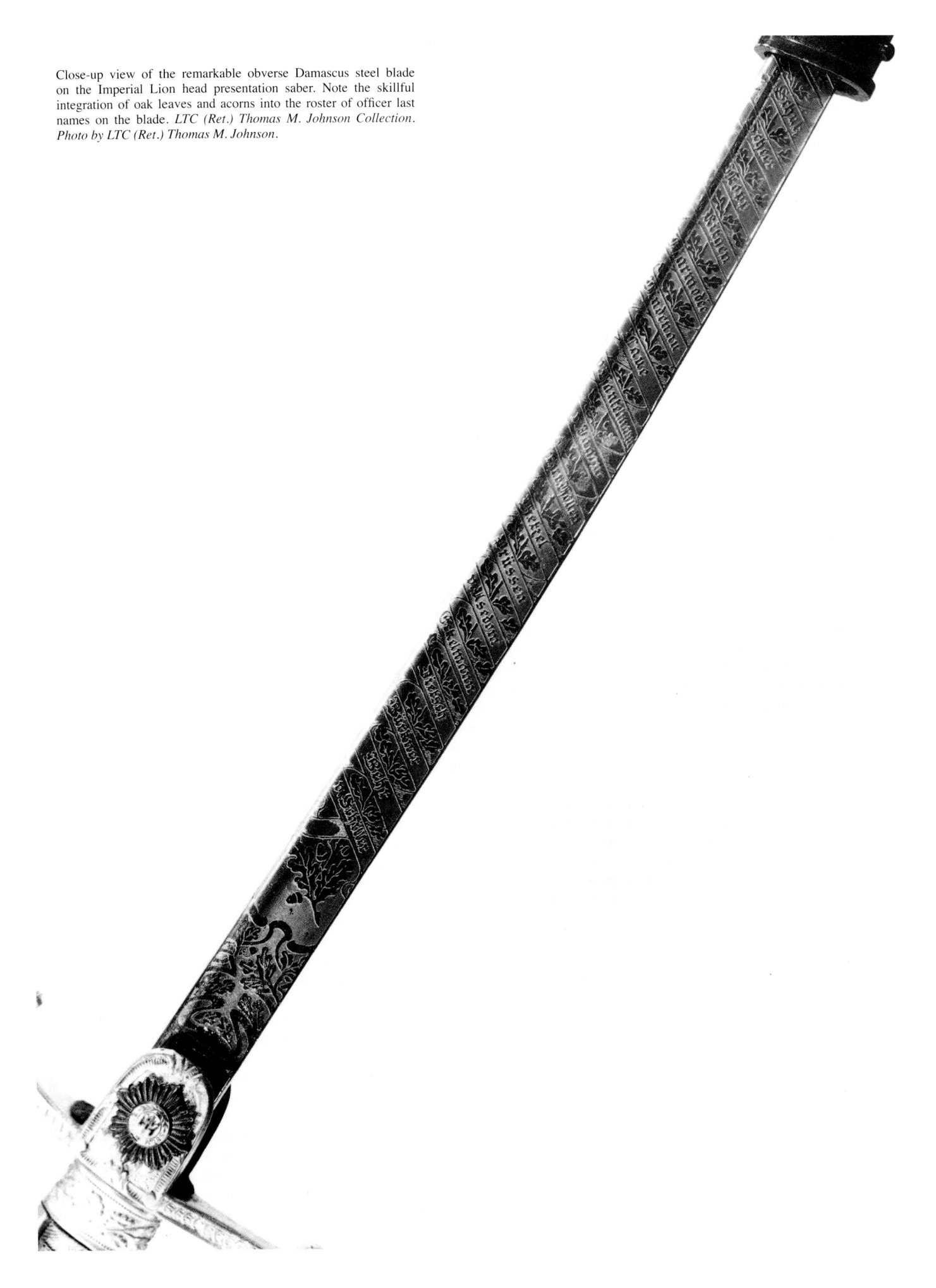

Close-up view of the remarkable obverse Damascus steel blade on the Imperial Lion head presentation saber. Note the skillful integration of oak leaves and acorns into the roster of officer last names on the blade. *LTC (Ret.) Thomas M. Johnson Collection. Photo by LTC (Ret.) Thomas M. Johnson.*

Imperial German Edged Weaponry

Unattributed Imperial Lion head saber similar to the WK&C model sword designated as model Nr.194, *Sächsischer Infanterie-Offizier Interims-Löwenkopf-Säbel*. This pommel is complete with red glass eyes, and the grip is wrapped in sharkskin. *LTC (Ret.) Thomas M. Johnson Collection. Photo by LTC (Ret.) Thomas M. Johnson.*

Reverse view of the hilt on the unattributed Imperial Lion head saber. The shield on the reverse langet has been left blank and does not bear the sword owner's initials. *LTC (Ret.) Thomas M. Johnson Collection. Photo by LTC (Ret.) Thomas M. Johnson.*

Imperial German Edged Weaponry

Extreme close-up view of the obverse crossguard on the unattributed Imperial Lion head saber. Note the hand embellishment on the ferrule and crossguard. *LTC (Ret.) Thomas M. Johnson Collection. Photo by LTC (Ret.) Thomas M. Johnson.*

Pictured is a portion of the obverse side of the double-etched blade on the unattributed Imperial Lion head saber. Under a loupe, the name *"Eisenhauer"* is detectable near the ricasso. *LTC (Ret.) Thomas M. Johnson Collection. Photo by LTC (Ret.) Thomas M. Johnson.*

Imperial German Edged Weaponry

Preussischen Armee und des XIII (Koniglich Württembergischen) Armeekorps für 1896 indicates that this ornate sword was presented by *Leutnant Breyer, 2. Württembergisches Feldartillerie-Regiment Nr.29 Prinz-Regent Luitpold von Bayern* to *Leutnant Freiherr (Baron) von Wollmarth – Lauterburg, Ulanen-Regiment Konig Wilhelm I. (2. Württembergisches) Nr.20*. Both officers first appear in the 1896 rank list. A sketch of this model rare sword is shown in the Imperial WK&C catalog as well as the publication *Waffengeschichte* as a *"Feiner Kavallerie u. Artillerie-Offizier Parderkopf-Sabel mit Eichenlaubbugel"*. LTC (Ret.) Thomas M. Johnson Collection. Photo by LTC (Ret.) Thomas M. Johnson.

The heavily chiseled langet with oak leaves and crossed cannon barrels retains much of the original fire gilt and is shown in close-up detail. Pinned to the langet is the silver Royal cypher (intertwined "LS" surmounted by a crown) of Crown Prince Luitpold of Bavaria, Regimental Chief of Artillery Regiment Nr.29. The black sharkskin grip is perfect with virtually no wear or damage and has its tight triple wire wrap intact. *LTC (Ret.) Thomas M. Johnson Collection. Photo by LTC (Ret.) Thomas M. Johnson.*

Imperial German Edged Weaponry

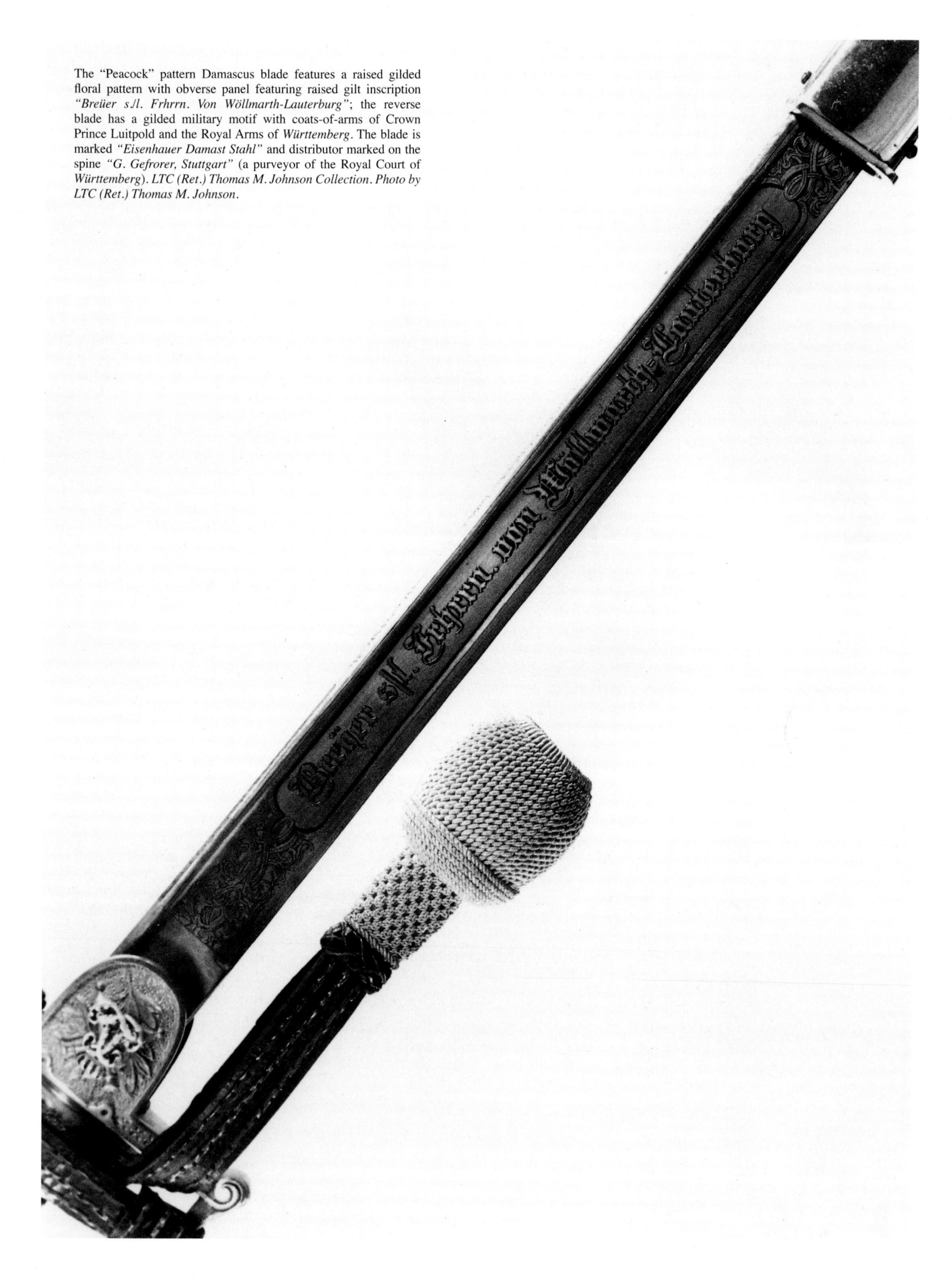

The "Peacock" pattern Damascus blade features a raised gilded floral pattern with obverse panel featuring raised gilt inscription *"Breüer s./l. Frhrrn. Von Wöllmarth-Lauterburg"*; the reverse blade has a gilded military motif with coats-of-arms of Crown Prince Luitpold and the Royal Arms of *Württemberg*. The blade is marked *"Eisenhauer Damast Stahl"* and distributor marked on the spine *"G. Gefrorer, Stuttgart"* (a purveyor of the Royal Court of *Württemberg*). LTC (Ret.) Thomas M. Johnson Collection. Photo by LTC (Ret.) Thomas M. Johnson.

48

Extreme close-up view of the gilt seal of the *Württemberg* German State. Note the exceptional condition of both the Damascus steel blade and the accompanying *Württemberg* sword knot. *LTC (Ret.) Thomas M. Johnson Collection. Photo by LTC (Ret.) Thomas M. Johnson.*

Imperial German Edged Weaponry

Pictured in color is an unusual Presentation Imperial Lion head sword with Damascus steel blade. This unique sword was presented by *Leutnant von Gaffron* and *Oberstradem* to *Leutnant von Plänckner* while both officers were assigned to the *Grenadier-Regiment König Wilhelm I (2. Westpreussisches) Nr.7*. The sword most likely was presented during 1891, as both officers appear as members of this regiment in the 1891 rank list, while *Leutnant von Plänckner* was serving in a different regiment in the 1892 rank list. The obverse langet features a heavily-chiseled profile of Athena, the Roman Goddess of War. The gorgeous "modified peacock" pattern Damascus blade bears the inscription, "von Gaffron und Oberstradem s./l. von Plänckner" in shadowed gilt Gothic letters. *Richard R. Williams Collection. Photo by Dick Scott Fine Photography, Houston.*

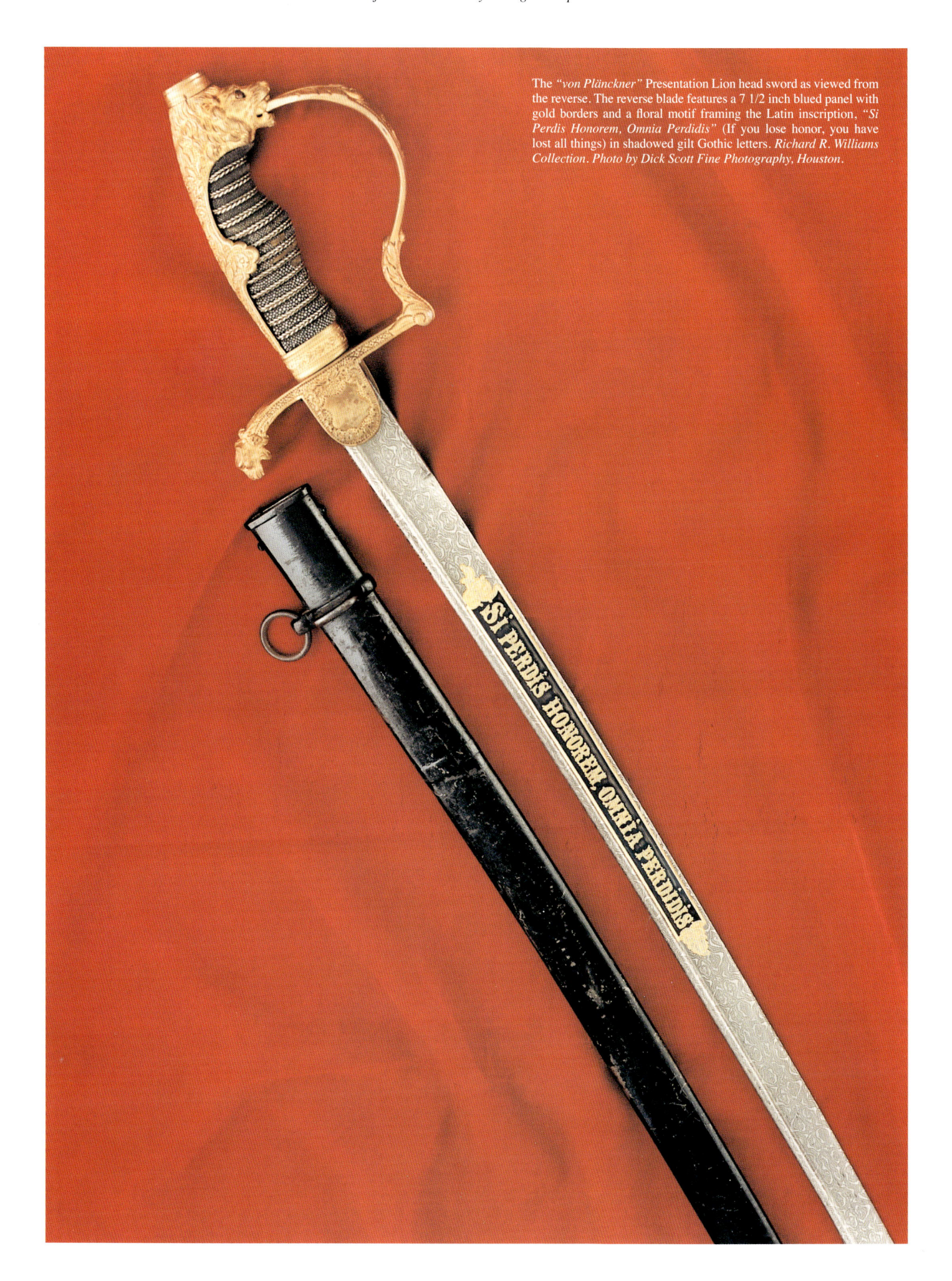

The *"von Plänckner"* Presentation Lion head sword as viewed from the reverse. The reverse blade features a 7 1/2 inch blued panel with gold borders and a floral motif framing the Latin inscription, *"Si Perdis Honorem, Omnia Perdidis"* (If you lose honor, you have lost all things) in shadowed gilt Gothic letters. *Richard R. Williams Collection. Photo by Dick Scott Fine Photography, Houston.*

Excellent close-up view of the obverse hilt on the *"von Plänckner"* Presentation Lion head Damascus sword. The obverse langet features a heavily chiseled profile of Athena, the Roman Goddess of War. The top of the heavily chiseled Lion head pommel has been hand fitted to accept an *M89* pattern pommel cap which features the *von Plänckner* coat-of-arms. Note the Royal cypher of Wilhelm I surmounted by a Prussian Crown on the sharkskin grip. *Richard R. Williams Collection. Photo by Dick Scott Fine Photography, Houston.*

Swords of the German Army during the Imperial Era

Pictured is the outer knucklebow of the *"von Plänckner"* Presentation Lion head sword. The top of the Lion head pommel has been hand-fitted to accept an *M89* pattern pommel cap which featured a deeply-engraved *von Plänckner* family coat-of-arms. Although not visible in this photograph, the sharkskin grip bears the Royal cypher of Wilhelm I surmounted by a Prussian Crown. The spine of the blade is marked in gilt letters on a blued panel, *"Ed Schultze, Hoflieferant, Pottsdam."* Richard R. Williams Collection. Photo by Dick Scott Fine Photography, Houston.

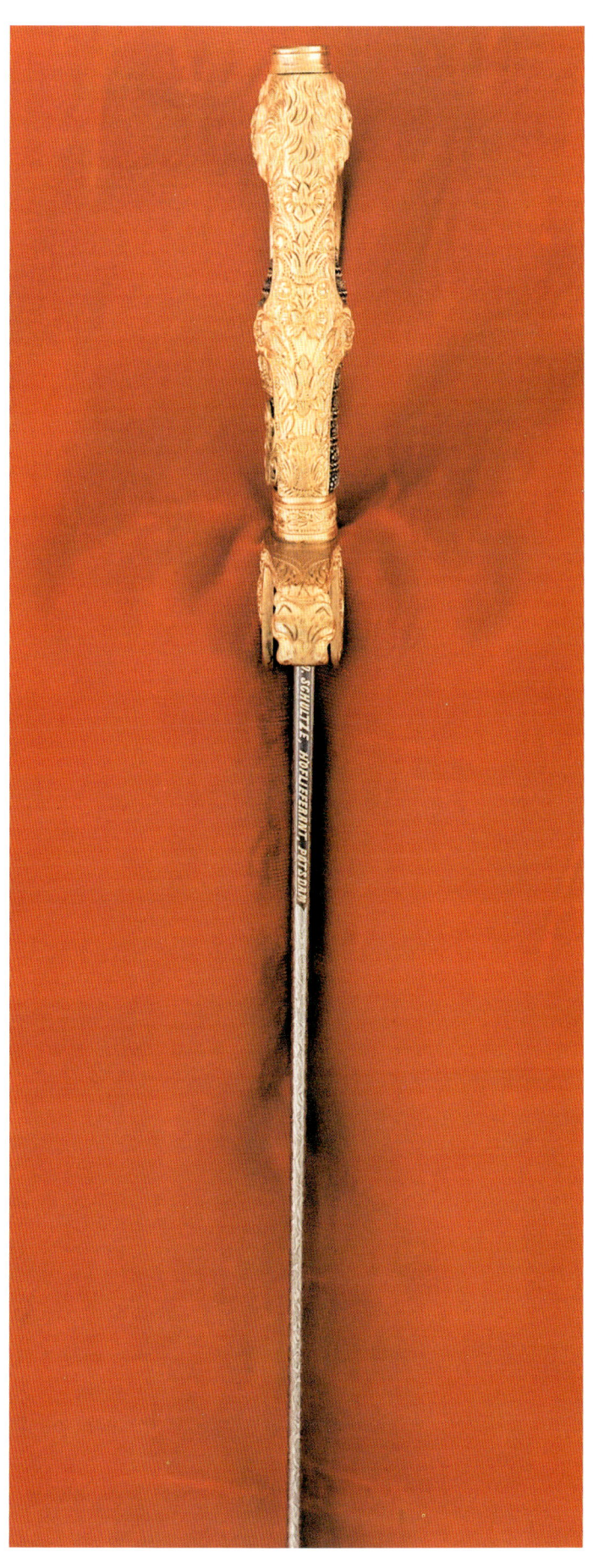

The spine of the blade on the Lieutenant *von Plänckner* Presentation Imperial Lion head Damascus sword is marked in gilt letters on a thin blued panel, *"Ed Schultze, Hoflieferant, Pottsdam."* Richard R. Williams Collection. Photo by Dick Scott Fine Photography, Houston.

Imperial German Edged Weaponry

Pictured in color is another spectacular Imperial *"Grosser"* Presentation Lion head sword, complete with a genuine Damascus steel blade. While the blade is totally void of a maker's trademark, the distributor's name, *"M. Neumann Hoflieferant, Berlin"* appears in raised gold lettering on the spine. The sword was veteran acquired with the attached sword knot. *Major General (Ret.) Theodore W. Paulson Collection. Photo by Major General (Ret.) Theodore W. Paulson.*

Color view of the reverse hilt on the *"Grosser"* Presentation Lion head sword with genuine Damascus steel blade and no manufacturer's trademark. The grip is sharkskin, dyed black. The scabbard is black metal with a single ring. *Major General (Ret.) Theodore W. Paulson Collection. Photo by Major General (Ret.) Theodore W. Paulson.*

Imperial German Edged Weaponry

The near mint obverse Damascus steel blade on the *"Grosser"* Presentation Lion head sword without a manufacturer's trademark features a raised gold presentation panel dated with the years "1910-1914". *Major General (Ret.) Theodore W. Paulson Collection. Photo by Major General (Ret.) Theodore W. Paulson.*

Similar to many Imperial (and later Third Reich) presentation swords, the most spectacular component is often the reverse blade which can feature in raised gold the individual names of the officers making the presentation. The reverse blade on the Damascus *"Grosser"* Presentation Lion head sword without maker's mark includes the names of twenty-three (23) officers. *Major General (Ret.) Theodore W. Paulson Collection. Photo by Major General (Ret.) Theodore W. Paulson.*

A decorated Imperial infantry *Leutnant* is pictured proudly wearing his deluxe pattern Lion head saber. The single ring black lacquer scabbard and reverse langet of the saber hilt are easily seen. *LTC (Ret.) Thomas M. Johnson Photo Collection. Photo by Max Fieller, Göppingen.*

Imperial German Edged Weaponry

Heavy cavalry troopers and their NCOs pose for their annual portrait. A number of broadswords and early pattern cavalry sabers are seen in wear. The location is in a military *Kaserne* in Munich. *LTC (Ret.) Thomas M. Johnson Photo Collection.*

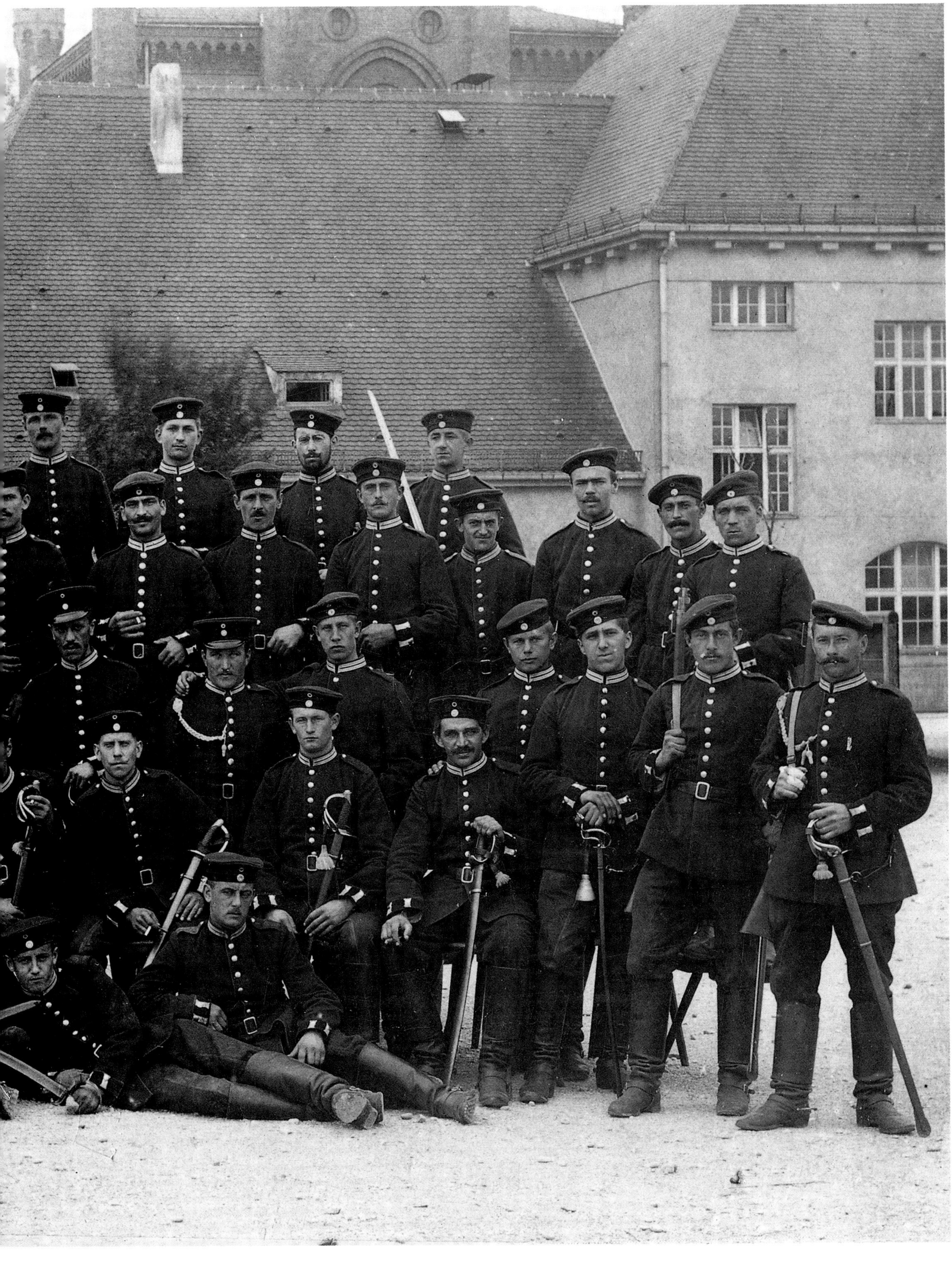

Imperial German Edged Weaponry

This *Prussian* Lieutenant is wearing a chiseled Lion head saber complete with a sword knot. The scabbard conforms to the regulations of 14 December 1910 which required it to be painted black and have the lower hanger ring removed. This scabbard has seen considerable wear by the 1916 date of this photo. The scabbard is nearly devoid of all of its paint and has a nasty bend near the drag. *LTC (Ret.) Thomas M. Johnson Photo Collection. Photo by Herm. Kniep, Straasburg.*

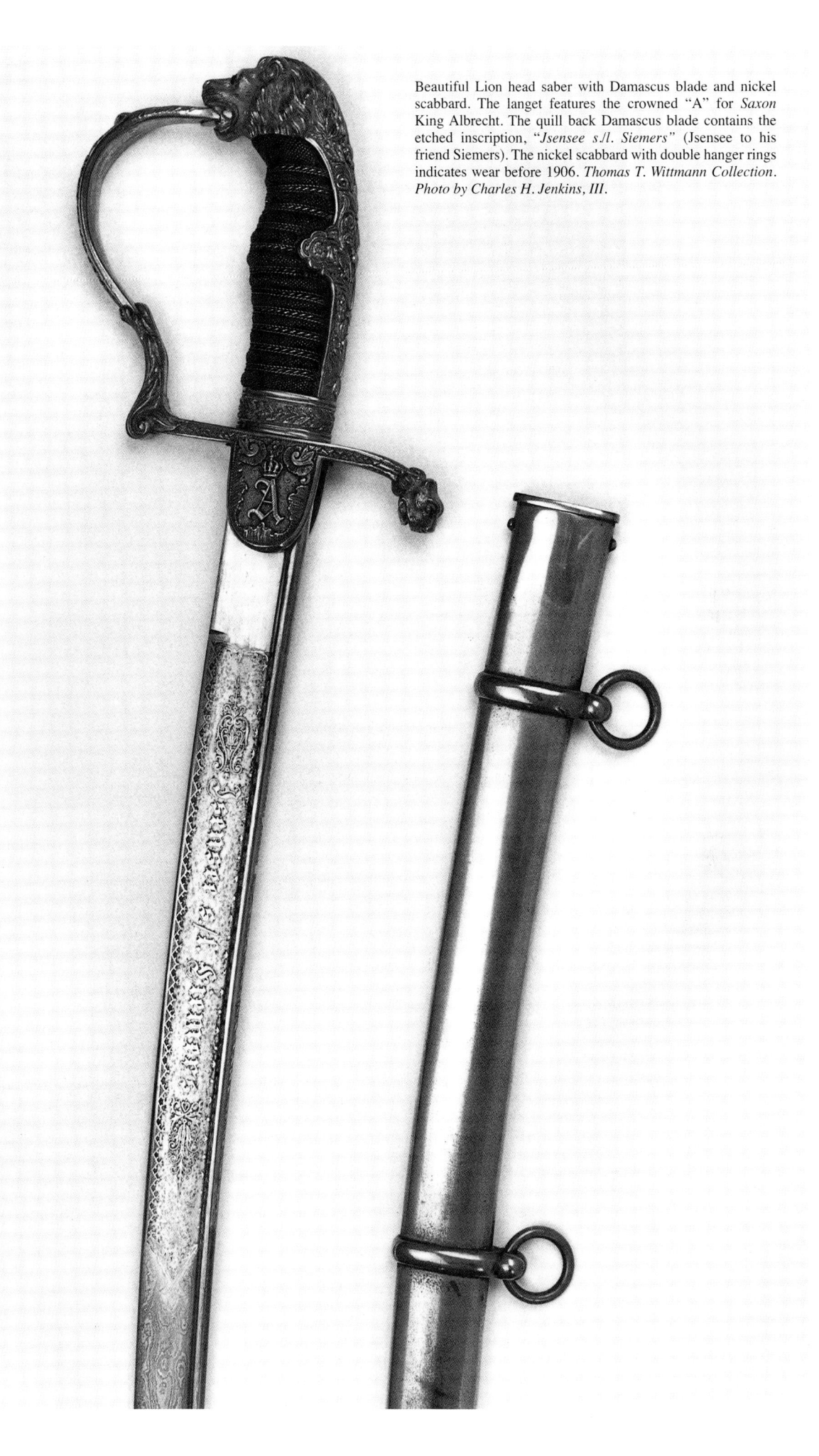

Beautiful Lion head saber with Damascus blade and nickel scabbard. The langet features the crowned "A" for *Saxon* King Albrecht. The quill back Damascus blade contains the etched inscription, *"Jsensee s./l. Siemers"* (Jsensee to his friend Siemers). The nickel scabbard with double hanger rings indicates wear before 1906. *Thomas T. Wittmann Collection. Photo by Charles H. Jenkins, III.*

Exquisite Lion head saber with oversized, *"Grosser"* hilt. The highly detailed work on the hilt is typical of the outstanding quality of weapons bearing the mark of retailer *M. Neumann Hoflieferant-Berlin*. The langet contains the cypher of the *Kaiser*. The wide quill-back blade is nickeled and bears the scrolled *"Eisenhauer"* designation. *LTC (Ret.) Thomas M. Johnson Collection. Photo by LTC (Ret.) Thomas M. Johnson.*

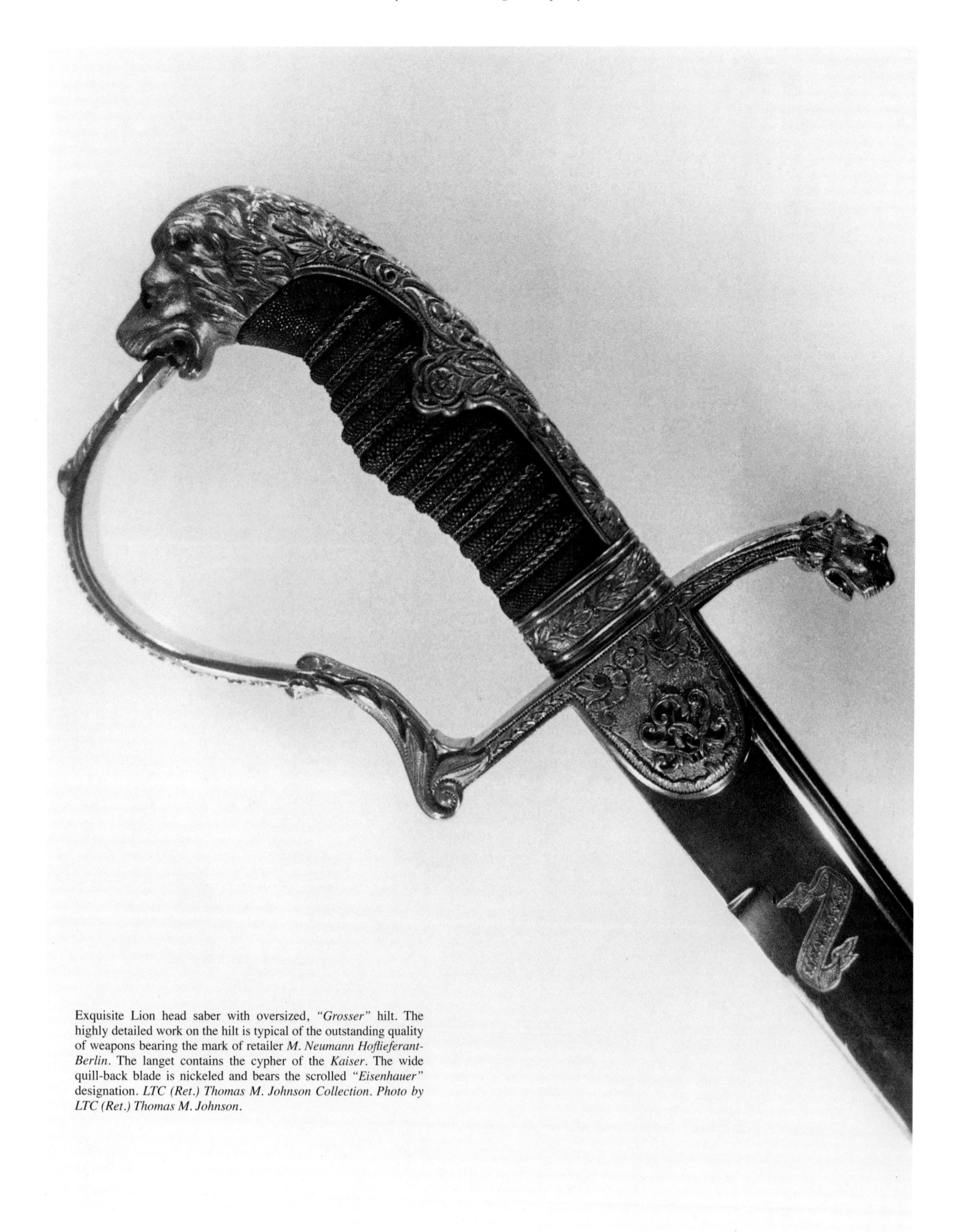

Close-up view of the crossguard and langet of the Lion head saber with *"Grosser"* hilt. The langet contains the cypher of the *Kaiser*. Note that the obverse blade bears the word *"Eisenhauer"* in a scroll. *LTC (Ret.) Thomas M. Johnson Collection. Photo by LTC (Ret.) Thomas M. Johnson.*

An interesting group on a horse-drawn carriage is off to the party. The driver is wearing a *"Grosser"* pattern Lion head saber complete with sword knot. The photograph is dated 15 May 1891. *LTC (Ret.) Thomas M. Johnson Collection. Photo by Rohrbek Photographie, Berlin.*

Swords of the German Army during the Imperial Era

Imperial Lion head presentation sword by Clemen und Jung. This saber features an unusual knucklebow dedication which reads, *"Fredrich Prinz zu Wittegenstein dem Wachmeister Scheel"*. The reverse langet bears *Prinz Fredrich's* coat-of-arms. The blade is a beautiful "maiden hair" Damascus steel, with raised gold floral design. *James Brown Collection. Photo Courtesy of James Brown.*

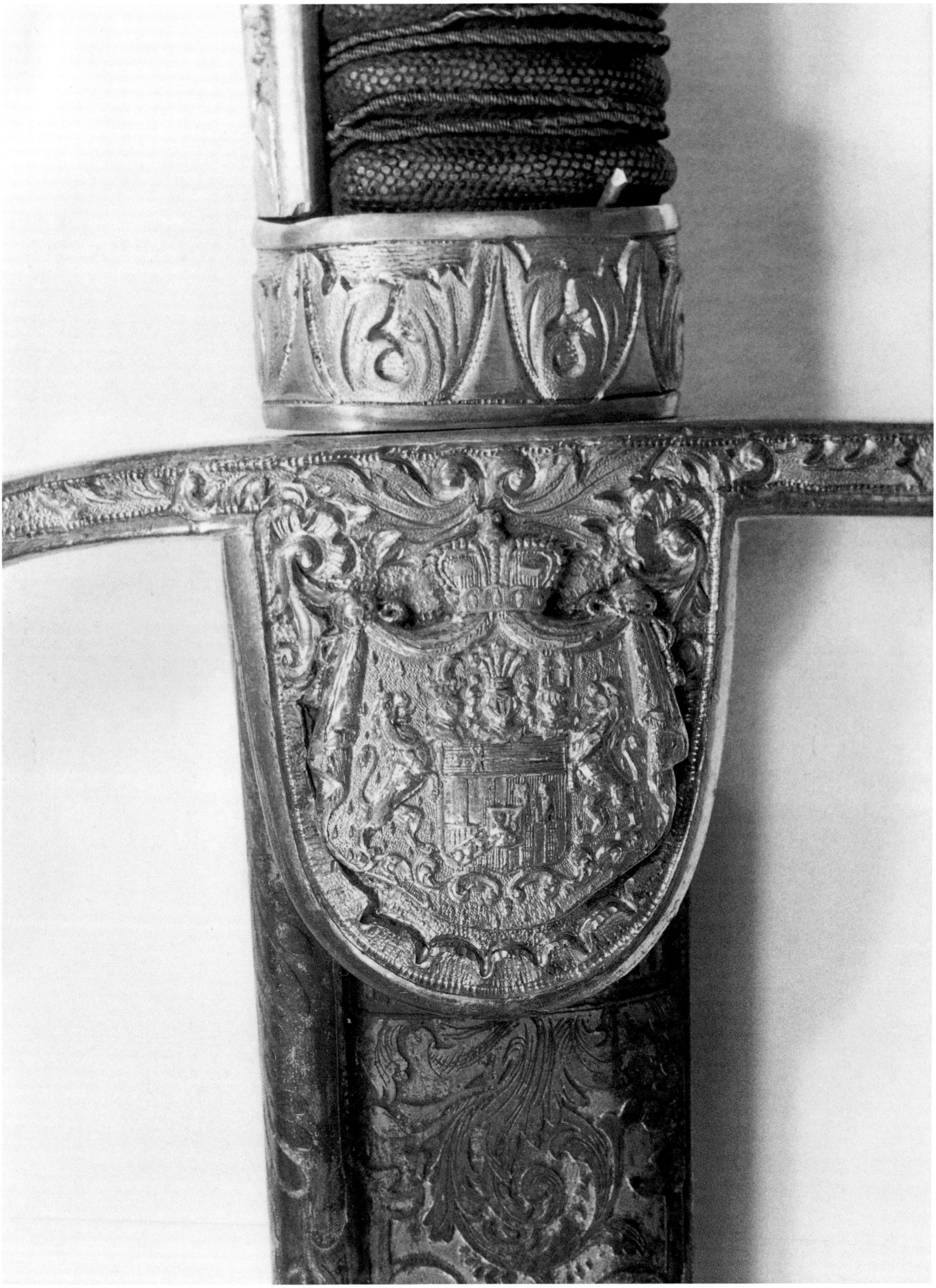

The Imperial Lion head saber is shown being worn very uncomfortably under the overcoat on the far right. The saddle has no provisions for hanging the saber from the mount. *LTC (Ret.) Thomas M. Johnson Photo Collection.*

OPPOSITE
Extreme close-up of the *Prinz Fredrich's* coat-of-arms appearing on the reverse langet of the Personalized Lion head sword. The detail on both the langet and blade could only have been achieved by master craftsmen. *James Brown Collection. Photo Courtesy of James Brown.*

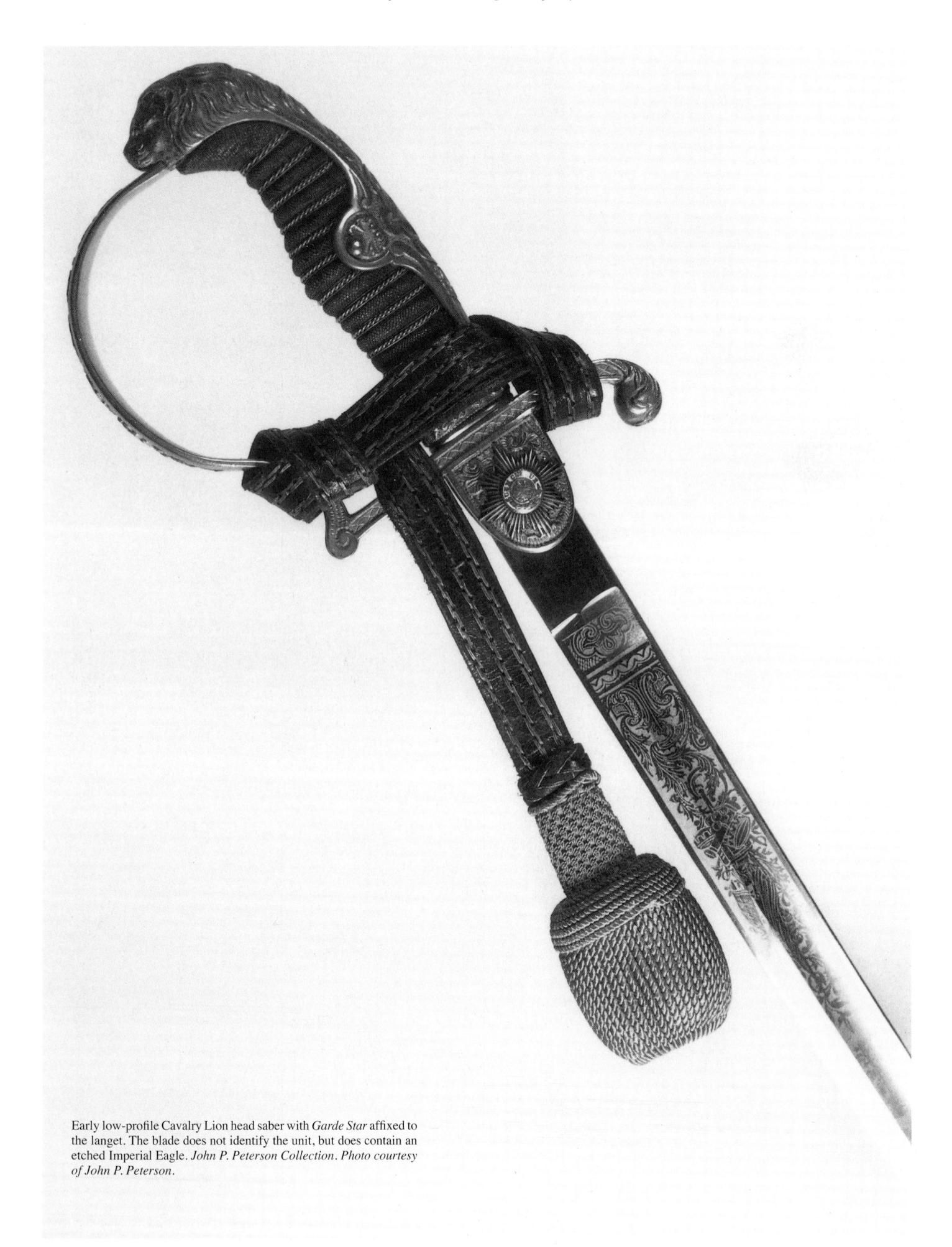

Early low-profile Cavalry Lion head saber with *Garde Star* affixed to the langet. The blade does not identify the unit, but does contain an etched Imperial Eagle. *John P. Peterson Collection. Photo courtesy of John P. Peterson.*

A *Hessen* cavalry officer is photographed wearing a custom ordered private purchase Lion head saber with highly chiseled alternate knucklebow. The officer's name is *"Spruner"* and the photograph is dated March 1898. *LTC (Ret.) Thomas M. Johnson Photo Collection. Photo by W. Pöllok, Darmstadt.*

A cavalry *Unteroffizier* proudly carrying his dovehead saber with blackened scabbard. The leather strapped *Faustriemen* and suspension strap are easily observed in this photograph. *LTC (Ret.) Thomas M. Johnson Photo Collection. Photo by Karl Bauer Studio, Karlsrühe.*

Bavarian infantry officer with an unusual Lion head saber with folding guard. Many Bavarian officers, when purchasing a Lion head saber, specified a nickel or silver hilt instead of gold, in keeping with their state and uniform colors. *SSGT (Ret.) T. Wayne Cunningham (USAF) Photo Collection. Photo by Charles H. Jenkins, III.*

A decorated *Saxon* veteran poses for a studio portrait with his wife wearing his Lion head saber in this 31 December 1924 dated photograph taken in Ebersbrich, Germany. *LTC (Ret.) Thomas M. Johnson Photo Collection.*

A most instructive period photograph of a cavalry man with his saber attached to his saddle. *LTC (Ret.) Thomas M. Johnson Photo Collection.*

Pictured is a full-length obverse view of an outstanding Imperial Damascus steel presentation sword presented to *Freiherr von Barnekow*. The overall sword length is 40 1/2 inches and the impressive Damascus blade is approximately thirty-five inches. *Major General (Ret.) Theodore W. Paulson Collection. Photo by Harry Bellows.*

Swords of the German Army during the Imperial Era

Pictured in color is the obverse hilt of a spectacular *"Grosser"* Presentation Lion head *Ehrendegen* (Honor Sword) presented to *General der Infanterie* (General of the Infantry) *Freiherr von Barnekow*. General Barnekow became the *Kommandierender General des l. Armee Korps*. The sword was presented in 1871 by selected members of his unit in honor of his 50th year of military service. *Major General (Ret.) Theodore W. Paulson Collection. Photo by Major General (Ret.) Theodore W. Paulson.*

Close-up view of the reverse hilt and upper portion of the fantastic Damascus blade on the *Freiherr von Barnekow* Imperial Presentation Sword. The reverse langet is engraved with *"15 Mai 1866 bis 23 Mai 1871"*. The reverse blade markings are as outstanding as the obverse. From the top of the blade is a panel with *"1866"* and the names of the major campaigns participated in during the Austrian-Prussian War. Under the *"1870/1871"* inscription are two sections – the first containing the names of major campaigns, two per loop. The second section contains the names, two per loop, of less significant campaigns. *Major General (Ret.) Theodore W. Paulson Collection. Photo by Major General (Ret.) Theodore W. Paulson.*

Swords of the German Army during the Imperial Era

Close-up view of the obverse hilt and upper portion of the outstanding Damascus Presentation steel blade on the *Freiherr von Barnekow* Imperial Presentation Sword. The obverse langet is engraved with *"Ostreich 1866, Frankreich 1870-71"*. The raised inscriptions on the obverse blade include a *Demtapfern Oberst Freiherrn von Barnekow* panel followed by sixteen (16) intertwined ribbon loops and twenty-six (26) names and titles engraved within the loops. The majority of the names appear to be from nobility. *Major General (Ret.) Theodore W. Paulson Collection. Photo by Major General (Ret.) Theodore W. Paulson.*

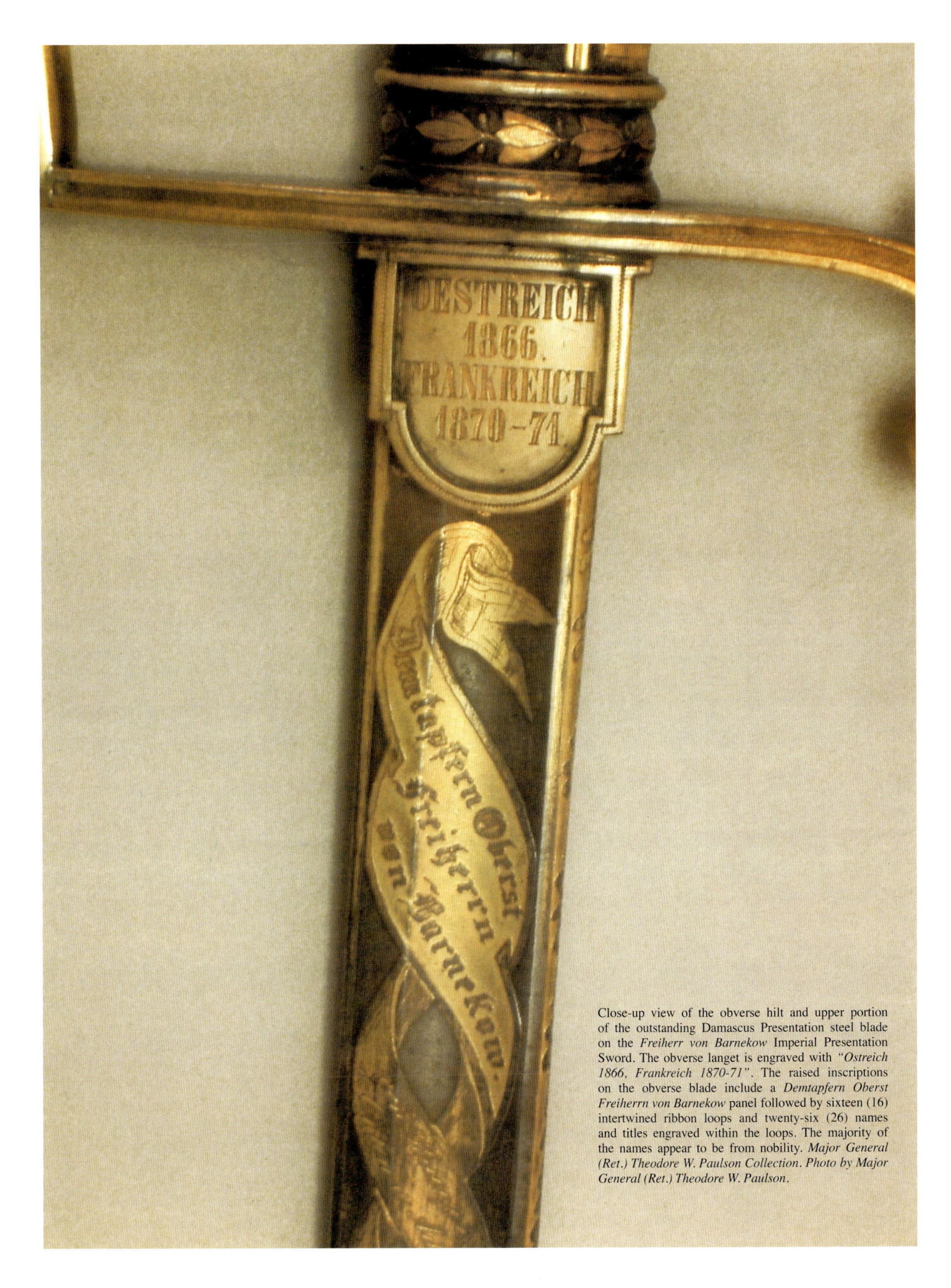

The impressive outer knucklebow on the beautiful *Freiherr von Barnekow* sword features a raised gilt Roman soldier, complete with lance and bow and arrows. The grip is solid ivory stained black. *Major General (Ret.) Theodore W. Paulson Collection. Photo by Major General (Ret.) Theodore W. Paulson.*

A more impressive or embellished sword hilt backstrap is not to be found than the beautiful backstrap decorating the unique *Freiherr von Barnekow* Presentation Damascus Sword. Note the attractive family crest. The raised gold lettering on the spine of the blade reads, *"Echtdamast Eisenhauer"* (Best quality genuine Damascus steel). *Major General (Ret.) Theodore W. Paulson Collection. Photo by Major General (Ret.) Theodore W. Paulson.*

Swords of the German Army during the Imperial Era

Field Marshal *Herzog Albert von Württemberg* was Commander in Chief of the *Grenadier* Regiment Queen Olga Nr.119. The Field Marshal is shown wearing a *"Grosser"* pattern Lion head saber complete with Guard Star on the langet. The private purchase *"Grosser"* pattern Lion head saber is one of the most desirable Imperial edged weapons. The photo is dated July 1916. *LTC (Ret.) Thomas M. Johnson Photo Collection.*

This decorated Imperial officer is wearing the rarely seen Eagle head pommel officer saber. This model was worn exclusively by the *Mecklenburg* Artillery units. This rare Imperial sword was WK&C Model Nr.275. *LTC (Ret.) Thomas M. Johnson Photo Collection.*

In this wedding photograph, the groom, an Imperial German Army Officer, wears what appears to be a *Mecklenburg* Artillery Officer's basket hilt sword with Eagle head pommel. Under close examination, the grenade motif is visible on the obverse langet. Note the highly polished *Pickelhaube* clutched in the officer's left hand. Although the photograph is undated, it is obviously late in World War I, as the officer is wearing the 1915 pattern field gray *Bluse*. Photo courtesy of SSGT (Ret.) T. Wayne Cunningham, (USAF).

Fürst Leopold zu Lippe.

Fürst Leopold zu Lippe is pictured wearing the ultra-rare highly chiseled Eagle head Imperial saber. Lippe is a very small principality comprised of less than 500 square miles. *LTC (Ret.) Thomas M. Johnson Photo Collection. Photo by E. Bleber, Hamburg.*

Artillery Officer's Lion head sword. Etched blade example features heavy chiseled hilt design with crossed cannons decorating the langet. Scabbard is blued steel with brass scabbard band. Grip is blue sharkskin. *Robert Johnston Collection. Photo by Charles H. Jenkins, III.*

Artillery sergeant with *"Grosser"* pattern Lion head saber. The tie of the sword knot and the deeply cast cannons on the langet are easily visible. *LTC (Ret.) Thomas M. Johnson Photo Collection. Photo by H. Dallmann, Iserlohn.*

OPPOSITE
Wartime photo of an Imperial NCO in the Field Artillery Regiment No.20. The crossed cannons and officer sword portepee are readily visible in the photograph. *LTC (Ret.) Thomas M. Johnson Photo Collection. Photo by Kruse & Carstensen, Thorn.*

A *Vizefeldwebel* in the *2nd Hannover Feldartillerie Regiment No.26*. The NCO is wearing a beautiful Lion head saber with crossed cannons on the langet complete with officer sword knot. The scabbard is painted black and has only one ring as directed by regulations in 1910. *LTC (Ret.) Thomas M. Johnson Photo Collection. Photo by F. Renrichhausen, Hannover.*

Swords of the German Army during the Imperial Era

A magnificent artillery officer's Lion head saber. The blade is of the English Rod Back variety (quill back), and is marked *"Eisenhauer"* (iron cutting blade). The cast Lion head has ruby glass eyes. The knucklebow is highly engraved, ending in a Panther head quillon end. The langet features the typical crossed cannons. The fishskin grip is double silver wire-wrapped. The cloth officer's knot is typical of the type seen before 1896. After that period, most officer knots contained a leather strap. *Edward M. Owen, Jr. Collection. Photo by Edward M. Owen, Jr.*

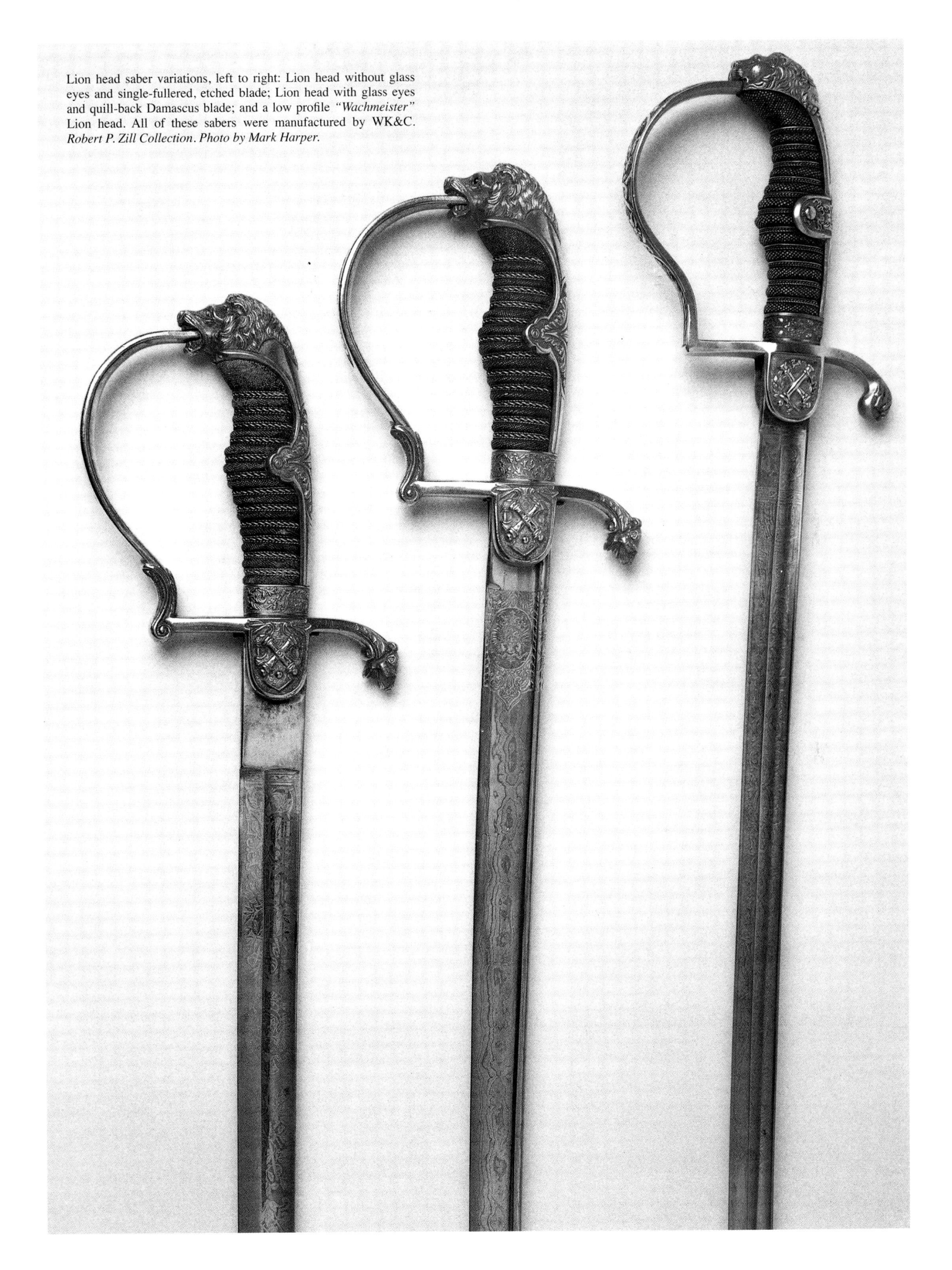

Lion head saber variations, left to right: Lion head without glass eyes and single-fullered, etched blade; Lion head with glass eyes and quill-back Damascus blade; and a low profile *"Wachmeister"* Lion head. All of these sabers were manufactured by WK&C. *Robert P. Zill Collection. Photo by Mark Harper.*

Imperial German Edged Weaponry

This photograph provides an excellent view of the obverse hilt on a highly detailed Imperial Lion head artillery saber. Note the raised crossed cannons on the obverse langet and the small Lion head at the tip of the crossguard. *LTC (Ret.) Thomas M. Johnson Collection. Photo by LTC (Ret.) Thomas M. Johnson.*

Extreme close-up photograph of the obverse crossguard and langet on the exquisite Imperial Deluxe Lion head artillery sword. Note the beautiful chased work on each and every metal component to include the grip ferrule. The grip is wrapped in black sharkskin. *LTC (Ret.) Thomas M. Johnson Collection. Photo by LTC (Ret.) Thomas M. Johnson.*

Shown is the exceptional knucklebow on the Imperial Deluxe Lion head artillery saber. Compare this exquisite workmanship to the more commonly seen plain knucklebow. The reverse langet is void of the original owner's crest or initials. *LTC (Ret.) Thomas M. Johnson Collection. Photo by LTC (Ret.) Thomas M. Johnson.*

ABOVE: A Sergeant in the *Field Artillery Regiment von Scharnhorst, (1st Hannover) No.10* is pictured wearing his deluxe pattern Lion head Artillery saber with portepee. The knucklebow and quillon end of this pattern saber allow the leather strap *Prussian* portepee to be easily tied and handsomely displayed. This period photograph provides an exceptional view of the accouterments associated with the Imperial Artillery saber. *LTC (Ret.) Thomas M. Johnson Photo Collection. Photo by Aug. Nolte, Hannover.*

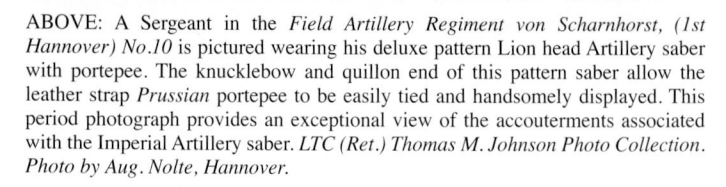

TOP RIGHT: A *Prussian Leutnant* (Lieutenant) of Artillery poses with his own Lion head saber with officer sword knot. The Artillery crossed cannons on the obverse langet are very discernible in this clear period photograph. *LTC (Ret.) Thomas M. Johnson Photo Collection.*

RIGHT: A 1918 photograph of a newly commissioned officer in the *Laurenburg Foot Artillery Regiment, No.20*. The Lion head saber is without glass eyes and carries a langet featuring crossed sabers, rather than the expected crossed cannons. *LTC (Ret.) Thomas M. Johnson Photo Collection.*

Pictured is a museum quality Imperial Damascus Shooting Award Sword presented to *Herrn Ernst Wolkertz* for his 1897-1898 service. This superb example shows the highest caliber swordsmaker art, and the engraving is spectacular. The exceptional grip is a perfect example of what the Germans refer to as "*Hochfein Ziseliert*" (superfine chiseling). The obverse langet features crossed cannon barrels. The sharkskin grip is in perfect condition with a tight triple wire wrap. *Richard R. Williams Collection. Photo by Dick Scott Fine Photography, Houston.*

Imperial German Edged Weaponry

Reverse color view of the magnificent "*Ernst Wolkertz*" Imperial Damascus Shooting Award Sword. The reverse blade features the inscription, "*Gewidmet von Wilh. Ernst Wolkertz 1897-1898*". The sword was presented from fellow officer Morsbach to Wolkertz. The dent-free nickel scabbard is complete with two brass scabbard bands. *Richard R. Williams Collection. Photo by Dick Scott Fine Photography, Houston.*

Close-up view of the obverse blade on the outstanding "*Wolkertz*" Lion head Damascus Shooting Award Sword. The obverse blade is a beautiful large "rosebud" pattern and contains the following raised inscription in silver lettering: "*Unsem Verehrten Schutzenkonig Herrn Ernst Wolkertz 1897-1898*" (Presented to the Shooting King Mr. Ernst Wolkertz 1897-1898). *Richard R. Williams Collection. Photo by Dick Scott Fine Photography, Houston.*

The reverse blade on "*Wolkertz*" Lion head Damascus Shooting Award Sword contains the inscription "*Gewidmet von Wilh. Küll. H. Morsbach*" in raised silver lettering. *Richard R. Williams Collection. Photo by Dick Scott Fine Photography, Houston.*

Imperial German Edged Weaponry

Close-up color view of the *"Grosser"* obverse hilt of the *"Wolkertz"* Artillery Shooting Sword. Note the exceptional workmanship displayed throughout the entire hilt. The Lion head hilt is complete with red glass "ruby" eyes. The ricasso of the presentation "rosebud" Damascus steel blade bears both *"Eisenhauer"* (Best quality steel) and *"Echt Damast"* (Genuine Damascus) in ribbon panels. *Richard R. Williams Collection. Photo by Dick Scott Fine Photography, Houston.*

Swords of the German Army during the Imperial Era

The reverse view of the hilt of the *"Wolkertz" Grosser* Artillery Shooting Sword shows the original owner's initials intertwined on a plain shield on the reverse langet. Note the exceptional "large rosebud" Damascus pattern on the reverse blade. *Richard R. Williams Collection. Photo by Dick Scott Fine Photography, Houston.*

The outer knucklebow on the Imperial Damascus Shooting Award Sword without maker features an intricately sculptured Royal crown. The Imperial factory sales catalogs describe work of this quality as *"Hochfein Ziseliert"* (superfine chiseling). Note the extra large red glass eyes mounted in the Lion head pommel. *Richard R. Williams Collection. Photo by Dick Scott Fine Photography, Houston.*

A decorated Field Artillery officer wearing the preferred Lion head saber with attached sword knot. The artillery crossed cannons are easily seen on the obverse langet. *LTC (Ret.) Thomas M. Johnson Photo Collection.*

Prussian Artillery Officer with Lion head saber. The Lion Head is without ruby glass eyes. The crossed cannons are clearly visible on the langet, and the sword knot shows the standard "tie" for this saber. The under-the-tunic hanger with Lion head strap is also pictured. *LTC (Ret.) Thomas M. Johnson Photo Collection. Copy Photo by Charles H. Jenkins, III.*

Pictured in color is an obverse view of the Lieutenant Von Ribbentrop Presentation Imperial Lion head Sword by the *Clemen und Jung* firm in Solingen. This superb Imperial presentation sword features a museum quality Damascus steel blade. This sword was presented to *Leutnant von Ribbentrop* by *Leutnant Freiherr von Wangenheim* while they both were assigned to the Field Artillery Marksmanship School Training Regiment at *Jüterbog* (of Berlin). *Richard R. Williams Collection. Photo by Dick Scott Fine Photography, Houston.*

Imperial German Edged Weaponry

Reverse color view of the *Leutnant von Ribbentrop* Presentation Imperial Lion head Sword by *Clemen und Jung*. The near-mint reverse Damascus blade features a 20-inch long blue and gilt panel inscribed, *"Frhr. Von Wangenheim s./l. von Ribbentrop"*. Richard R. Williams Collection. Photo by Dick Scott Fine Photography, Houston.

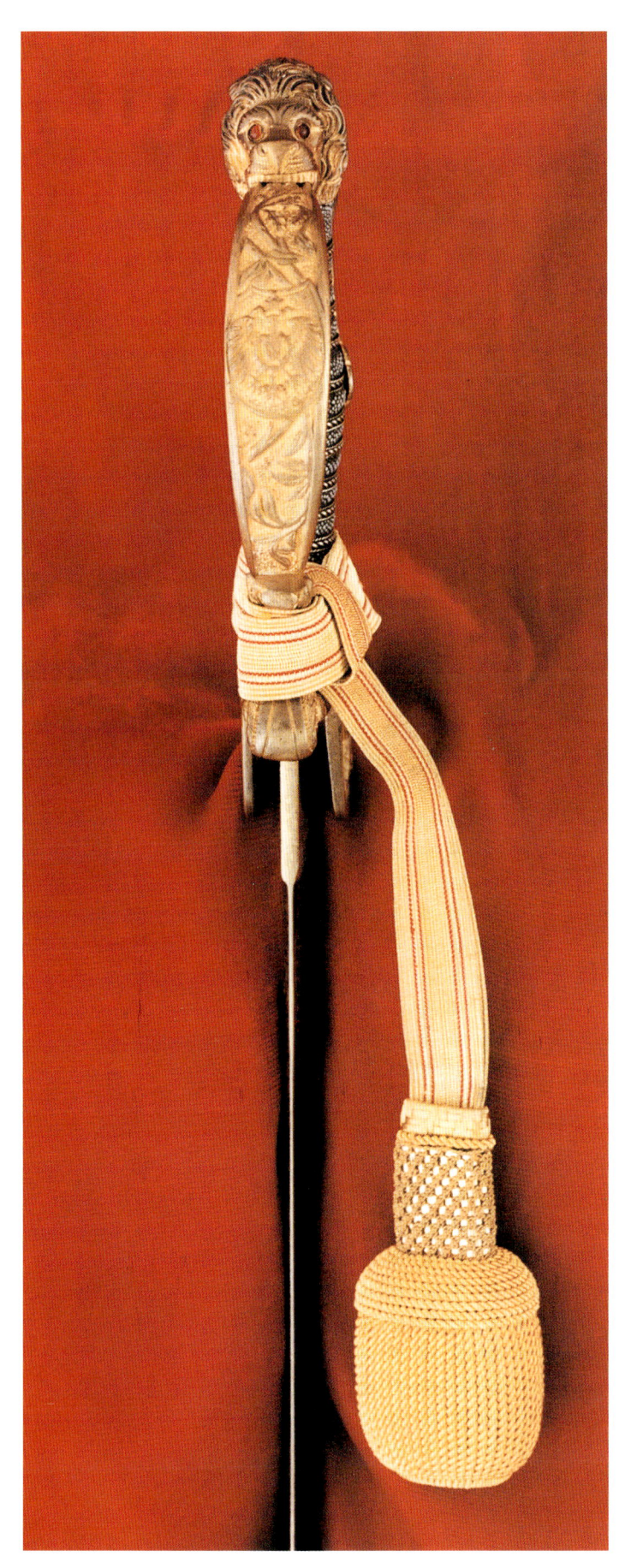

Swords of the German Army during the Imperial Era

The unique knucklebow on the *Leutnant von Ribbentrop Clemen und Jung* Imperial Lion head Sword features a central motif of a raised Imperial German eagle beneath the Imperial crown. The underside of the crossguard is stamped, *"Geschutz Müster"* (sample) beside the *Clemen und Jung* company trademark. Richard R. Williams Collection. Photo by Dick Scott Fine Photography, Houston.

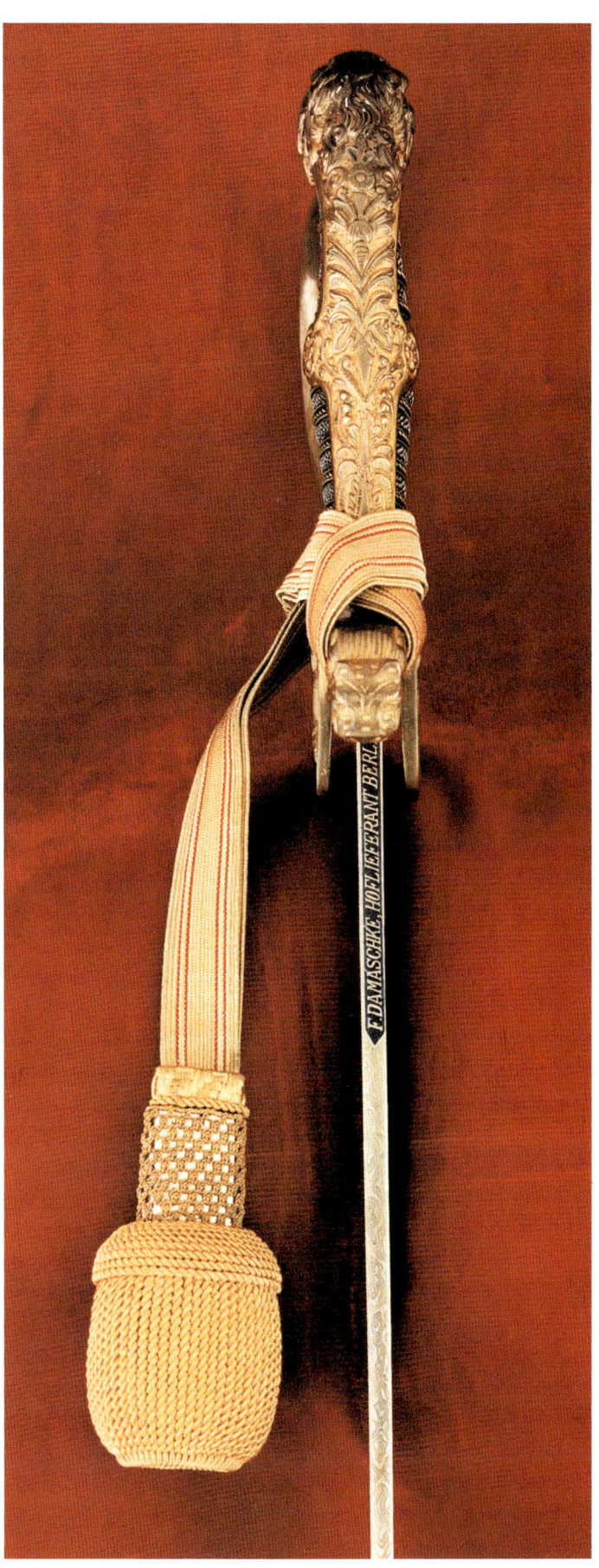

The spine of the Damascus steel blade on the *Clemen und Jung "Lt. Von Ribbentrop"* Imperial Lion head Sword features, *"F. Damaschke, Hoflieferant, Berlin"* in raised gold letters on a dark blue background. The sword is complete with its original Imperial sword knot. Richard R. Williams Collection. Photo by Dick Scott Fine Photography, Houston.

Presentation *"Grosser"* Artillery Lion head sword with Damascus blade. This ornate Imperial sword features a heavily-chiseled, gilded brass hilt without glass eyes, a floral and oak leaf embellished backstrap, oak leaf and acorn detailed knucklebow and crossguard. The obverse langet features a floral pattern background with a pinned-on silver artillery motif badge, which features crossed artillery barrels interlaced with an oak leaf wreath. The obverse blade bears the presentation, *"von Ditfurth s./l. Winkler"* (von Ditfurth to his dear friend Winkler). The sword was presented on or about 1898. *Richard R. Williams Collection. Photo by Dick Scott Fine Photography, Houston.*

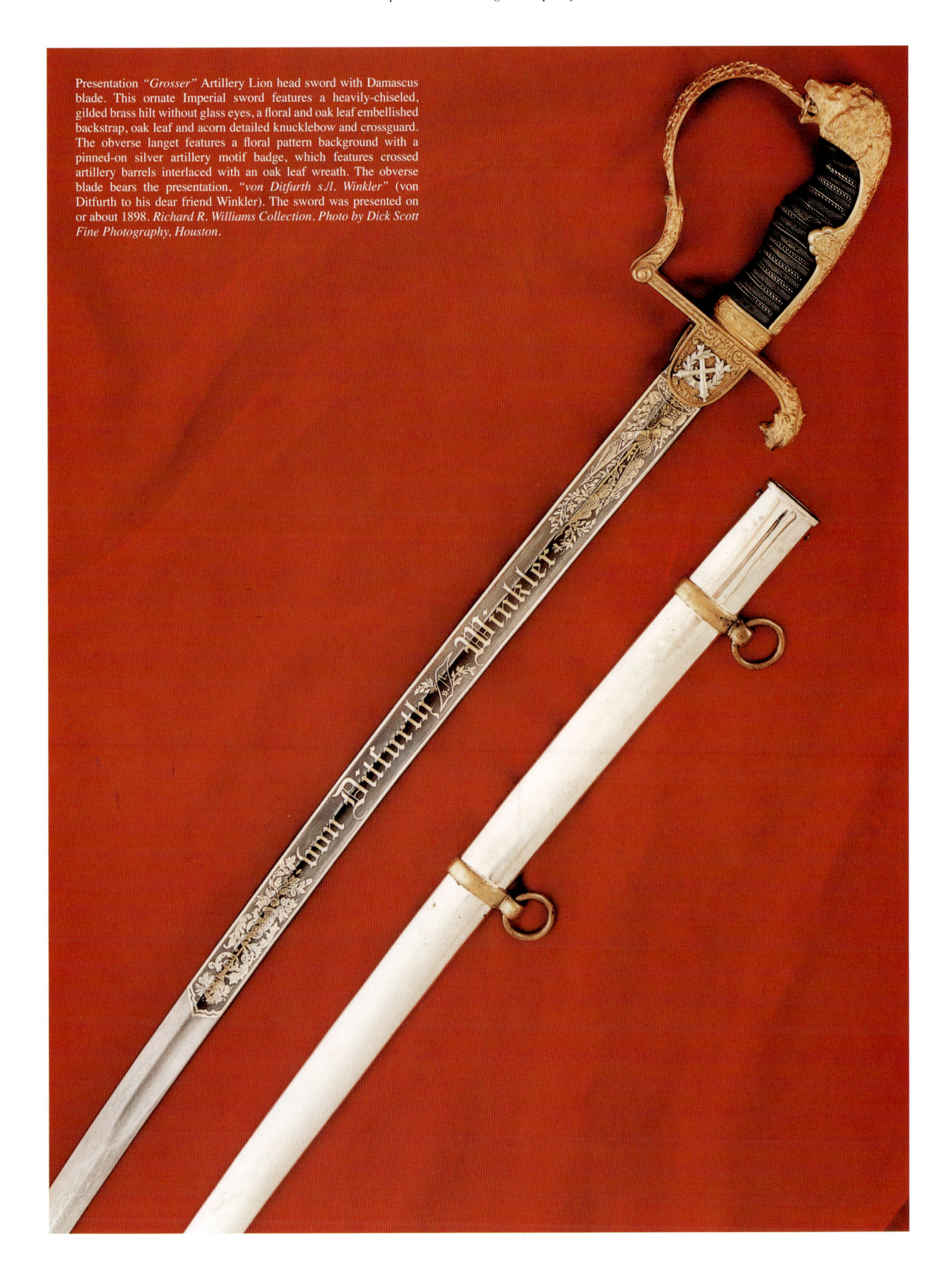

Reverse view of the exquisite *"Winkler"* Presentation Artillery Lion head Sword with Damascus blade. The reverse blade is inscribed, *"Feldartill.=Rgt. (Schleswigsches) Nr.9 General=Feldmarschall Graf Waldersee"*, flanked on each end by a floral pattern and military motif. The nickel-plated scabbard is complete with double brass suspension rings. *Richard R. Williams Collection. Photo by Dick Scott Fine Photography, Houston.*

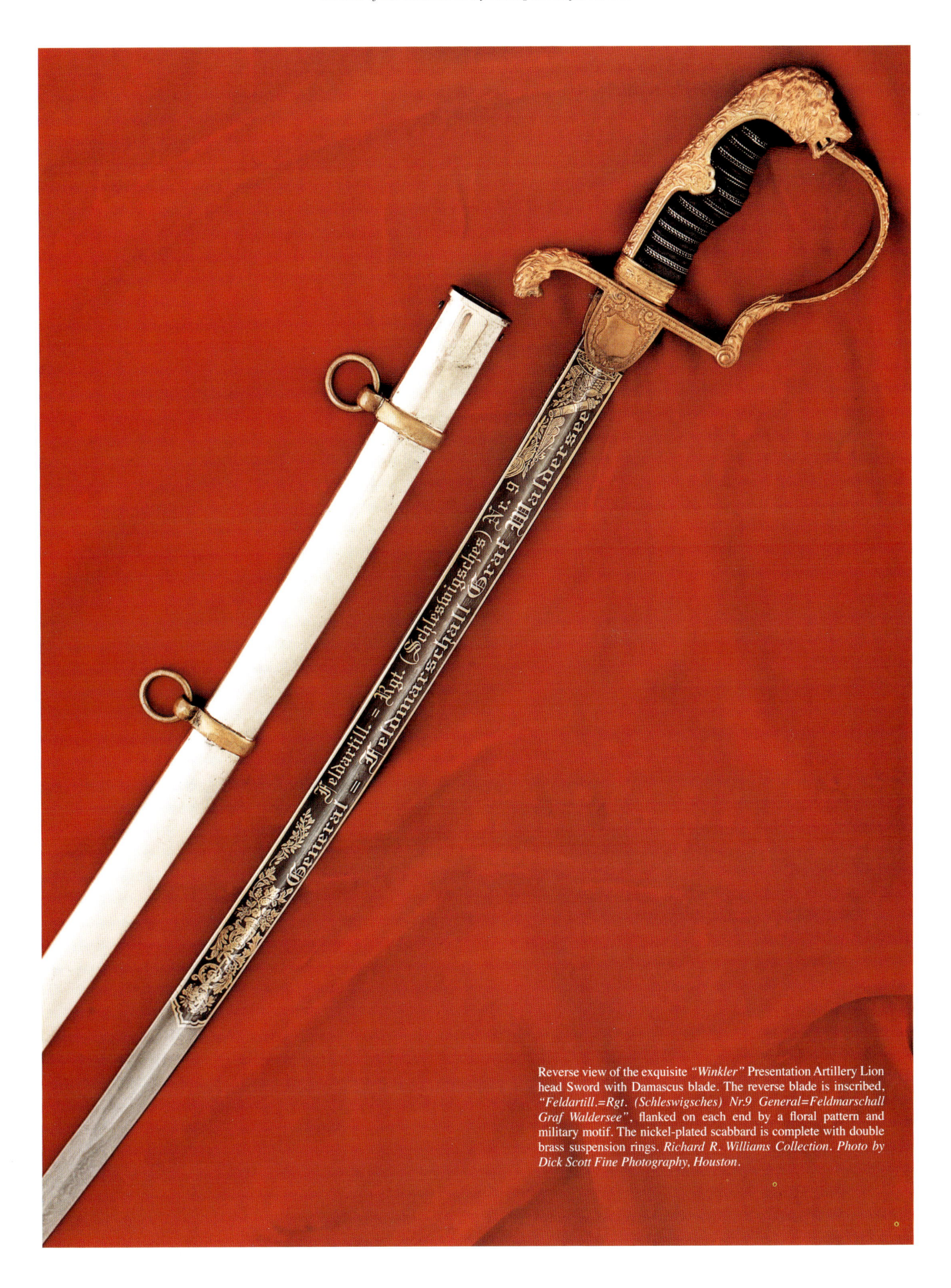

Imperial German Edged Weaponry

Excellent close-up view of the obverse hilt on the *"Winkler"* Presentation *"Grosser"* Lion head Damascus Sword. The silver artillery cannons and wreath are pinned to the obverse langet. Note also the artillery motif displayed on the upper obverse blade. *Richard R. Williams Collection. Photo by Dick Scott Fine Photography, Houston.*

Pictured is a close-up view of the heavily chiseled oak leaf and acorn-detailed outer knucklebow on the *"Winkler"* Presentation Artillery Lion head Sword with Damascus blade. The sharkskin grip is complete with the standard tight triple-wire wrap. *Richard R. Williams Collection. Photo by Dick Scott Fine Photography, Houston.*

ABOVE: This formal studio period photograph provides an excellent view of an Artillery saber "in-wear". Note the crossed cannons on the obverse langet and the nickel single-ring scabbard. *LTC (Ret.) Thomas M. Johnson Photo Collection. Photo by R. Fender's Studio, Magdeburg.*

TOP RIGHT: A wartime Lion head saber worn by an officer in the Royal *Saxon* 2nd Field Artillery Regiment Nr.28. Notice the crossed cannons clearly seen on the obverse langet of his sword. *LTC (Ret.) Thomas M. Johnson Photo Collection. Photo by Alex Möhlen, Hannover.*

RIGHT: An artillery General Major is pictured wearing his Great Coat. The fine detail of his exquisite Lion head saber is observed. The silver crossed cannons on the langet are pinned to the hilt. *LTC (Ret.) Thomas M. Johnson Photo Collection. Photo by H. Noack, Berlin.*

Prussian artillery and infantry Regimental officers observe a field artillery unit during the annual "*Kaiser*" Maneuvers" of 1907. The artillery officers with their ball top spiked helmets prefer the Lion head saber in the *"Wachmeister"* pattern, and the crossed cannons are clearly seen on the langets. The weapon of choice of the infantry officers, is the infantry officer *Degen* model 1889 with fixed clamshell. The correct tie of the sword knot is easily observed. *LTC (Ret.) Thomas M. Johnson Photo Collection. Photo by Oscar Teligmann, Eschwege.*

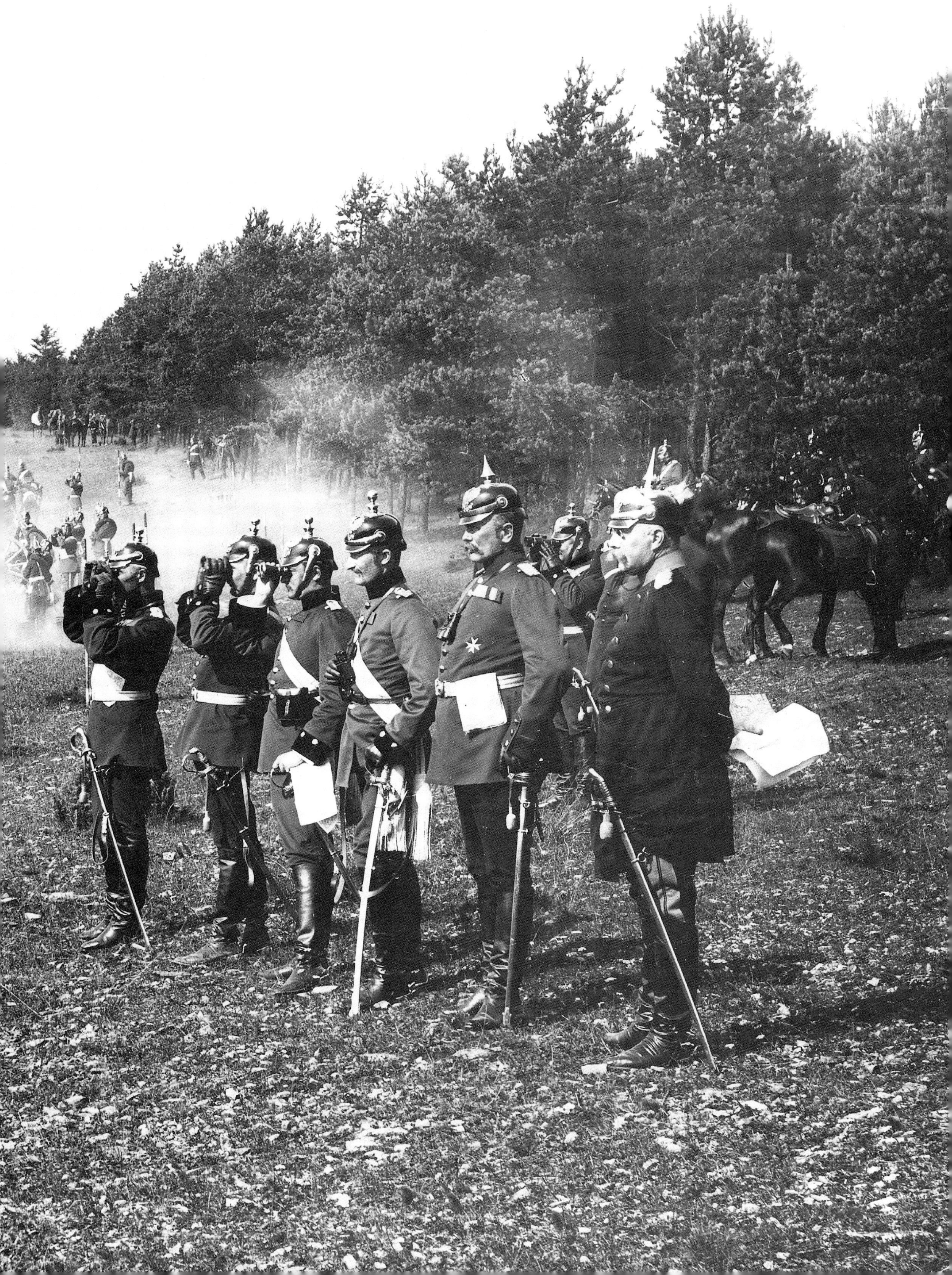

Imperial German Edged Weaponry

Presentation *"von Ravensburg" Grosser* Artillery Lion head Imperial Damascus Sword. This sword was presented by *Leutnant Brinkman* to *Leutnant Göler von Ravensburg* to commemorate their 1891/1892 time at the *Kriegschule* at Metz. The maker is WK&C, Solingen. The sword is complete with its original sword knot. *Richard R. Williams Collection. Photo by Dick Scott Fine Photography, Houston.*

Swords of the German Army during the Imperial Era

Pictured in color is the reverse view of the magnificent *"Grosser"* Presentation Imperial Lion head artillery sword by WK&C. The massive 1 3/8 inch wide curved, double-etched quillback Damascus blade features gilt raised laurel leaves surrounding a blued three-ribbon presentation panel inscribed in raised gilt Gothic letters, *"Brinkmann s./l. Göler v. Ravensburg, Metz 1891/1892"* (Brinkmann to his dear friend von Ravensburg, Metz (city) 1891/1892). This sword was apparently presented by *Leutnant* Brinkmann to his close friend *Leutnant* Göler von Ravensburg to commemorate their two years together at the *Kriegschule* in Metz. *Richard R. Williams Collection. Photo by Dick Scott Fine Photography, Houston.*

Imperial German Edged Weaponry

The *"Menzel"* Presentation *"Grosser"* Artillery Lion head Damascus sword is a magnificent Imperial *"Grosser"* Lion head sword with much fine chiseling and hand enhancing along the knucklebow, backstrap, and crossguard. The front of the knucklebow contains the seldom seen on edged weapons Imperial motto, *"Gott Mit Uns"* cast into the knucklebow. The obverse langet contains an unusual Lion head with crossed silver artillery barrels containing flaming projectiles. The reverse langet has a shield with the intertwined initials of Fritz Menzel. The gold knot on the sword has, obviously, been attached for a long time but does not appear to be Imperial German but possibly 1890s American Navy. The sword was presented circa May 1900. Note that the scabbard still has its nickel finish and the unusual ornate scabbard bands. The beautiful "maiden hair" Damascus blade features a 12 inch panel of blue gray and gold with military equipment at one end and a floral design at the other. In the middle of gilt gothic lettering is the presentation, *"Umbeck s./ l. Menzel"* (Umbeck to his dear friend Menzel). *Richard R. Williams Collection. Photo by Dick Scott Fine Photography, Houston.*

Close-up color view of the obverse hilt of the magnificent *"Menzel"* Presentation Artillery Lion head sword. Note the highly unusual obverse langet which features a three-dimensional Lion head and crossed silver artillery barrels with flaming balls. The unusual sword knot is not believed to be of German origin, but it has apparently been on this sword for many years. *Richard R. Williams Collection. Photo by Dick Scott Fine Photography, Houston.*

Imperial German Edged Weaponry

Close-up color view of the reverse hilt of the spectacular *"Menzel"* Presentation Artillery Lion head sword. The reverse langet shows the original owner's initials intertwined on a shield. The stunning blue and gold reverse blade ricasso shows that the blade is superior genuine Damascus steel. Obviously, an old-world Solingen swordsmith crafted this beautiful masterpiece. *Richard R. Williams Collection. Photo by Dick Scott Fine Photography, Houston.*

The reverse blade on the *"Menzel"* Presentation Artillery Lion head Damascus sword features a raised gold inscription on a gray background which reads, *"Für Ehr und Pflicht bis Herz und Klinge bricht"* (For honor and duty until heart and sword break). Note that the scabbard still has its nickel finish and unusually ornate scabbard bands. *Richard R. Williams Collection. Photo by Dick Scott Fine Photography, Houston.*

This outstanding color photograph provides the reader with a clear view of the *"Menzel"* Presentation *"Grosser"* Artillery Lion head Damascus Sword. The seldom seen on edged weapons Imperial motto, *"Gott Mit Uns"* is cast into the mint condition knucklebow. The impressive *"Grosser"* Lion head hilt is complete with red glass eyes. The gold sword knot is not original to the piece. *Richard R. Williams Collection. Photo by Dick Scott Fine Photography, Houston.*

Imperial German Edged Weaponry

The obverse blade of a splendid Lion head Artillery Saber by WK&C. A translation of the obverse blade dedication reads, "*Lubner* to his dear friend, *Baum*". Stephen Wolfe Collection. Photo Courtesy of Stephen Wolfe.

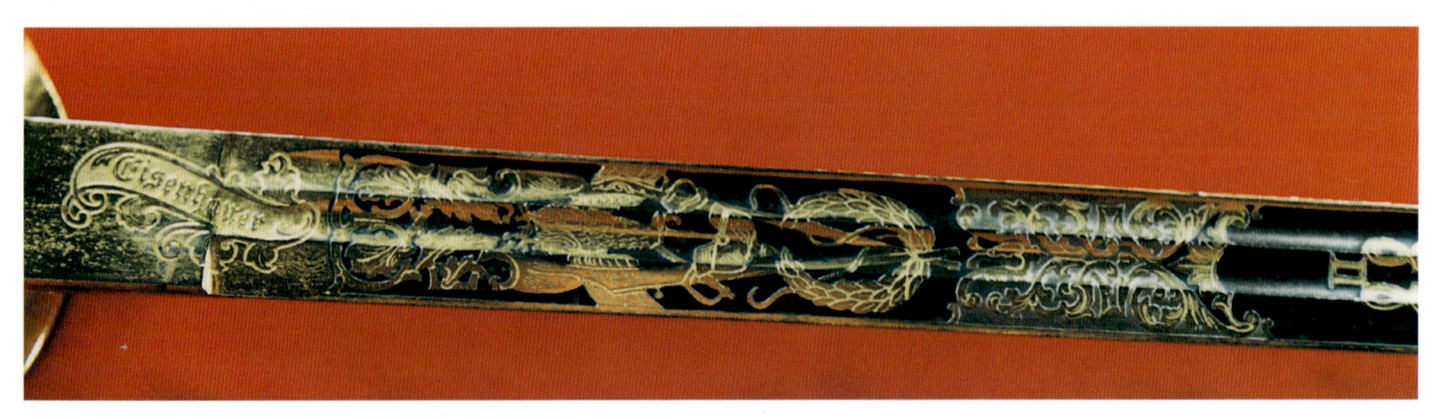

Honor Prize *Degen*. The *"Grosser"* size Infantry Officer *Degen* is fitted with a magnificent fullered Damascus blade. The obverse blued and gilded panel features military equipment and the Royal cypher. The scrolled *"Eisenhauer"* blade designation is also in gold. The blade is marked "WK&C" on the spine. Stephen Wolfe Collection. Photo Courtesy of Stephen Wolfe.

The reverse panel exclaims the universal axiom, "One for All, All for One". The saber is attributed to the firm of Weyersberg, Kirschbaum and Company (WK&C). WK&C was Solingen's most famous edged weapon producing concern during the Imperial era. The company was founded in 1883 by the joining of *Gebrüder Weyersberg* and *W. R. Kirschbaum & Cie*. Stephen Wolfe Collection. Photo Courtesy of Stephen Wolfe.

OPPOSITE
Obverse hilt of an Imperial Presentation Lion head Artillery Saber with genuine Damascus steel blade. Note the raised crossed cannons on the obverse langet and the small Lion head on the tip of the crossguard. The large Lion head pommel is complete with red glass eyes. The sword is seated in a nickel scabbard. LTC (Ret.) Thomas M. Johnson Collection. Photo by LTC (Ret.) Thomas M. Johnson.

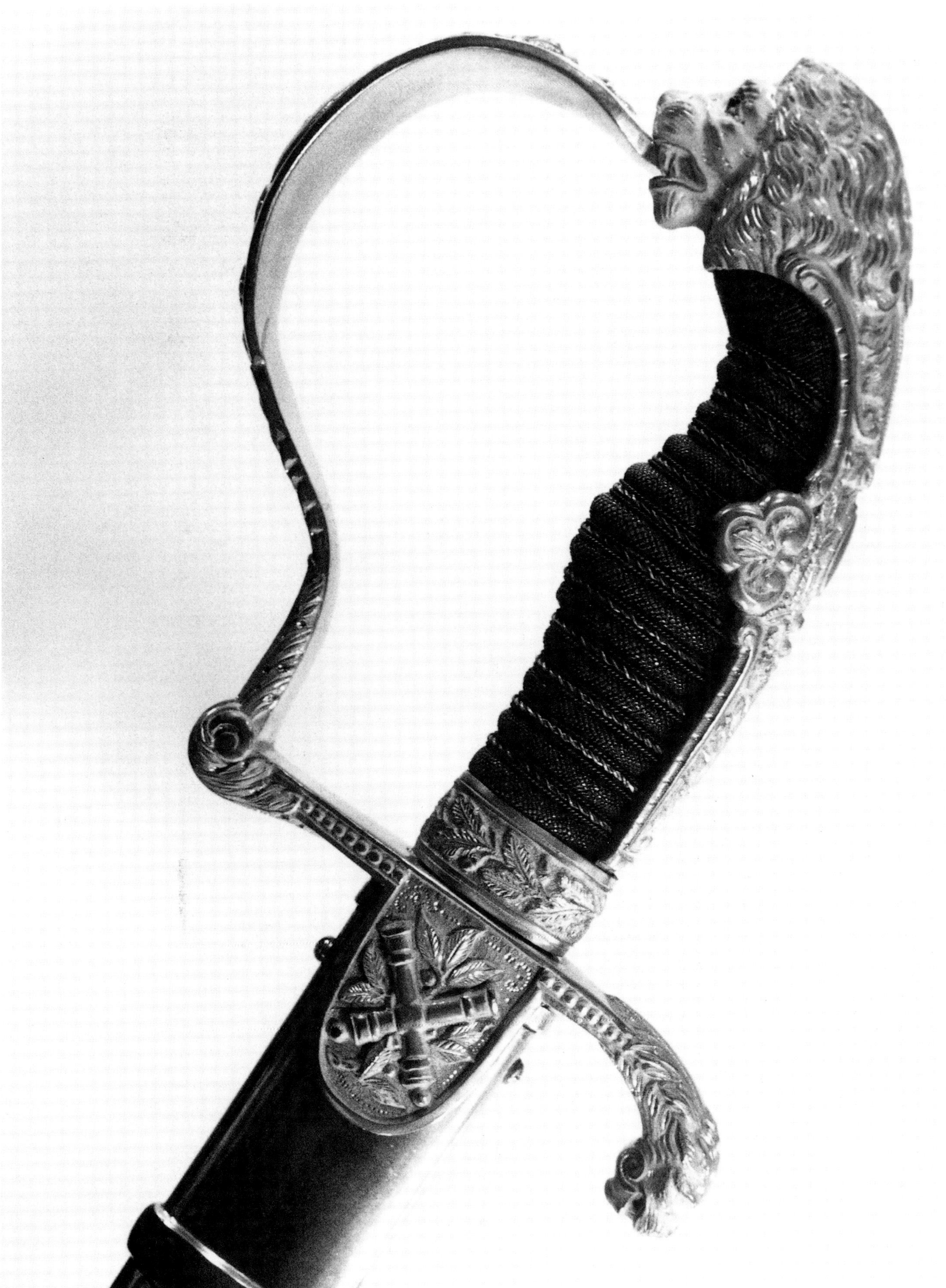

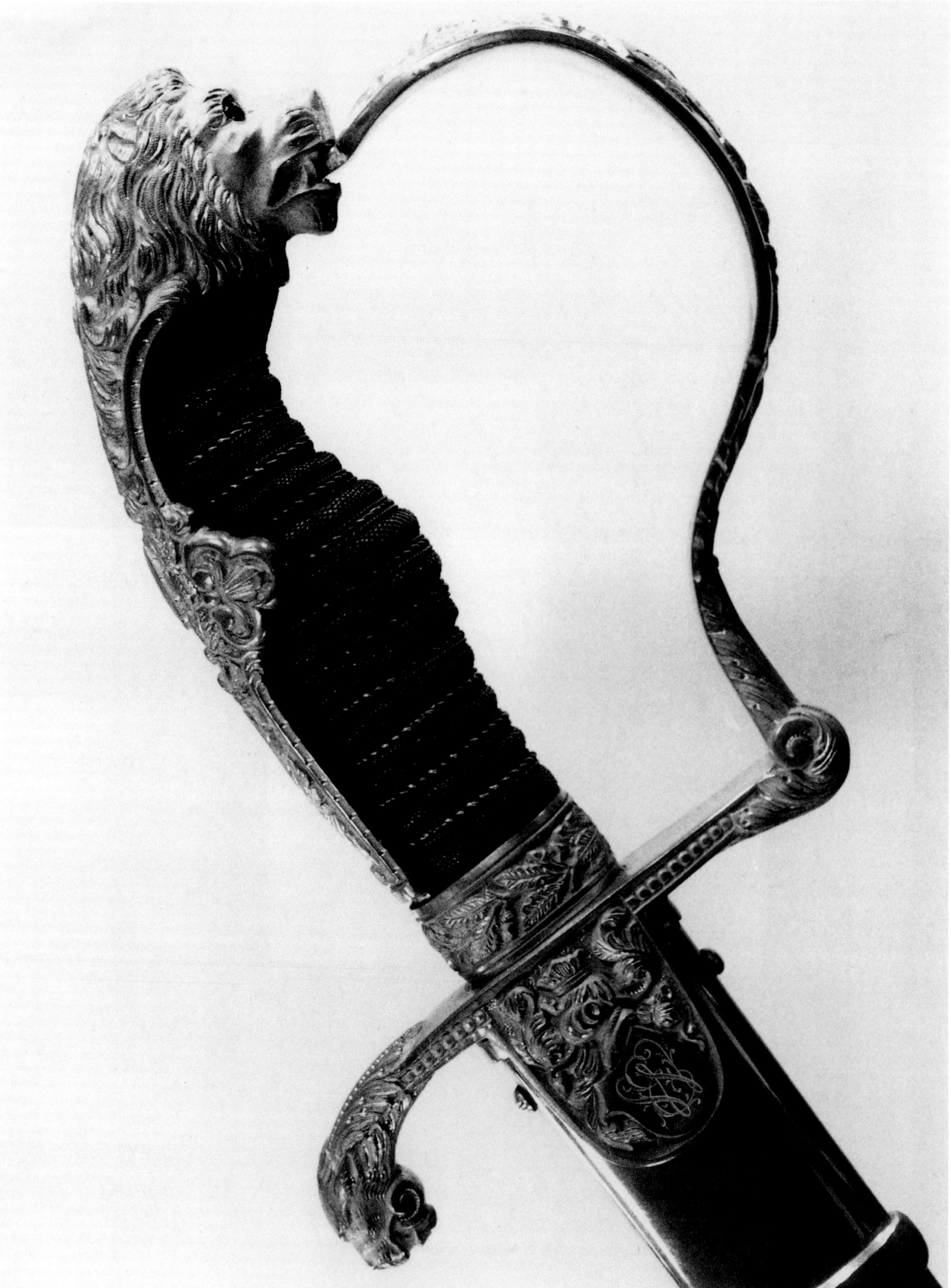

OPPOSITE
Reverse view of the Imperial Lion head Presentation Artillery Saber with genuine Damascus steel blade. Both the original owner's family crest or city crest and initials are displayed on the reverse langet. This high-quality Artillery sword is in exceptional condition. *LTC (Ret.) Thomas M. Johnson Collection. Photo by LTC (Ret.) Thomas M. Johnson.*

Close-up black and white view of the obverse genuine Damascus steel blade on the Imperial Lion head Presentation Artillery Saber. The blade dedication provides not only the original owner's full name but also the date of the presentation. The *Echt-Damast* in a ribbon denotes a top quality Damascus blade. *LTC (Ret.) Thomas M. Johnson Collection. Photo by LTC (Ret.) Thomas M. Johnson.*

Close-up black and white view of the dedication on the reverse Damascus steel blade on the Imperial Lion head Presentation Artillery Saber. The presenter's full name is highlighted in a panel on the reverse blade. *LTC (Ret.) Thomas M. Johnson Collection. Photo by LTC (Ret.) Thomas M. Johnson.*

Pictured is a close-up view of the obverse tip of the genuine Damascus steel blade on the Imperial Lion head Presentation Artillery Saber. The name of the Damascus steel blade pattern is "Large Rosebud". *LTC (Ret.) Thomas M. Johnson Collection. Photo by LTC (Ret.) Thomas M. Johnson.*

No. 806.
Natürl. Grösse.

Preussischer Kavallerie- und Artillerie-Offizier-Säbel mit Parderkopf- und Augen, hochfein ziseliert.

The Carl Eickhorn factory Imperial Edged Weaponry sales catalog depicts the company's Model #806 in actual size. The accompanying caption reads, *"Preussischer Kavallerie-und Artillerie-Offizier-Säbel mit Parderkopf und Augen, hochfein ziselier"*. (Prussian Cavalry and Artillery Officer Saber with Lion head and eyes, finely chiseled.) *Johnson Reference Books & Militaria Archives.*

Swords of the German Army during the Imperial Era

Pictured is a very interesting Franco Prussian Lion head presentation saber presented to a Major Hübsch by the officers of *Regiment #15,3. Schliesisches Dragoner.* Of special note is the highly unusual steel scabbard with an individual crowned eagle forming each of the two scabbard bands. *Jason P. Burmeister Collection. Photo by Charles H. Jenkins, III.*

Imperial German Edged Weaponry

The ornate Franco Prussian Lion head presentation saber is pictured out of its scabbard. The beautiful blue and gold Damascus steel blade features the names of the unit officers. The last name on the listing belonged to the unit *Wachmeister* or Senior NCO of the regiment. The word *"Eisenhaur"* (best quality steel) appears in a banner just under the mounted horseman. *Jason P. Burmeister Collection. Photo by Charles H. Jenkins, III.*

Swords of the German Army during the Imperial Era

Reverse view of the interesting Franco Prussian Lion head presentation saber given to Major Hübsch upon his departure. Note that the crowned eagle's motif on the scabbard bands is repeated on the scabbard reverse. *Jason P. Burmeister Collection. Photo by Charles H. Jenkins, III.*

Imperial German Edged Weaponry

Swords of the German Army during the Imperial Era

OPPOSITE
Reverse view of the ornate Franco Prussian Lion head presentation saber pictured out of its scabbard. The reverse side of the outstanding blue and gold Damascus steel blade features the dates "1870" and "1871" and the names of various campaigns that the unit participated in. The two years of 1870 and 1871 most likely represent the length of service time for the recipient before his departure. The words, *"Echt Damast"* (genuine Damascus) appear directly under the figure of winged victory on the reverse blade. INSET: Extreme close-up detail of one of the highly unusual crowned eagle motif scabbard bands on the interesting Franco Prussian Lion head presentation saber. *Jason P. Burmeister Collection. Photo by Charles H. Jenkins, III.*

This Franco Prussian War veteran is wearing his Lion head saber with early leather and nickel mounted scabbard. An early bullion knot adorns the hilt. *LTC (Ret.) Thomas M. Johnson Photo Collection. Photo by Ateuer Ehrlich, Dresden.*

Imperial German Edged Weaponry

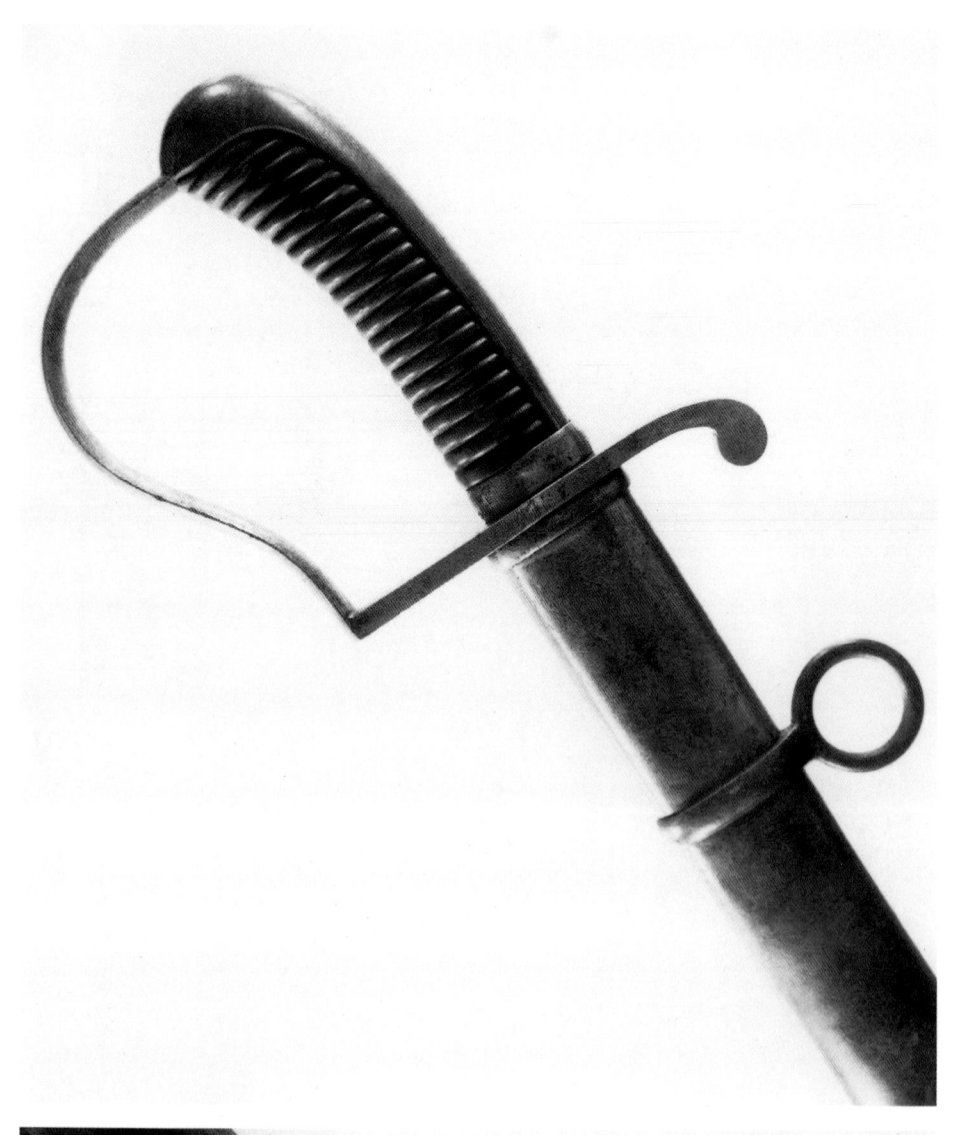

Close-up view of the hilt and upper scabbard of an enlisted *Saxon* Artillery sword. The black composition grip is ribbed while the reverse "P" guard's quillon terminates in a disc finial. The back strap is iron with a smooth pommel cap. A single 5/8 inch fuller runs nearly the length of the slightly curved 29 5/8 inch blade. A crowned, unidentified to date, monogram is highlighted on the spine. The iron scabbard has a single fixed carrying ring while the scabbard drag is stamped. *LTC (Ret.) Thomas M. Johnson Collection. Photo by LTC (Ret.) Thomas M. Johnson.*

View of the blade ricasso of the *Saxon* enlisted sword showing the manufacturer's name and location (WK&C, Solingen). *LTC (Ret.) Thomas M. Johnson Collection. Photo by LTC (Ret.) Thomas M. Johnson.*

If the soldier came to the photo studio without a personal sidearm, the studio would provide one. On occasion the photo studio "prop" sword for a formal portrait resulted in the sword being too long for the young soldiers being photographed. *LTC (Ret.) Thomas M. Johnson Photo Collection.*

Gefreiter in the *Royal Saxon 2nd Field Artillery Regiment No.28* wearing his nickel Artillery saber with *Faustriemen*. As can be seen, the slot in the guard for attaching the sword knot was rarely, if ever, used. *LTC (Ret.) Thomas M. Johnson Photo Collection. Photo by H. Schulze, Bautzen.*

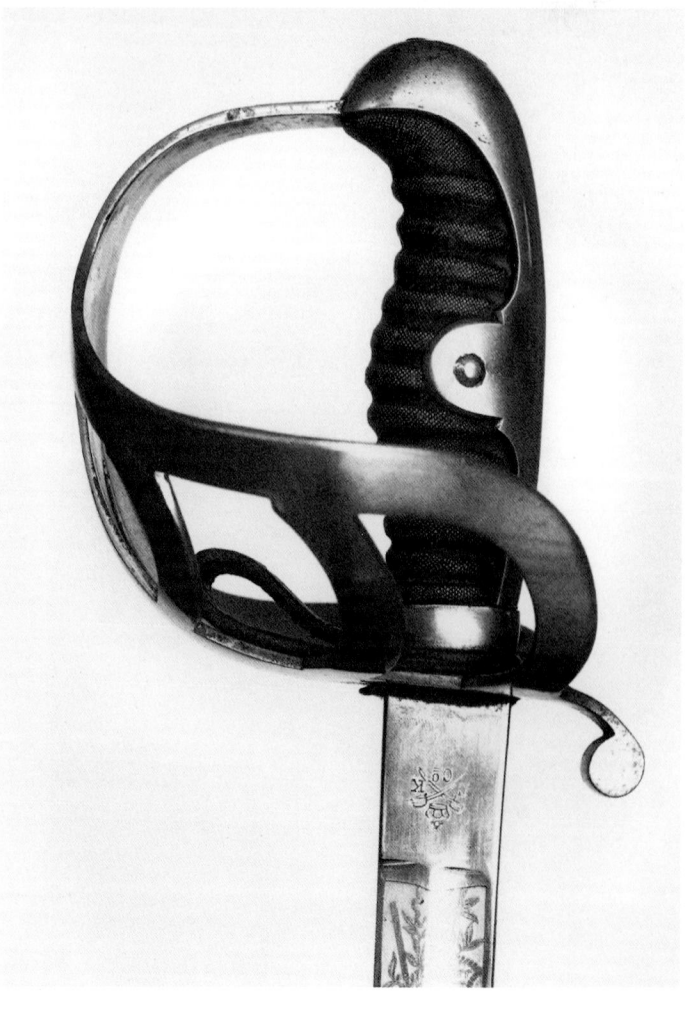

ABOVE: Bavarian private who is a member of the *9th Infantry Regiment "Wrede"* is pictured wearing for this portrait a heavy cavalry saber complete with *Faustriemen*. Note the severe dents in the scabbard. *LTC (Ret.) Thomas M. Johnson Photo Collection.*

TOP RIGHT: An Imperial artilleryman is pictured wearing the seldom seen *Prussian* Artillery *"Extra-Saber"* with a wide 28 mm wide blade and artillery *Faustriemen* knot. *LTC (Ret.) Thomas M. Johnson Photo Collection. Photo by Alfred Hirrlinger, Stuttgart.*

RIGHT: Train basket hilt saber with double-etched blade. The massive nickel hilt with sheetmetal sidebars is very distinctive. The blade is marked, "Carl Kaiser and Company" (circa 1875-1896). The obverse blade is etched for the 10th Hannover Train Battalion. The reverse blade contains the patriotic slogan, "With God for King and Fatherland". The silver grip wire has been removed. *Edward M. Owen, Jr. Collection. Photo by Edward M. Owen, Jr.*

Swords of the German Army during the Imperial Era

Blade etchings applied to the Hannover Train Batallion saber.

These cavalry troopers, many of whom are one-year volunteers, are wearing their basket-hilt sabers. The saber knot, or *Faustriemen,* contains a red leather strap. It is certain that these *Kameraden,* on other occasions, raised many a beer stein to the Fatherland! The standing collar and Swedish cuff is standard for the Cavalry tunic. The one-year volunteer is recognized by the black and white "candy stripe" trim on the shoulder boards. *LTC (Ret.) Thomas M. Johnson Photo Collection.*

Imperial German Edged Weaponry

Excellent black and white photograph of a *Prussian M89 Degen* with a fine quality hand chiseled hilt and genuine steel blade. The grip is black sharkskin, and the obverse blade ricasso is stamped *"Damast Stahl Eisenhauer"* in a ribbon. *Brian Rich Collection. Photo by Steven Colardeau.*

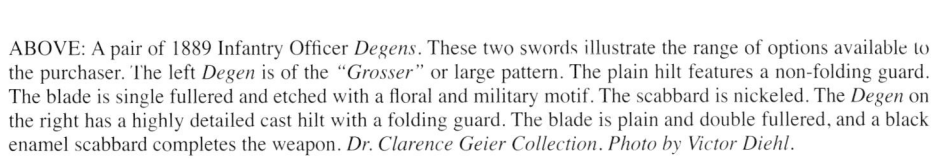

ABOVE: A pair of 1889 Infantry Officer *Degens*. These two swords illustrate the range of options available to the purchaser. The left *Degen* is of the *"Grosser"* or large pattern. The plain hilt features a non-folding guard. The blade is single fullered and etched with a floral and military motif. The scabbard is nickeled. The *Degen* on the right has a highly detailed cast hilt with a folding guard. The blade is plain and double fullered, and a black enamel scabbard completes the weapon. *Dr. Clarence Geier Collection. Photo by Victor Diehl.*

TOP RIGHT: 1915 dated photo of *"Onkel Authur"*. He is wearing his *IOD89* complete with officer knot. The folding clamshell is very detailed, and the sword is in new condition. *LTC (Ret.) Thomas M. Johnson Photo Collection.*

RIGHT: Imperial Infantry *Unteroffizier* wearing his *IOD89 Degen* with folding clamshell. The attached officer sword knot has become, over time, unwrapped. *LTC (Ret.) Thomas M. Johnson Photo Collection. Photo by Max Grutzner, Jauer.*

Imperial German Edged Weaponry

An NCO in the *Queen Augusta Grenadier Guard No.4* with an exquisite *IOD 1889*. Close examination of the grip reveals the cypher of *Kaiser* Wilhelm and the highly sought after Guard Star. The hilt of the *Degen* features the standard non-folding clamshell with *Prussian* eagle and sword knot wrapped in a standard configuration. Historically the German eagle dates to the 1300s. *LTC (Ret.) Thomas M. Johnson Photo Collection. Photo by C. Euen, Berlin.*

128

Imperial Infantry NCO wearing the *IOD89 Degen* with officer sword knot attached as permitted by his senior ranking. *LTC (Ret.) Thomas M. Johnson Photo Collection.*

A decorated Imperial infantry sergeant wearing his field tunic and Infantry Officer *Degen* with folding *Prussian* eagle clamshell. The cypher of *Wilhelm* is clearly visible on the obverse grip. *LTC (Ret.) Thomas M. Johnson Photo Collection. Photo by Georg Wiele, Ludwigshaven.*

A Sergeant in the *Bremen Infantry Regiment Nr.75*. He is holding an issue pattern *IOD89 Degen*, however, with the addition of triple wire grip wrap. The clamshell is the non-folding type. The officer sword knot "tie" provides an excellent view of the three rows of "darning stitches" in the leather strap as well as the acorn core. *LTC (Ret.) Thomas M. Johnson Photo Collection.*

RIGHT: Reverse view of the unusual WK&C *M89 Degen* manufactured with a totally black hilt. Note the mint condition of the leather *Fingerschlauf* (finger loop). The standard steel scabbard is painted with black lacquer. BELOW: Pictured in color is a highly unusual *Prussian* Infantry *M89 Degen* by WK&C manufactured with a totally black hilt. The condition of this unusual Imperial *Degen* is mint, and remains complete with the original leather finger loop and red felt blade buffer pad. The WK&C "single knighthead" logo is stamped into the obverse blade and is clearly visible in the photograph. *"Rockie" Blunt Collection. Photo Courtesy of "Rockie" Blunt.*

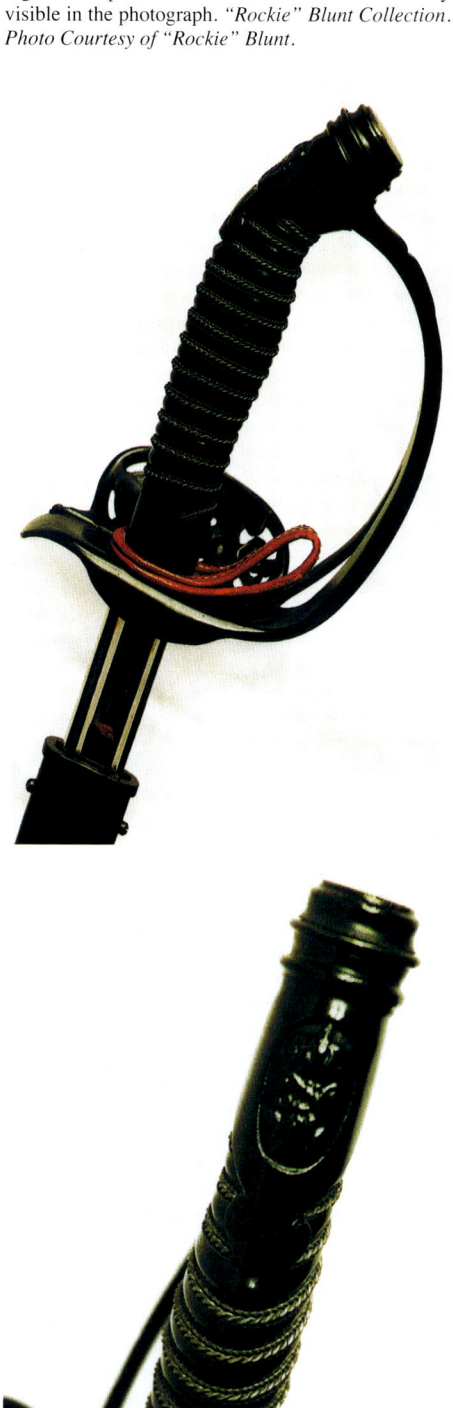

LEFT: Top side view of the unusual black hilt Infantry *M89 Degen* reposing in the collection of World War II veteran and best selling author Roscoe "Rockie" Blunt of Shrewsbury, Massachusetts. *"Rockie" Blunt Collection. Photo Courtesy of "Rockie" Blunt.*

Imperial German Edged Weaponry

An Imperial Officer in the 8th Regiment poses for his formal studio portrait. His blued *IOD89* is rarely seen. *LTC (Ret.) Thomas M. Johnson Photo Collection. Photo by Marcel Schmitter, Berlin.*

OPPOSITE
TOP: Pictured in color is another high-quality Deluxe Presentation *M89* Infantry *Degen* by the Carl Eickhorn firm in Solingen. The large gold acorn sword knot is original to the sword. The steel scabbard is the standard black, single ring version. *Major General (Ret.) Theodore Paulson Collection. Photo by Major General (Ret.) Theodore Paulson.*

BOTTOM: The beautifully etched presentation panel on the Carl Eickhorn Deluxe Imperial *M89 Degen* includes the years of service, "1897-99". The trademark is the early Eickhorn "C. E." logo. *Major General (Ret.) Theodore Paulson Collection. Photo by Major General (Ret.) Theodore Paulson.*

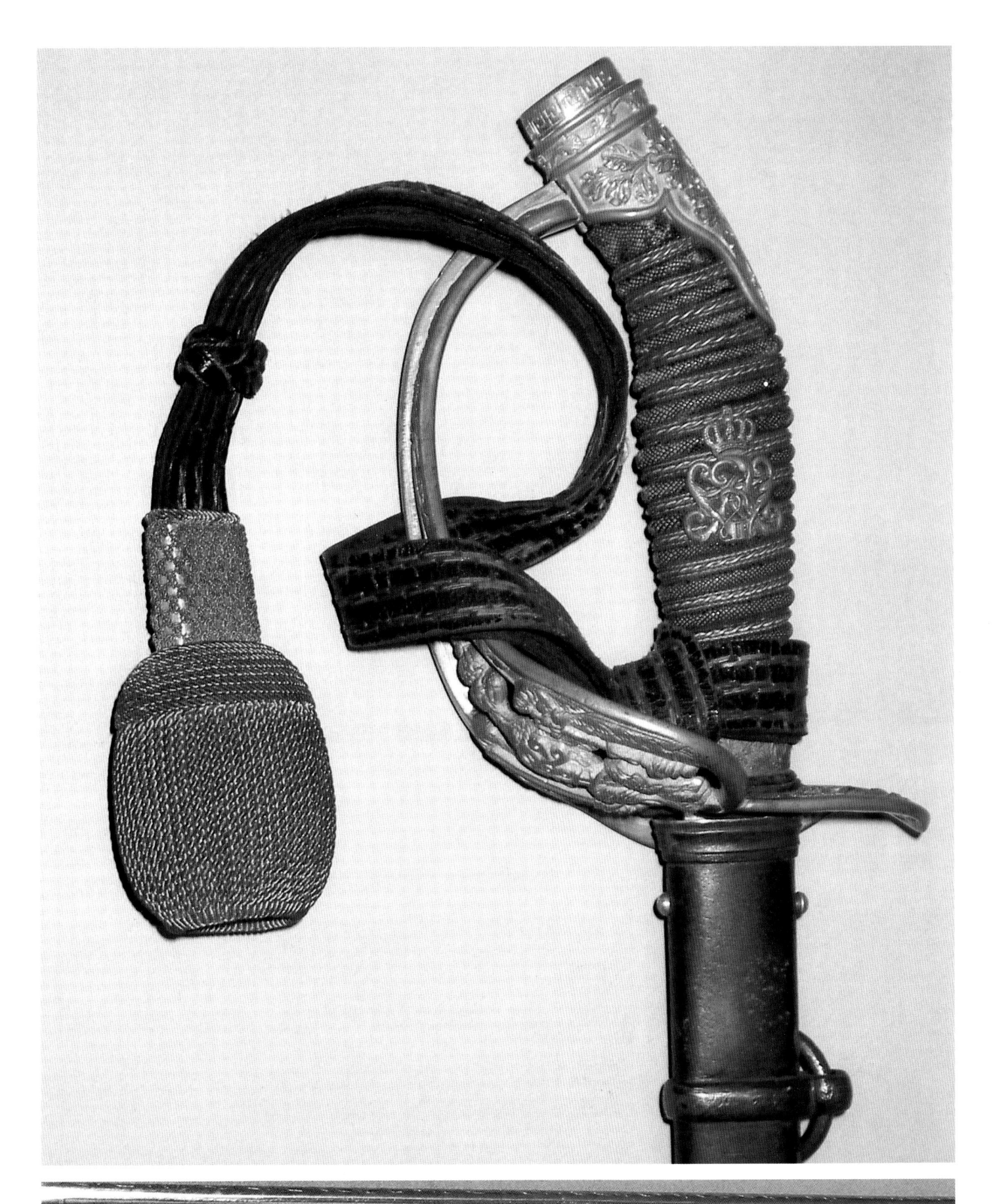

Gewidmet v.d. ausscheidendem Jahrgang 1897-99.

Imperial German Edged Weaponry

Pictured in black and white is the obverse hilt on the outstanding Presentation *M89* Infantry *Degen* with Damascus steel blade and gilt/blue presentation panels by *Weyersberg, Kirschbaum & Cie* (WK&C), Solingen. This sword was presented to *Oberleutnant* (1st Lieutenant) E. Gazert by the Officer Corps of Reserve District Meiningen on 1 October 1899. Lt. Gazert was, subsequently, promoted to Captain and Major, but was killed in action on 28 October 1914. The Gazert *Degen* is complete with the original Imperial sword knot and leather finger loop. The pommel cap is jeweler-engraved with the owner's initials "*EG*". *Richard Williams Collection. Photo by LTC (Ret.) Thomas M. Johnson.*

BELOW: The beautiful obverse genuine Damascus steel blade on the Lt. Gazert Imperial Presentation *M89* Infantry *Degen* features a 13 1/2 inch long panel with a central presentation inscription in raised Gothic letters on a gray background stating, *"Dem Oberleutnant Gazert das Offizier-Corps des Landwehrbezirks Meiningen, 1 October 1899"*. This central presentation panel is flanked on each end by blued panels with gilt floral designs and a depiction of Imperial military equipment. *Richard Williams Collection. Photo by LTC (Ret.) Thomas M. Johnson.*

A Senior NCO in the 3rd West *Prussian* Infantry Regiment No.125. His pre-war Infantry *Degen* has been removed from the regain hook on his belt for this photograph which provides the reader an excellent study of his uniform, spiked helmet, belt and belt buckle, as well as his Imperial sword and accompanying accouterments. *LTC (Ret.) Thomas M. Johnson Photo Collection. Photo by H. Schmuckler, Friedenau.*

Prussian Sergeant in the *Infantry Regiment Count Werder (4th Rhenish) No.30* with his *Frau* (wife). The senior NCO is wearing the Infantry Officer *Degen 89* with much preferred folding clamshell. *LTC (Ret.) Thomas M. Johnson Photo Collection. Photo by Heinz Maurer, Coblenz.*

A senior Non-Commissioned Officer in the *Hesse-Hamburg Infantry Regiment Nr.166*. The sword being worn is the *IOD M89* with folding clamshell and post-1910 scabbard. *LTC (Ret.) Thomas M. Johnson Photo Collection. Photo by Max Bollon, Walsrode.*

TOP LEFT: A Senior Imperial Army NCO in the *2nd Garde Dragoon Regiment* poses with his sweetheart. Both the *Garde Star* and officer sword knot are evident on the *Degen* hilt. *LTC (Ret.) Thomas M. Johnson Photo Collection. Photo by P. Eitelsberg, Berlin.*

ABOVE: A member of the *Garde Regiment Zu Fuss* in full dress uniform. He is wearing the *M1895*-tunic with *Garde Litzen* at collar and cuffs. He is also wearing an Infantry Officer *Degen* with sword knot. The grip contains the *Garde Star* affixed on the center of the sharkskin grip. *LTC (Ret.) Thomas M. Johnson Photo Collection. Photo by Sellin Hofphotograph, Berlin.*

LEFT: An Infantry *Vizefeldwebel* with his wife poses for a formal photograph. He is wearing a pre-war Infantry Officer *Degen* complete with portepee, showing that he is a Senior NCO. *LTC (Ret.) Thomas M. Johnson Photo Collection. Photo by Gebr. Liebe, Stettin.*

Prussian Guard *Grenadier Regiment* Senior Non-Commissioned Officer with marksmanship lanyard and high quality Infantry Officer *Degen*. The *IOD89* has a non-folding clamshell and Guard Star affixed to the fishskin grip. *"Grenadiers"* made their first appearance in the 1600s. Originally they were large, powerful men especially selected to throw hand grenades. In later years as military tactics changed *Grenadier* units were no longer used, but the name was retained to designate particularly outstanding infantry units. *LTC (Ret.) Thomas M. Johnson Photo Collection. Photo by Robert Wiener, Berlin.*

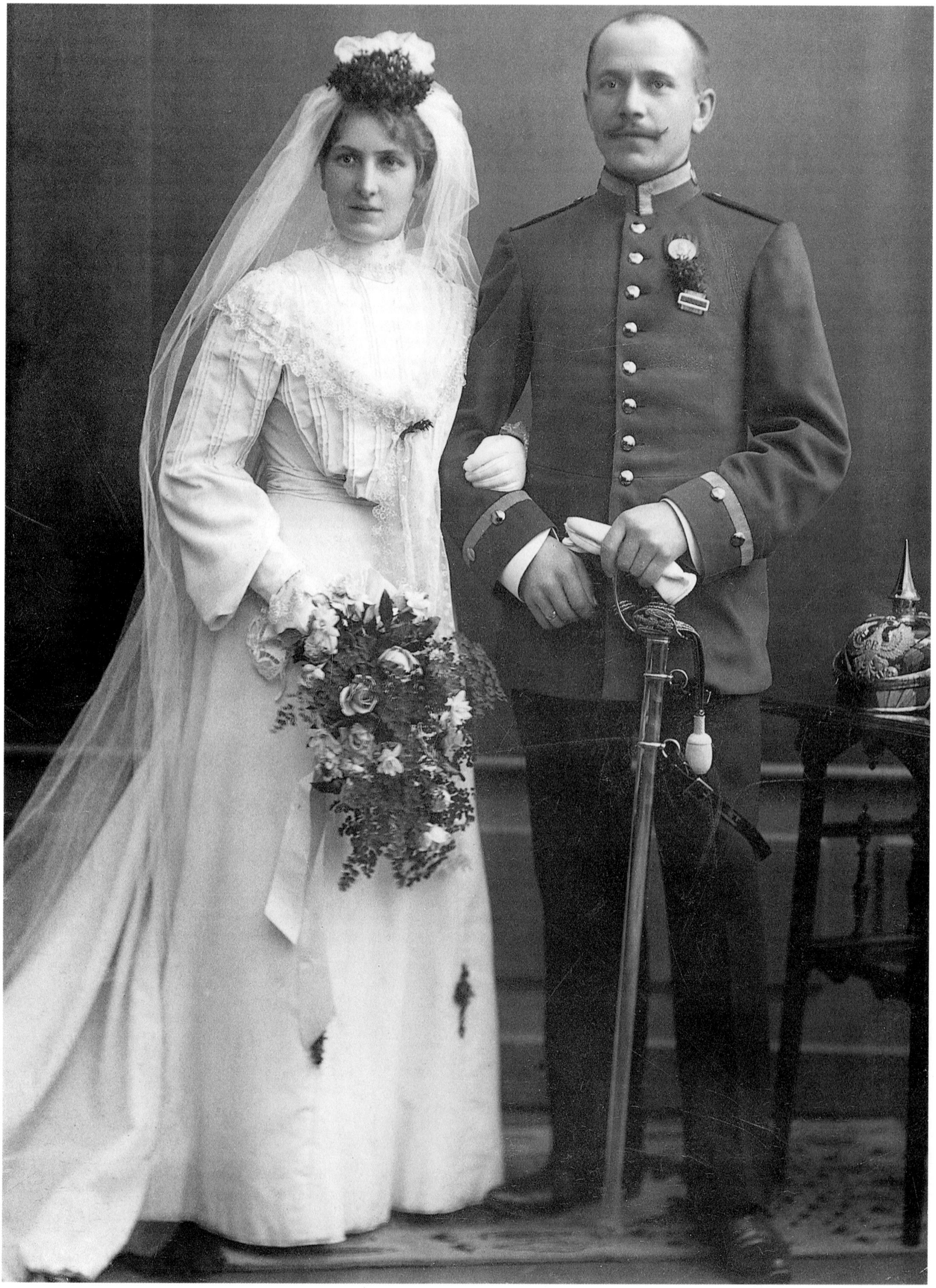

Pictured is an outstanding *Prussian* Infantry Deluxe Officer *Degen (IOD)* Model 89 belonging to an Infantry officer assigned to the Infantry Regiment Prince Louis Ferdinand from Prussia. *LTC (Ret.) Thomas M. Johnson Collection. Photo by LTC (Ret.) Thomas M. Johnson.*

Pictured is the obverse blade on the Deluxe *IOD89 Prussian* Infantry Officer *Degen* belonging to an officer in the Infantry Regiment Prince Louis Ferdinand from Prussia. This inscription appears in raised gold letters on a dark blue panel. *LTC (Ret.) Thomas M. Johnson Collection. Photo by LTC (Ret.) Thomas M. Johnson.*

OPPOSITE
A senior Imperial Army NCO in the 1st Hannover Infantry Regiment on his wedding day. He proudly carries his Infantry Officer *Degen* with folding clamshell and portepee for his formal wedding studio portrait. His spiked helmet rests on the table on the right. *LTC (Ret.) Thomas M. Johnson Photo Collection. Photo by Atelier Blesius, Hamelin.*

A Telegraph Senior NCO with *IOD89 Degen*. The *Degen* hilt is decorated with a portepee signifying his rank. The gentleman obviously enjoys his cigars, even for a formal studio portrait. *LTC (Ret.) Thomas M. Johnson Photo Collection.*

For his wedding portrait this *Vizefeldwebel* (Sergeant Major) was shown with his *IOD89* complete with an accompanying pristine sword knot. *LTC (Ret.) Thomas M. Johnson Photo Collection. Photo by Paul Weich Studio, Breslau.*

Imperial Army *M89* Sword with deluxe hilt by the Weyersberg Company. This sword bears the configuration of the standard Imperial Army *M89* sword, but with ornate hilt fittings. Note the very elaborate pommel complete with knight's head, floral design, and so forth. The sword is pictured complete with its original Imperial gold sword knot. While Imperial *M89* swords are relatively common, one with the deluxe hilt is difficult to find. *LTC (Ret.) Thomas M. Johnson Collection. Photo by LTC (Ret.) Thomas M. Johnson.*

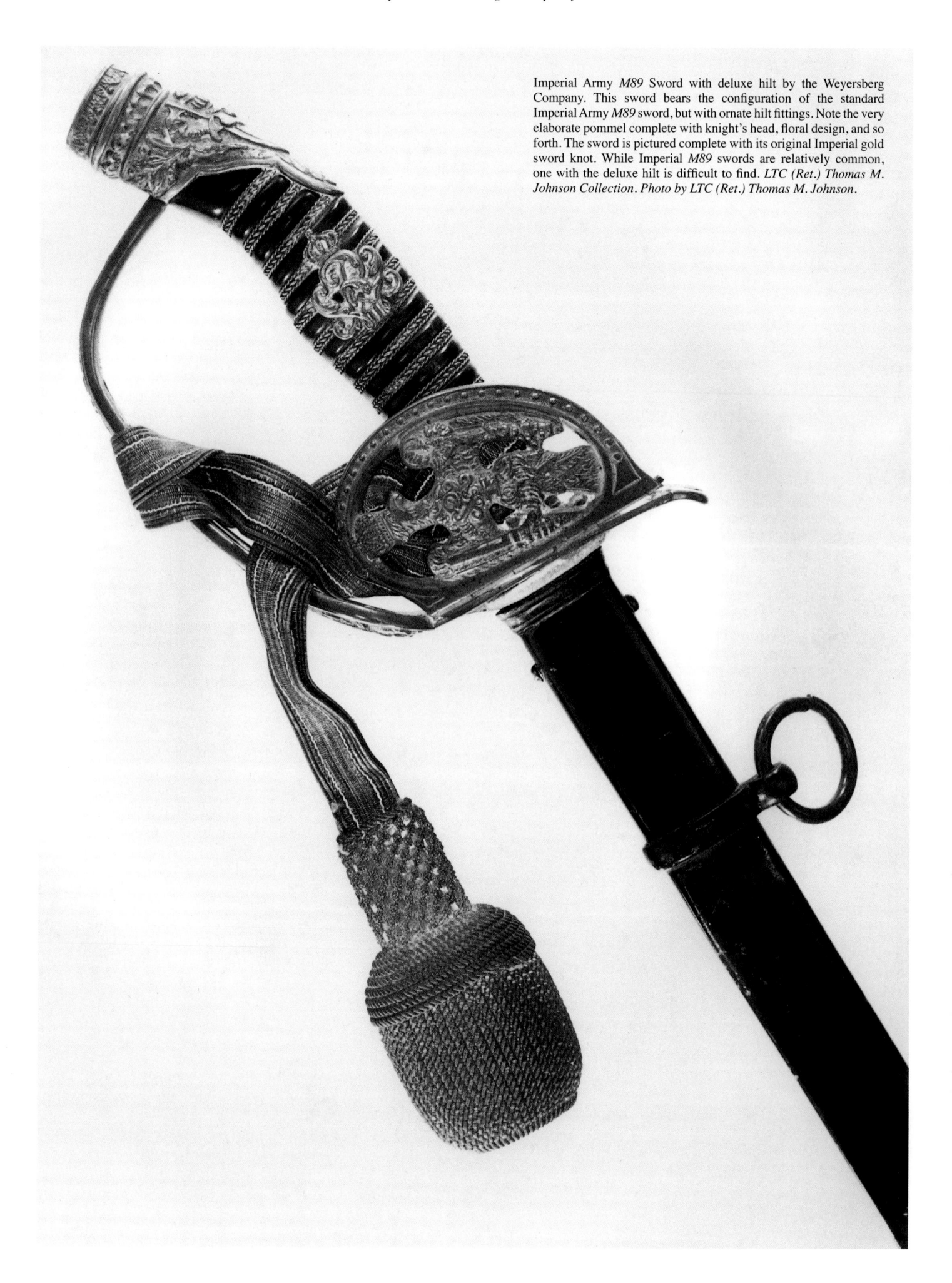

IOD Model 1889 retailers' pattern model. This top-of-the-line Infantry officer's sword contains a highly chiseled hilt with the pommel engraved with double *"S"*. The grip is custom ebony wood. The blade spine bears the name *"M. Neumann Hoflieferant"* (purveyors to the Royal household) *Berlin*. The blade is of the custom *"Ultra"* Damascus pattern. The extremely large presentation style ricasso has been left unetched. The blued scabbard contains gilded and crowned crossed *"B"*s. *Victor Diehl Collection. Photo by Victor Diehl.*

Imperial German Edged Weaponry

IOD89 retail model reverse. The highly engraved ferrule and *Fingerschlauf* are clearly visible. The wearer hooked his first and second fingers through the *Fingerschlauf* to prevent loss of the sword from his grasp. *Victor Diehl Collection. Photo by Victor Diehl.*

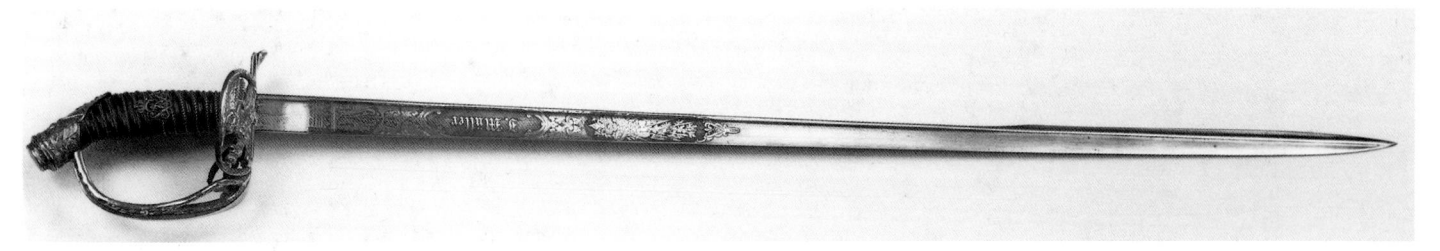

Pictured is a full-length obverse view of a rare named Imperial *M89* Damascus *Degen* with blue and gold panels on the blade presented to an Imperial Officer named *Müller*. Thomas T. Wittmann Collection. Photo by Charles H. Jenkins, III.

OPPOSITE
A *Weimar* NCO is pictured posing with an Imperial Infantry Officer's *Degen* with folding clamshell and officer knot. This *Degen* is most likely a family saber worn by a second generation soldier. *LTC (Ret.) Thomas M. Johnson Photo Collection.*

144

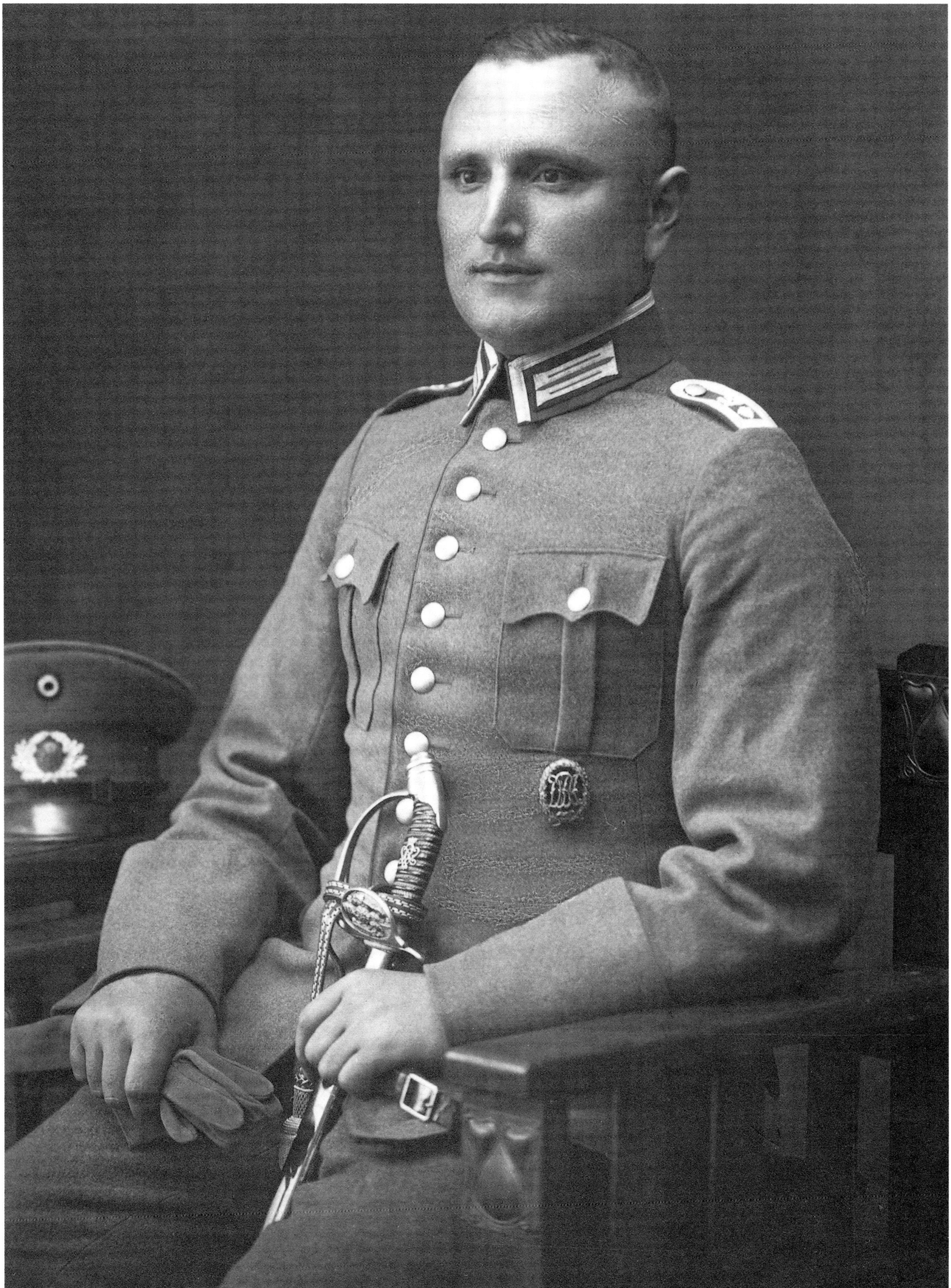

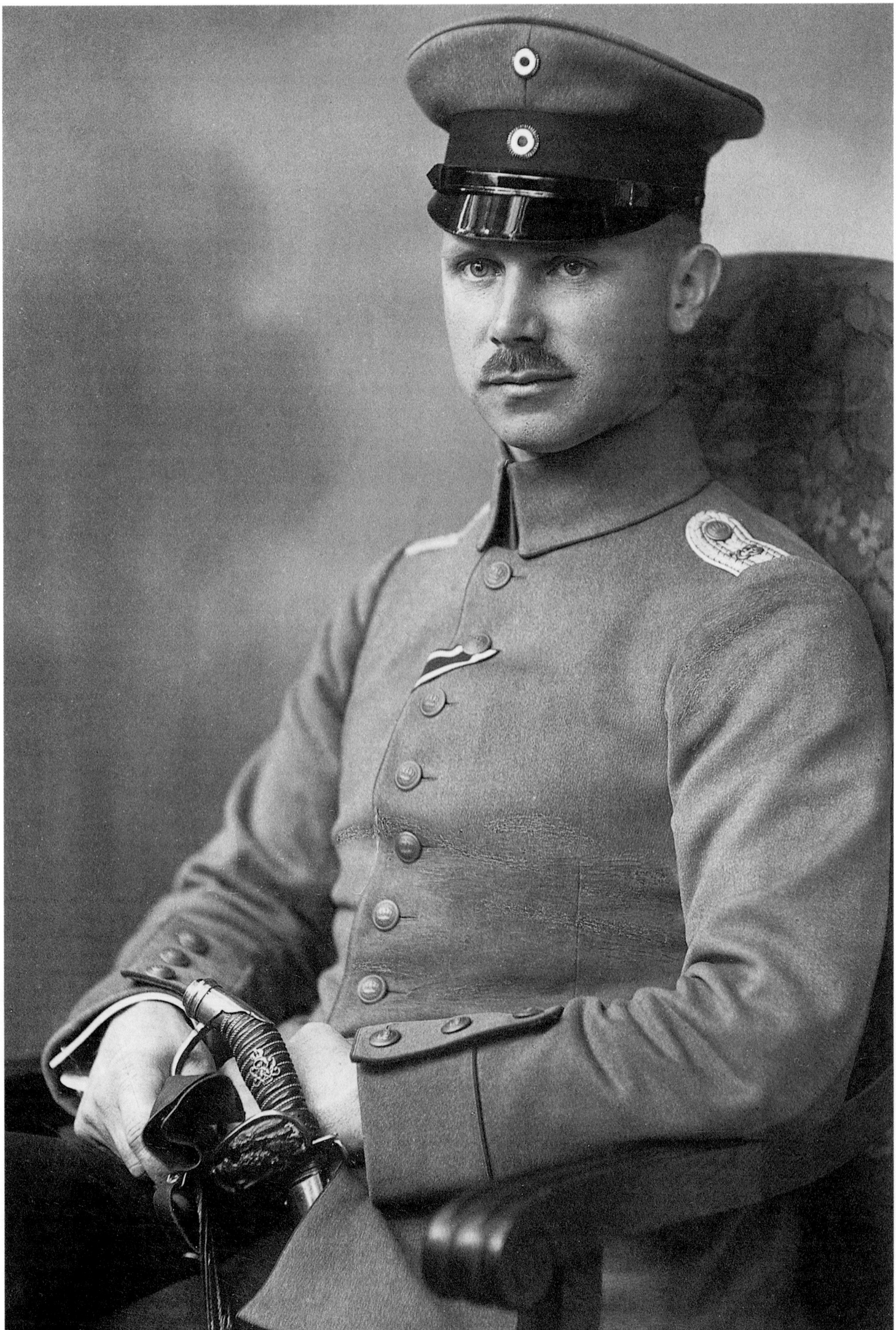

ABOVE: Three *Prussian* Infantry *Leutnants* and a *Feldwebel* (aspirant officer) proudly display their officer swords with portepees on 22 May 1915. The *Feldwebel* and two of the officers wear the *Prussian* infantry officer *Degen* with folding clamshell. The second officer from the left wears the nickeled *Baden* pattern infantry officer saber. All of the portepees are tied in the same manner, around the knucklebow and ferrule. The officer wearing the *Baden* saber wears the *Prussian* portepee with three silver stripes and black core rather than the *Baden* pattern that has a central red stripe on the strap and red core. *LTC (Ret.) Thomas M. Johnson Photo Collection.*

RIGHT: *Prussian* Infantry *Oberleutnant* (First Lieutenant) with *IOD89 Degen* with the post-1910 black lacquer sword scabbard. The folding guard, Royal cypher, and sword knot are clearly discernible. *LTC (Ret.) Thomas M. Johnson Photo Collection.*

OPPOSITE: A *Leutnant* in the 73rd Regiment proudly displays his *M89* Officer's *Degen* complete with sword knot. This *Degen* has an ebony grip and double folding clamshells. The knot displays the silver wire stitching on the leather strap in its typical "frayed" condition. The 73rd Regiment was officially titled *FUSILIERS REGIMENT, GENERAL FELDMARSCHALL PRINZ ALBRECHT von PREUSSEN (HANNOVER) Nr.73*. This regiment was formed in Hannover in 1803 and received military honors for its exploits under Wellington during the Peninsula and Waterloo campaigns. *LTC (Ret.) Thomas M. Johnson Photo Collection. Photo by Feldhoff-Meyer, Hannover.*

Imperial German Edged Weaponry

TOP LEFT: Christmas portrait sent by this Infantry Officer to his sister during the year 1915. The *IOD89* with portepee and *Kaiser* Wilhelm cypher on the grip are both easily seen. *LTC (Ret.) Thomas M. Johnson Photo Collection. Photo by Herm Bock, Alfred.*

LEFT: *Prussian* Infantry officer posing *"mit hund"*. The hanging straps and officer knot affixed to his 1889 Infantry Officer *Degen* are clearly visible. *LTC (Ret.) Thomas M. Johnson Photo Collection. Photo by Kersten-Sohn, Altenburg.*

ABOVE: Infantry officer holding his *IOD89* sword complete with sword knot. This pre-war *Degen* had, obviously, been maintained with pride and appears to be in mint condition. *LTC (Ret.) Thomas M. Johnson Photo Collection. Photo by Bernh. Günther, Goslar.*

OPPOSITE
LEFT: Infantry officer wearing the wartime *IOD 1889 Degen* with painted scabbard. His helmet cover is an example of the short-lived 1914 stone gray waterproof patterns. The belt being worn is the field sash for officers which was 4.3 cm wide. Photo is dated 1915 on the reverse. *LTC (Ret.) Thomas M. Johnson Photo Collection.*

RIGHT: Imperial Officer in the *2nd Degen Garde Regiment*. He is carrying an *IOD89* with *Garde Star* on the grip. The scabbard color and single hanger ring meet the regulations of 1910. This photo is undated; however, the leather boots are of the regulation of 1915. *LTC (Ret.) Thomas M. Johnson Photo Collection.*

Swords of the German Army during the Imperial Era

Imperial German Edged Weaponry

Standard Model 89 sword with floral pattern etch, blue panels, and Damascus blade presented to *Leutnant* (Lieutenant) *Cuno von Falkenhayn* in 1912. *Robert Johnston Collection. Photo by Charles H. Jenkins, III.*

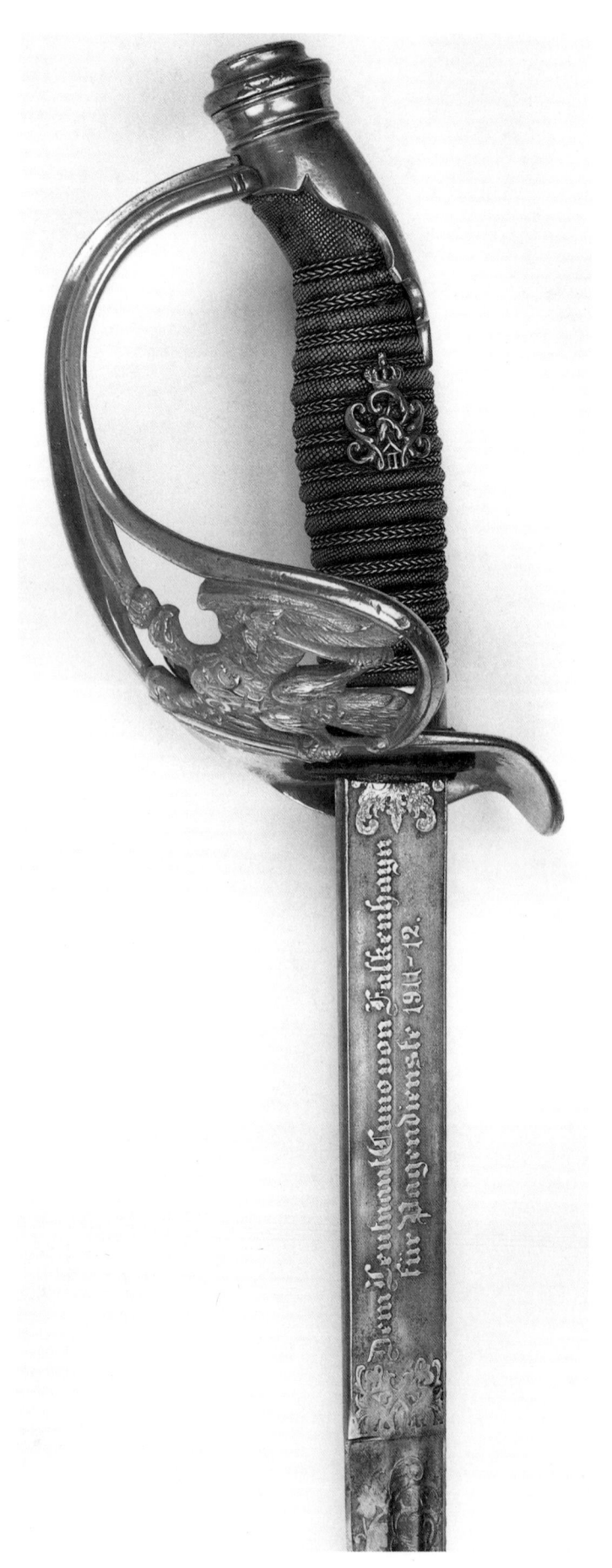

Reverse of Damascus-bladed Model 89 sword reveals this piece was a gift from *"Heinrich, Prinze von Preussen"*. Prince Heinrich was the *Kaiser's* brother, and an important personage highly visible during the *Kaiser's* heyday. *Robert Johnston Collection. Photo by Charles H. Jenkins, III.*

150

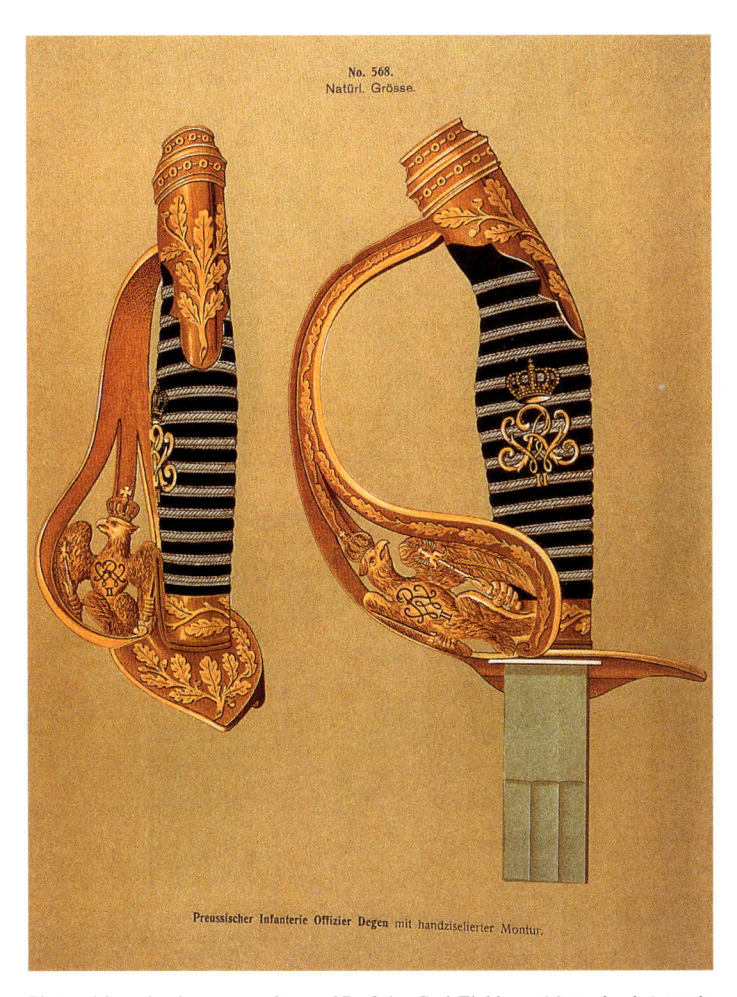

Pictured in color is a copy of page 27 of the Carl Eickhorn *Müsterbuch* (sample book). Shown in actual size is the hilt of the Eickhorn *Prussian* Infantry officer sword model number 568. *Johnson Reference Books & Militaria Archives.*

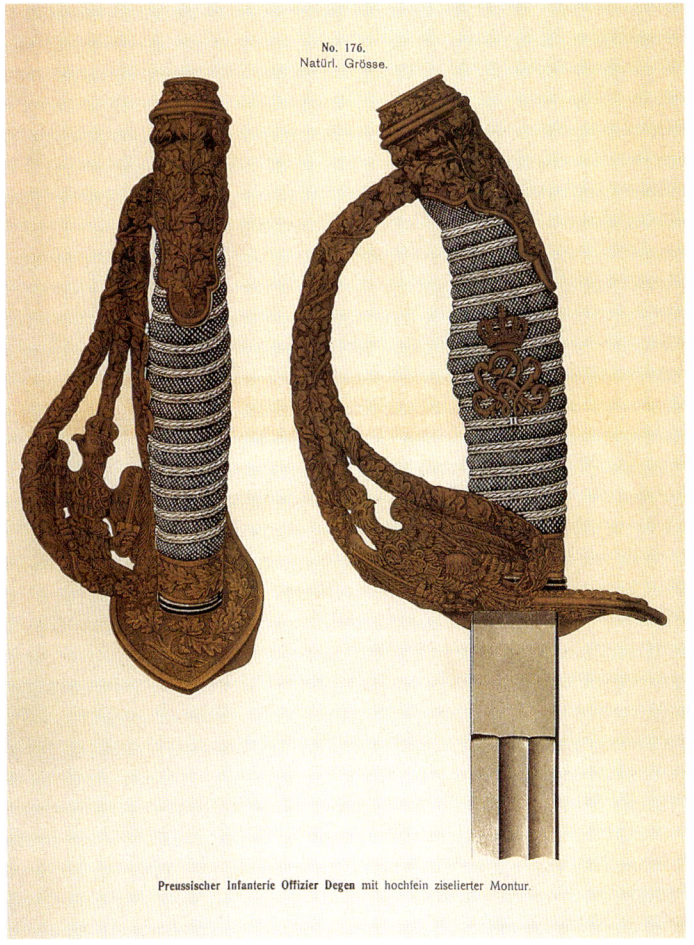

The Carl Eickhorn factory Imperial Edged Weapon Sales Catalog depicts the company's Model #176 in actual size. The accompanying caption reads, *"Preussischer Infanterie Offizier Degen mit hochfein ziselierter Montur"* (Prussian Infantry Officer Sword with finely chiseled hilt). *Johnson Reference Books & Militaria Archives.*

Imperial German Edged Weaponry

Another outstanding *"Grosser"* Presentation model 1889 sword manufactured by WK&C. This highly collectible sword was acquired by the present owner complete with the original sword knot (pictured) and sword belt with hangers. *Major General (Ret.) Theodore W. Paulson Collection. Photo by Major General (Ret.) Theodore W. Paulson.*

This color photograph provides an excellent view of the large *Prussian* eagle on the WK&C *"Grosser" M89 Degen*. Note the correct attachment of the accompanying sword knot. *Major General (Ret.) Theodore W. Paulson Collection. Photo by Major General (Ret.) Theodore W. Paulson.*

The obverse blade on the WK&C *"Grosser" M89 Degen* provides the original owner's unit, "Infantry Regiment Number 78", in raised silver lettering on a deep blue center panel. Also, featured on the obverse blade, is a profile of a horsehead on a second deep blue panel. *Major General (Ret.) Theodore W. Paulson Collection. Photo by Major General (Ret.) Theodore W. Paulson.*

The raised dedication on the reverse blade of the WK&C *"Grosser" M89 Degen* in a blued panel translates, "We Germans Fear God, but Nothing Else in the World". *Major General (Ret.) Theodore W. Paulson Collection. Photo by Major General (Ret.) Theodore W. Paulson.*

Pictured in color are the original fabric sword belt and hangers which accompanied the outstanding WK&C *"Grosser" M89 Degen*. Note that one hanger is brown leather, while the principal hanger has a silver bullion facing on a red leather backing. *Major General (Ret.) Theodore W. Paulson Collection. Photo by Major General (Ret.) Theodore W. Paulson.*

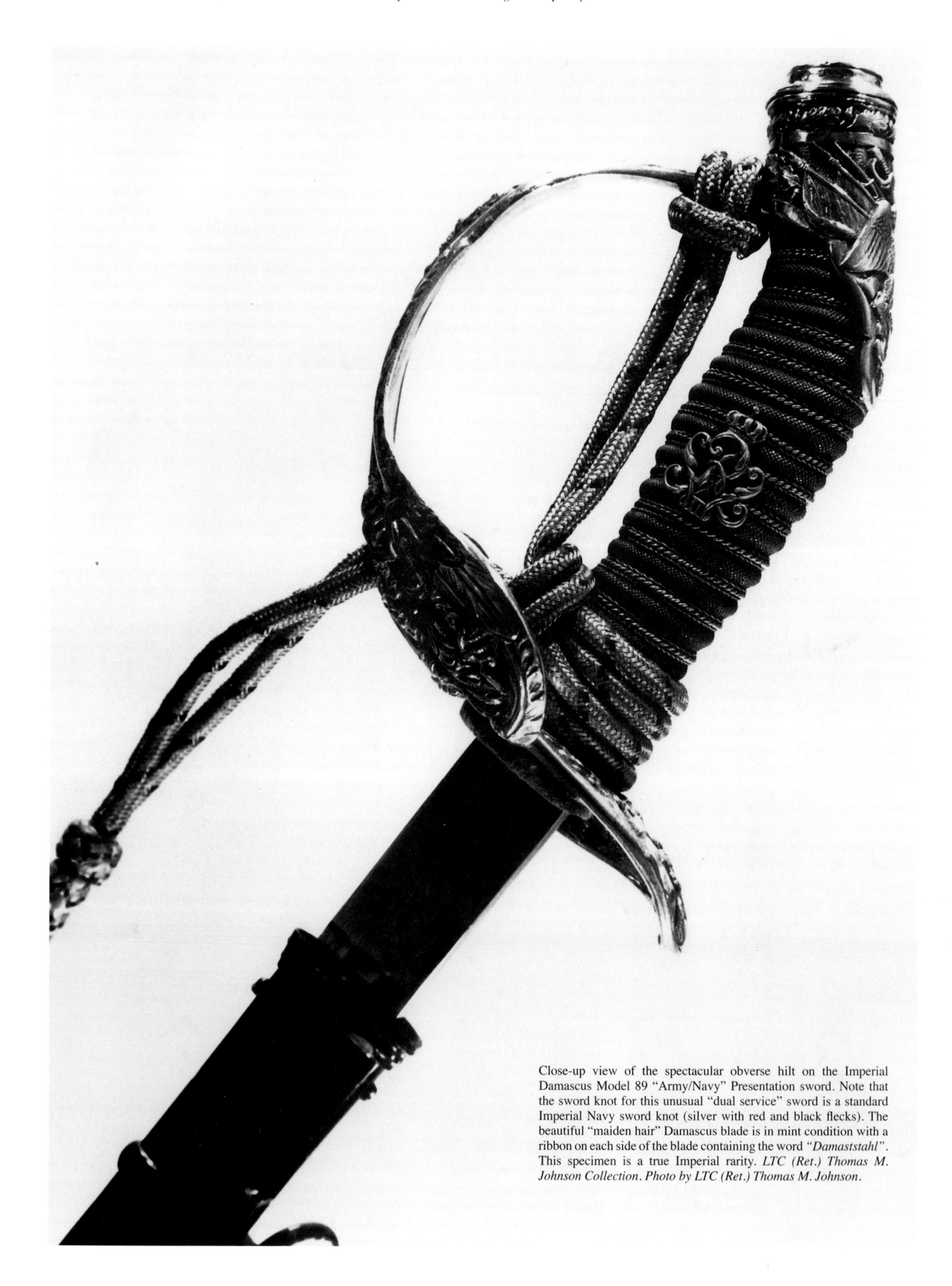

Close-up view of the spectacular obverse hilt on the Imperial Damascus Model 89 "Army/Navy" Presentation sword. Note that the sword knot for this unusual "dual service" sword is a standard Imperial Navy sword knot (silver with red and black flecks). The beautiful "maiden hair" Damascus blade is in mint condition with a ribbon on each side of the blade containing the word *"Damaststahl"*. This specimen is a true Imperial rarity. *LTC (Ret.) Thomas M. Johnson Collection. Photo by LTC (Ret.) Thomas M. Johnson.*

Close-up view of the reverse hilt on the Imperial Damascus *M89* "Army/Navy" Presentation sword. It is interesting to note that this sword knot had to be applied prior to the final assembly of the sword, as the cord passes around the upper hilt and through a slot in the knuclebow and could not have been added after the sword was assembled. *LTC (Ret.) Thomas M. Johnson Collection. Photo by LTC (Ret.) Thomas M. Johnson.*

The upper portion of the front crossguard on the Imperial Damascus *M89* "Army/Navy" Presentation sword features a raised Royal crown and a *Naval* fouled anchor surrounded by an oak leaf and acorn motif. Again, note the highly unusual "tie" of the portepee. *LTC (Ret.) Thomas M. Johnson Collection. Photo by LTC (Ret.) Thomas M. Johnson.*

The top of the pommel cap on the Imperial Damascus *M89* "Army/Navy" Presentation sword is deeply jeweler engraved with the family crest of the original recipient and pictures a 7-point crown above a crest with three quarter moons enclosed. Research reveals that this crest is attributed to the *Von Hansteins*. Further research reveals that a *Frhr. Von Hanstein* was assigned to the 2nd Sea Battalion. Upon reviewing information available in *"Auszienert Unsere Marine"*, it was discovered that the officers of the 2nd Sea Battalion were presented with an Honor Saber on 1 April 1914 by Prince *Egan von Furstenverg*. This was presented in recognition of the 25th anniversary of the 2nd Sea Battalion on 1 April 1914. The sword shown is obviously one of these RARE Honor Sabers. *LTC (Ret.) Thomas M. Johnson Collection. Photo by LTC (Ret.) Thomas M. Johnson.*

Officer of the 63rd Infantry Regiment. The *Brandenburg* cuff is seen on a number of Imperial infantry uniforms. He is carrying the *IOD89 Degen* complete with officer portepee. *LTC (Ret.) Thomas M. Johnson Photo Collection. Photo by Julius Standt, Berlin.*

ABOVE: An officer in the Infantry Regiment *von Horn* which was garrisoned in Trier. The *IOD* has a folding clamshell and the grip contains the cypher of Wilhelm II. The officer's portepee dates to the 1700s. *LTC (Ret.) Thomas M. Johnson Photo Collection.*

TOP RIGHT: This highly decorated *Weimar* officer is pictured wearing his *IOD* 1889 *Degen* with *Garde Star* on the handle. The Imperial sword portepee continues to be worn in this 1920 studio photograph. *LTC (Ret.) Thomas M. Johnson Photo Collection. Photo by Georg Kishn, Spandau.*

RIGHT: Infantry officer in the Infantry Regiment *Prinz Moritz von Auhalt – Dessau No.42*. His *IOD89* is standard issue with folding clamshell. The officer portepee is correctly tied. The officer's peaked cap shows the popular "50 mission crush". The boots he is wearing were worn about 1915. *LTC (Ret.) Thomas M. Johnson Photo Collection. Photo by H. Wiese, Stralsund.*

Imperial German Edged Weaponry

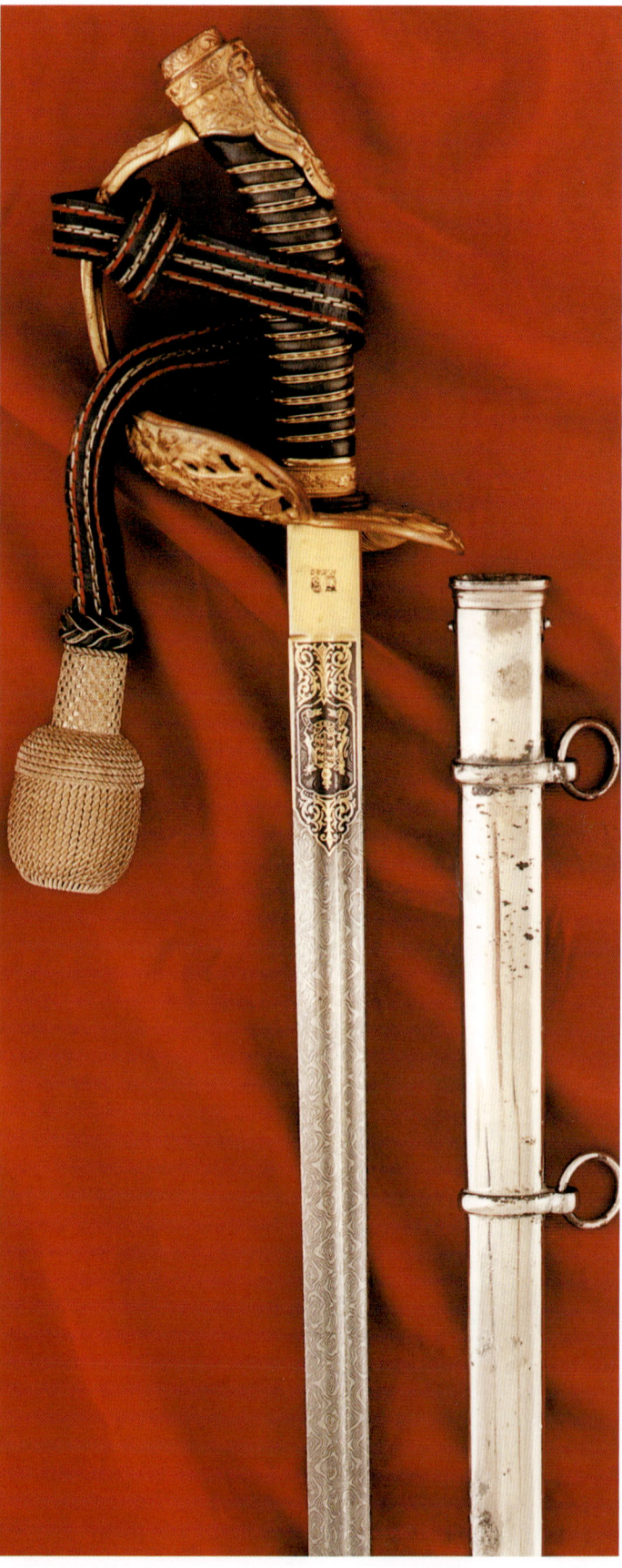

The Model 89 *Württemberg* Infantry *Degen* with Damascus blade by WK&C, Solingen, is pictured in color. Based upon the configuration of the hilt, this sword most likely was carried by an officer assigned to Infantry Regiment *"Konig Wilhelm I (6 Württemberg) Nr.124"*. The deluxe *M89* pattern hilt features a deeply chiseled pommel with the cypher of *Württemberg* King Karl (1864-1891), a pommel cap with a deeply engraved crown and *"W"* (Wilhelm I), and a three finger knucklebow and non-folding handguard with the Royal *Württemberg* crest. In the upper side of the quillon, to the front of the ferrule, is a raised shield engraved with a standing knight in armor (possibly part of the family crest of the original owner). A facsimile of the Royal *Württemberg* crest decorates the obverse "peacock" pattern Damascus steel blade. RIGHT: Reverse view of the *M89 Württemberg* Infantry *Degen* by WK&C. The reverse Damascus blade features a floral motif surrounding the standard inscription *"Eisenhauer Damaststahl"*. The spine of the blade is distributor-marked, *"Hans Romer, Hoflieferant München."* Richard R. Williams Collection. Photo by Dick Scott Fine Photography, Houston.

Pictured in color is a top-of-the-line Deluxe Presentation *M89* Prussian Infantry *Degen*. While no manufacturer's trademark is evident, the name of the distributor, *"Schultze Hoflieferant Potsdam"* is engraved on the spine of the blade. The obverse blade features a four-line presentation panel to *Oberstleutnant* (Lieutenant Colonel) *von Holtzendorff* of Infantry Regiment No.32. The entire sword is in near mint condition. *Major General (Ret.) Theodore W. Paulson Collection. Photo by Major General (Ret.) Theodore W. Paulson.*

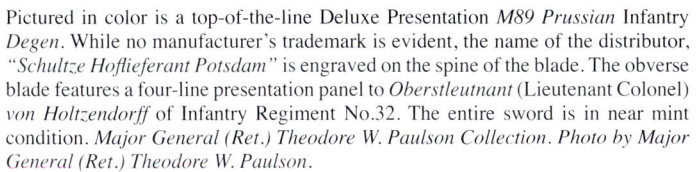

Reverse view of the *Oberstleutnant von Holtzendorff* Deluxe Presentation *M89 Degen*. The reverse blade panel highlights *von Holtzendorff's* service period from 15 December 1881 – 17 June 1897. Note that the leather finger hook remains intact. The grip is wrapped in black leather, and the scabbard is the nickel double-ring version. *Major General (Ret.) Theodore W. Paulson Collection. Photo by Major General (Ret.) Theodore W. Paulson.*

Prussian infantry officer with standard *Degen* with non-folding clamshell. The 1916 metal spike helmet was probably supplied by the studio for the photograph as the chin scales have been reversed. *LTC (Ret.) Thomas M. Johnson Photo Collection. Photo by Carl Thies, Hannover.*

An Imperial Army officer is pictured wearing his *IOD* Model 1889 sword with folding clamshell and officer portepee. *LTC (Ret.) Thomas M. Johnson Photo Collection.*

OPPOSITE
LEFT: Imperial Infantry officer with his personal *Degen* featuring a standard folding clamshell guard and officer portepee. *LTC (Ret.) Thomas M. Johnson Photo Collection.*

RIGHT: A proud Infantry *Oberleutnant* in full Imperial dress uniform with epaulets and *"Sharpe"* or full parade sash. His infantry officer *Degen* with folding clamshell is correctly wrapped with the black and silver striped officer portepee. *LTC (Ret.) Thomas M. Johnson Photo Collection. Photo by F. Wenning, Lichtenfels.*

Swords of the German Army during the Imperial Era

Imperial German Edged Weaponry

This photo is identified on the reverse as "members of the 22nd Division Medical School, 1904-1905". The officers in front are carrying the *IOD89* swords, while the NCO on the right is wearing his Imperial 1871 bayonet. *LTC (Ret.) Thomas M. Johnson Photo Collection.*

Prussian Infantry officer pictured with his officer *Degen*. This officer has chosen a rather plain hilted sword, with a folding clamshell. The folding clamshell was generally left open during wear. The officer portepee completes the presentation and provides the reader an excellent view of the correct method of tie. *LTC (Ret.) Thomas M. Johnson Photo Collection. Photo by Herm. Kniep, Straasburg i/Els.*

Three generations of the *Henser* family serving in the *8th Rhenish Infantry Regiment No.70*. The 1900 dated photograph clearly shows three infantry *Degens* being worn. The grandson selected the standard model with stationary clamshell, while his father selected the folding clamshell variety. Other interesting items in this photo include the *Kaiser* style mustache and the *Kaiser* Centennial Medal worn by the grandson and the diminutive Reservist Cross worn on the peaked hat of the grandfather. *LTC (Ret.) Thomas M. Johnson Photo Collection. Photo by Theo Schafgans, Bonn.*

Excellent close-up view of the near-mint *M89* Imperial *Württemberg* Damascus Infantry *Degen* by WK&C. The beautiful peacock pattern Damascus blade features the *Württemberg* coat-of-arms and the WK&C company (king's head/knight's head) trademark. *Richard R. Williams Collection. Photo by Dick Scott Fine Photography, Houston.*

Imperial German Edged Weaponry

Outstanding original studio photograph of an Imperial Infantry officer in dress uniform complete with sash and *Pickelhaube*. He is wearing the Infantry Officer *Degen* with *Prussian* officer sword knot. The metal helmets were wartime issue. *LTC (Ret.) Thomas M. Johnson Photo Collection. Photo by Arno Graeb, Coblenz.*

OPPOSITE: Excellent example of *IOD89s* in wear. The highly chiseled hilt, wire wrapped grip with *Wilhelm's* cypher and portepee are clearly seen on the *Degen* on the left. Also, the clamshell on the *Degen* on the left is the non-folding variety. *LTC (Ret.) Thomas M. Johnson Photo Collection. Photo by Otto Petermann, Aachen.*

Swords of the German Army during the Imperial Era

Imperial German Edged Weaponry

Pictured in color is a private-purchase top-of-the-line *M89* Damascus Shooting Award sword by WK&C presented to an *Oberleutnant* (First Lieutenant) *Vollmer* during 1906. The black bone grip and the obverse blade contain the monogram of *Kaiser Wilhelm II*. Lt. *Vollmer* served as an officer in *Infantry Regiment Markgraf Karl (7th Brandenburgisches) Nr.60*. Richard R. Williams Collection. Photo by Dick Scott Fine Photography, Houston.

Swords of the German Army during the Imperial Era

Reverse view of the fantastic *M89* shooting sword presented to *Lt. Vollmer* of Infantry Regiment Nr.60. The "maiden hair" genuine Damascus blade with blued/gilded presentation panels measures 31 1/2 inches in length. The beautiful reverse blade features a gilded blade ricasso and is marked, *"Damaststahl"* in raised gold letters with a long blued ribbon panel featuring the inscription *"Ehrenpreis für hervorragende Schiessleisturngen 1906. dem Oberleutnant Vollmer vom Infanterie-Regiment Markgraf Karl (7th Brandenburg Nr.60)* (honor prize for outstanding shooting performance, 1906 to 1st Lieutenant Vollmer of Infantry Regiment Markgraf Karl (7th Brandenburg Nr.60). *Richard R. Williams Collection. Photo by Dick Scott Fine Photography, Houston.*

Imperial German Edged Weaponry

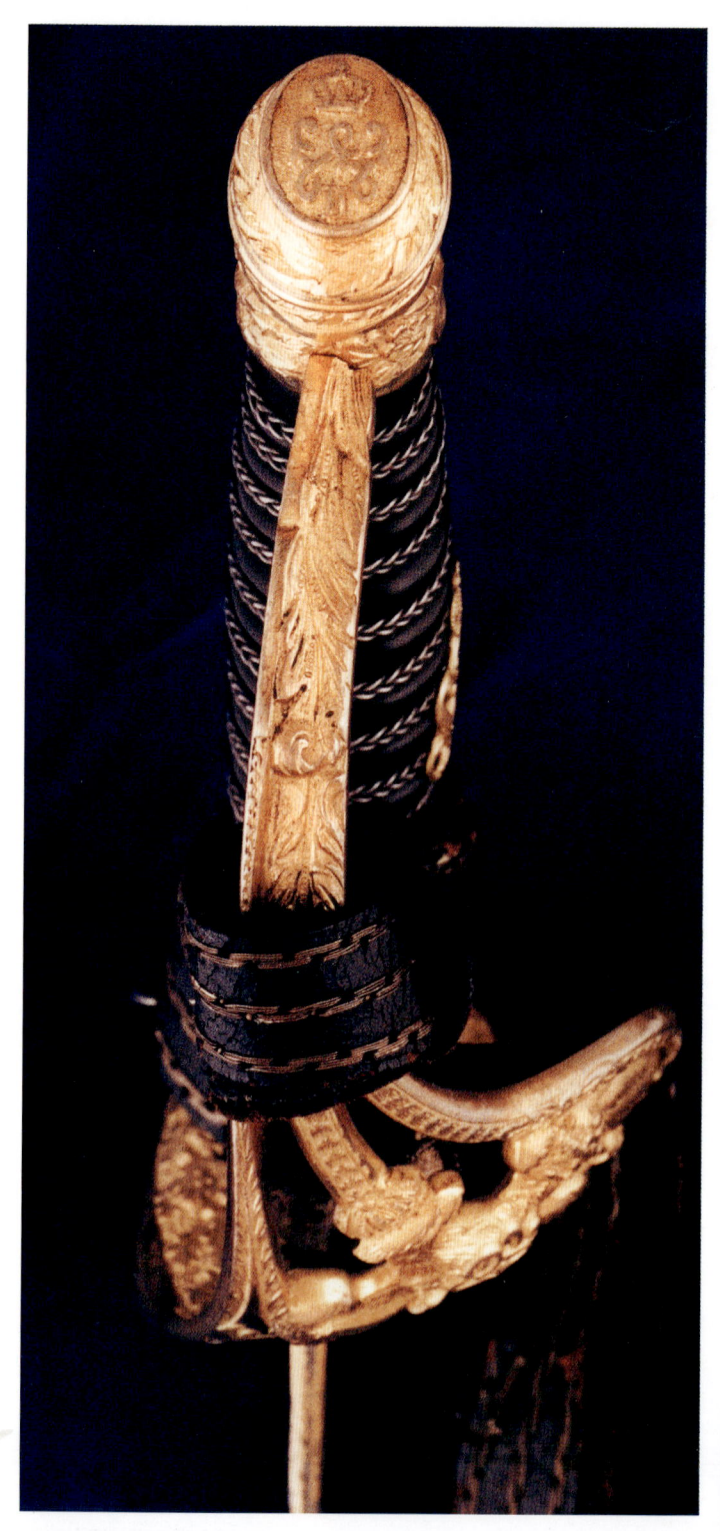

The pommel cap on the *"Lt. Vollmer"* M89 Presentation Damascus shooting award sword features a raised Imperial cypher. The deluxe, gilded-brass hilt fittings retain virtually 100% of the original fire gilding. The grip is complete with the original leather finger loop. *Richard R. Williams Collection. Photo by Dick Scott Fine Photography, Houston.*

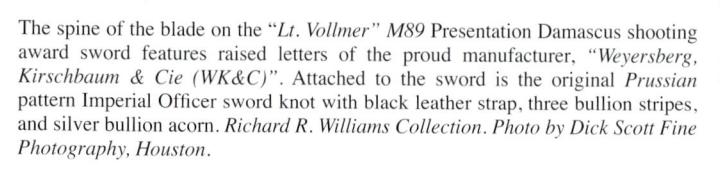

The spine of the blade on the *"Lt. Vollmer"* M89 Presentation Damascus shooting award sword features raised letters of the proud manufacturer, *"Weyersberg, Kirschbaum & Cie (WK&C)"*. Attached to the sword is the original *Prussian* pattern Imperial Officer sword knot with black leather strap, three bullion stripes, and silver bullion acorn. *Richard R. Williams Collection. Photo by Dick Scott Fine Photography, Houston.*

The Deluxe *Prussian M89* sword pictured above in color has the original owner's initial's *"A.K."* nicely engraved on a small circular plate on the upper front of the handguard. Note that the *Prussian* eagle has been "finished" on the inside as well as the outer side (a characteristic of many Imperial deluxe model swords). The grip is constructed of horn, and the scabbard is a black single-ring style. *Major General (Ret.) Theodore W. Paulson Collection. Photo by Major General (Ret.) Theodore W. Paulson.*

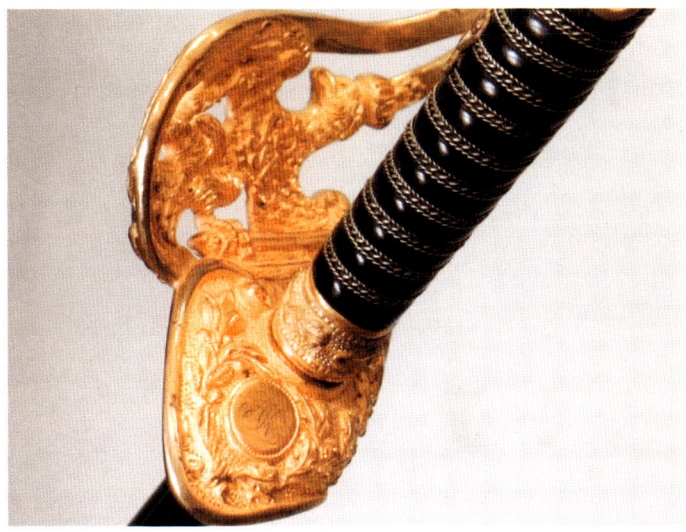

The Deluxe *Prussian M89* sword pictured above in color has the original owner's initial's *"A.K."* nicely engraved on a small circular plate on the upper front of the handguard. Note that the *Prussian* eagle has been "finished" on the inside as well as the outer side (a characteristic of many Imperial deluxe model swords). The grip is constructed of horn, and the scabbard is a black single-ring style. *Major General (Ret.) Theodore W. Paulson Collection. Photo by Major General (Ret.) Theodore W. Paulson.*

Both the obverse and reverse blade on this Deluxe *Prussian M89* sword are etched with a standard Imperial military motif. Additionally, a large "W" (Wilhelm) is etched on the upper reverse blade. The condition of the entire sword is near mint. *Major General (Ret.) Theodore W. Paulson Collection. Photo by Major General (Ret.) Theodore W. Paulson.*

IOD89 sword being worn in full dress by a member of the *Fusilier Regiment #80*, headquartered in Wiesbaden. This studio portrait provides an outstanding study of the complete Imperial dress uniform. *LTC (Ret.) Thomas M. Johnson Photo Collection. Photo by A. Mocsigay, Hamburg.*

Imperial German Edged Weaponry

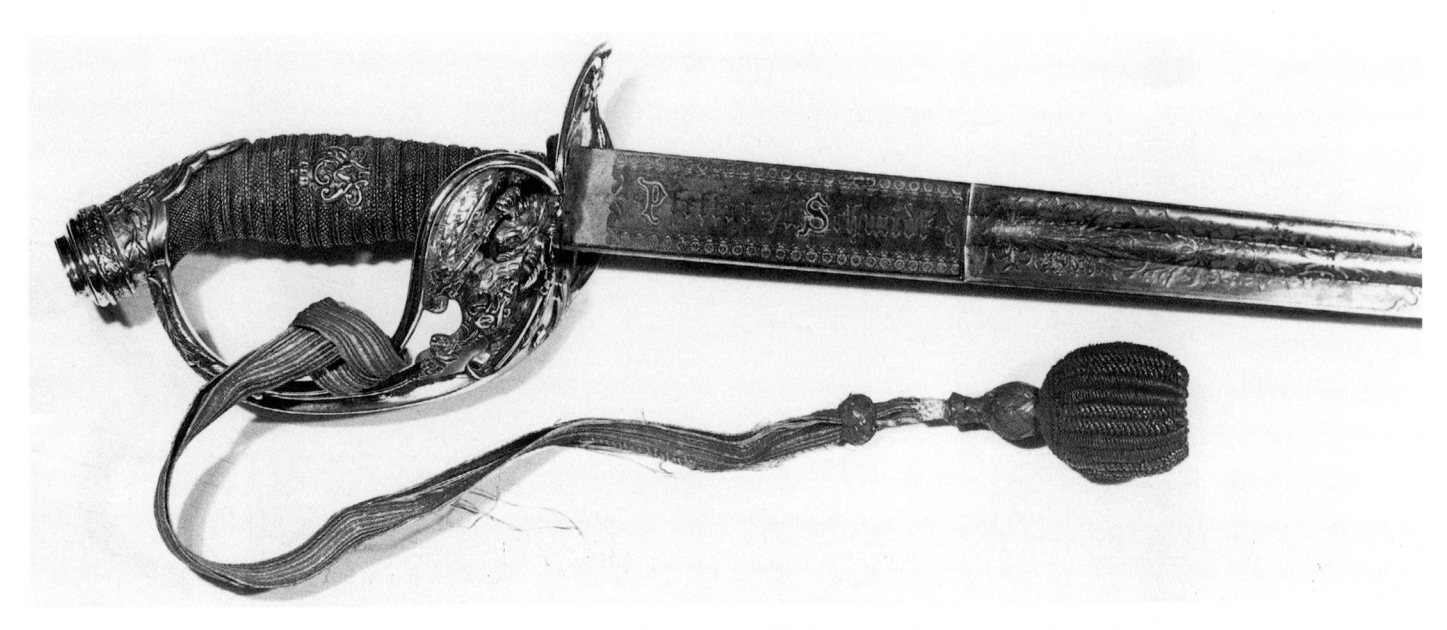

Pictured out of the scabbard is an outstanding Prussian *M89* Presentation Officer *Degen*. The acid etched Damascus steel blade features the presentation *"Pfeffer s./l. Schmidt"* (Pfeffer to his friend Schmidt) on the upper obverse blade. Approximately 60% of the gilt remains on the inscription and the floral design. The original sword knot is silver with blue thread. *Thomas Winter Collection. Photo Courtesy of Thomas Winter.*

The reverse upper blade on the *"Schmidt"* Prussian Officer *Degen* bears the raised gold inscription, *"Dem Feind Zum Trutz Der Ehre Schutz"*. While there is no maker's trademark, the distributor's name is raised on the spine. *Thomas Winter Collection. Photo Courtesy of Thomas Winter.*

The distributor's name, *"M. Neumann, Hoflierant, Berlin"* is prominently displayed in raised gold letters on the blade spine. *Thomas Winter Collection. Photo Courtesy of Thomas Winter.*

170

Swords of the German Army during the Imperial Era

This unidentified individual poses for a studio portrait in *Gelsenkirchen* wearing a standard *IOD89*, complete with an Imperial sword knot. *LTC (Ret.) Thomas M. Johnson Photo Collection. Photo by J. Volk, Gelsenkirchen.*

Imperial German Edged Weaponry

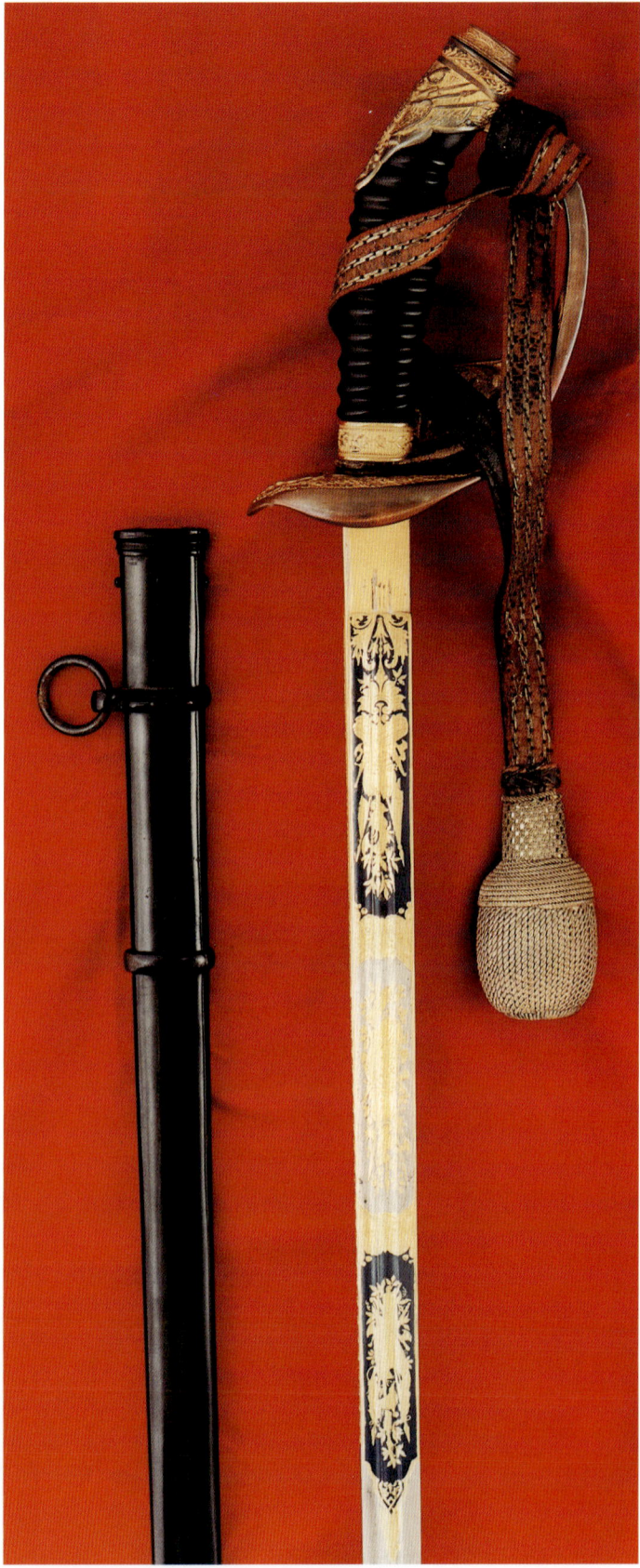

This outstanding *IOD89* Damascus sword by WK&C was presented to *Oberleutnant E. Gazert* by the Officer Corps of Reserve District Meiningen on 1 October 1899. An illustration of this same type sword with a heavily chiseled, oak leaf embellished pommel cap, pommel, and crossguard appears in the original Imperial *Weyersberg, Kirschbaum & Cie* company sales catalog as Pattern Number 6 as the *"Preussischer Infanterie Offizier-Degen, Fein Ciselirt, mit Trophänenkappe"*. *Oberleutnant Gazert* was killed in action (KIA) on 28 October 1914. RIGHT: The outstanding *"Lt. Gazert"* M89 Damascus *Degen* by WK&C is pictured in color, reverse view. The Imperial sword knot is original to the piece, but is, obviously, improperly tied. The reverse blade features a 13 1/2 inch long panel featuring a gilt floral design and a depiction of miscellaneous military equipment on a blue background. *Richard R. Williams Collection. Photo by Dick Scott Fine Photography, Houston.*

Close-up view of the outstanding Presentation Damascus blade on the *"Lt. Gazert"* M89 *Degen* by WK&C. The obverse blade is "maiden hair" Damascus with raised gilt presentation in Gothic lettering on a blue background: "Dem Oberleutnant Gazert das Offizier-Corps des Landwehrbezirks Meiningen 1. October 1899." *Richard R. Williams Collection. Photo by Dick Scott Fine Photography, Houston.*

The reverse blade on the *"Lt. Gazert"* Presentation *M89* Damascus sword by WK&C features a 13 inch long panel featuring a central raised gilt motif of military equipment atop a deep blue background. *Richard R. Williams Collection. Photo by Dick Scott Fine Photography, Houston.*

The heavily chiseled oak leaf pommel on the *"Lt. Gazert" Degen* is jeweler engraved with the recipient's initials, *"EG". Richard R. Williams Collection. Photo by Dick Scott Fine Photography, Houston.*

Prussian Infantry officers and NCOs from a line regiment in typical pre-war pose. Good example of the Model 89 *Degen* and the Model 1910 *Degen* pictured in wear. *LTC (Ret.) Thomas M. Johnson Photo Collection. Photo by Charles H. Jenkins, III.*

This truly beautiful Damascus Model 89 Presentation *Degen* by WK&C, Solingen, was presented to *Lt. Vonhoff* by fellow officer *Lt. K. Reckel* circa 1911. The sword is shown in color and complete with all accompanying accouterments including the original *Prussian* sword knot, doe skin storage bag, felt and brocade sword hanger. A rare and complete combination indeed! *Lt. Vonhoff* died of wounds sustained in combat on 11 February 1915. The reverse Damascus blade features the raised presentation inscription, *"K. Reckel s./l. Vonhoff"*. Richard R. Williams Collection. Photo by Dick Scott Fine Photography, Houston.

Swords of the German Army during the Imperial Era

A second color photograph is provided of the Presentation *M89* Infantry *Degen* with genuine Damascus blade by Weyersberg & Co., Solingen. This handcrafted specimen was purchased directly from the family of *Leutnant* Vonhoff of *Infanterie-Regiment Lubeck Nr.162*. The deluxe gilded brass hilt fittings feature heavy chiseling. The pommel cap is professionally engraved with the crest of the *Vonhoff* family. The obverse blade is inscribed in raised gothic letters, *"I. R. Hamburg – I. R. Lubeck"*. RIGHT: Color reverse view of the Weyersberg & Co., Solingen Presentation *M89* Infantry *Degen* with Damascus blade. Near the reverse ricasso is a gilded scroll panel with raised inscription, *"Echt Damast"* ("Genuine Damascus"). The reverse blade is inscribed in raised gilt letters, *"K. Reckel s./l. Vonhoff"*. In addition to the stamped trademark, the spine is marked in raised lettering, *"Weyersberg & Co., Solingen"*. The sword is complete with a *Prussian* Officer sword knot. *Richard R. Williams Collection. Photo by Dick Scott Fine Photography, Houston.*

175

Imperial German Edged Weaponry

A unique feature of the impressive Presentation *M89* Infantry *Degen* with Damascus blade presented to *Leutnant Vonhoff* is the fact that the pommel cap with the engraved *Vonhoff* family crest is constructed for removal by the original owner for use as a wax seal! *Richard R. Williams Collection. Photo by Dick Scott Fine Photography, Houston.*

This close-up photograph provides the reader with an excellent view of the top of the pommel cap, which is professionally engraved with the crest of the *Vonhoff* family. A unique feature of this particular *Degen* is the fact that the pommel cap is constructed for removal by the owner for use as a wax seal! Note that the inside of the folding clamshell is deeply and intricately sculptured. *Richard R. Williams Collection. Photo by Dick Scott Fine Photography, Houston.*

176

Excellent photo of the *IOD89* being worn in a saddle rig. The large frog and securing straps are easily seen in this period photograph which is an important picture for the serious Imperial edged weapon accouterments collector. *LTC (Ret.) Thomas M. Johnson Photo Collection.*

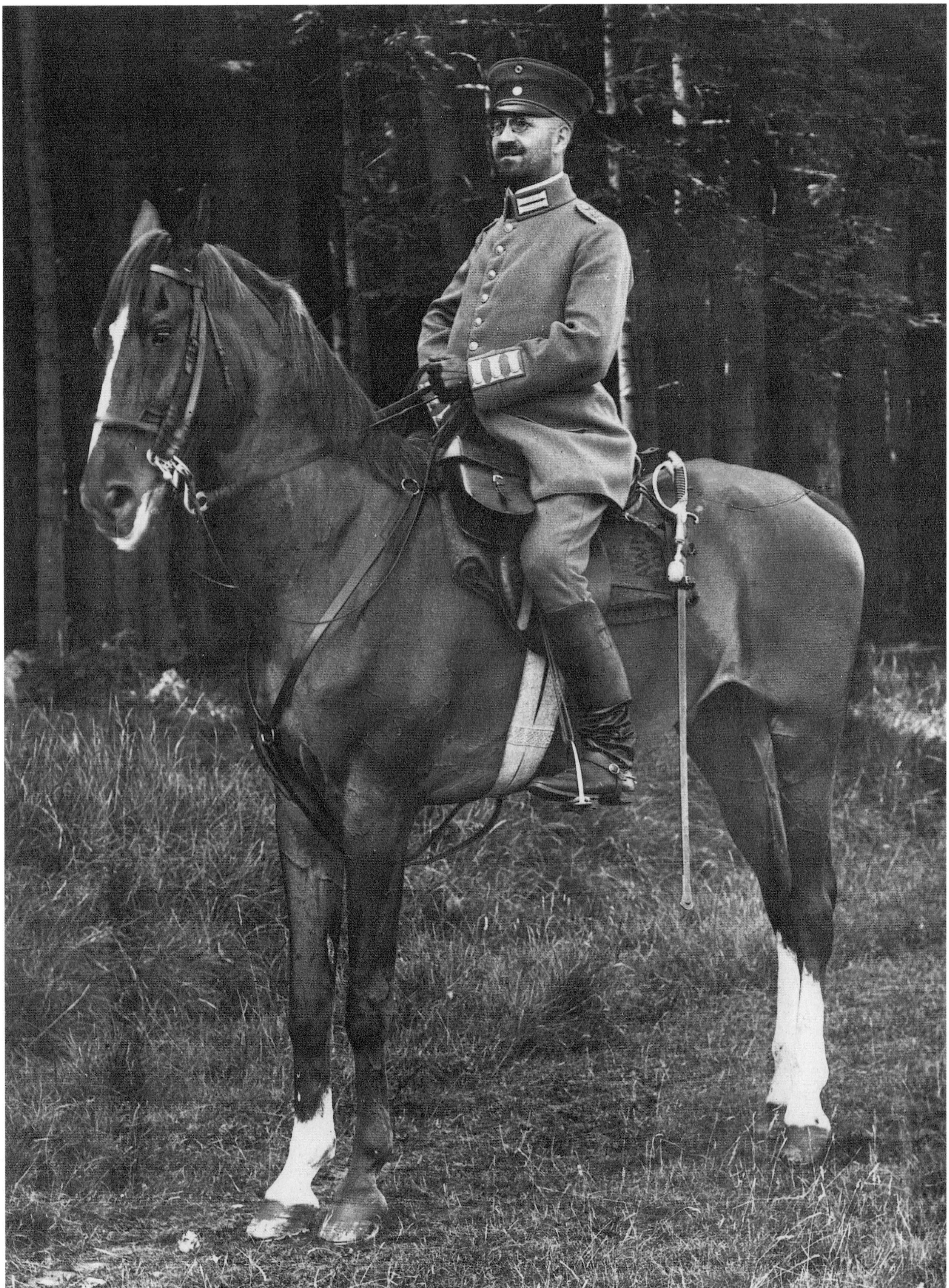

OPPOSITE: This outstanding period photograph shows an Imperial Model 89 *Degen* being carried in a mounted position on horseback. Mounted personnel were authorized by regulation to carry their sabers suspended from the rear of the saddle. *LTC (Ret.) Thomas M. Johnson Photo Collection.*

RIGHT: Mounted *Prussian* Infantry Officer. This officer with frock coat and riding boots is astride a splendidly groomed and obviously well-trained horse. Affixed behind the riding saddle is the officer's Infantry Officer's *Degen* with post-1910 scabbard. *SSGT (Ret.) T. Wayne Cunningham, (USAF) Photo Collection. Photo Courtesy of SSGT (Ret.) T. Wayne Cunningham, (USAF).*

BELOW: Mounted *Hannover* Officers with Model 89 Infantry Officer *Degens*. *LTC (Ret.) Thomas M. Johnson Photo Collection. Copy Photo by Charles H. Jenkins, III.*

Crown Prince Wilhelm in the *Garde* Infantry uniform. Wilhelm is wearing the Deluxe *IOD M89* with non-folding clamshell. A large *Garde Star* is affixed to the fishskin grip. This photo is dated 1907 and an advertisement on its reverse reads *"Unser Kronprinz"* ("Our Crown Prince"), price 8 marks per hundred copies. *LTC (Ret.) Thomas M. Johnson Photo Collection. Photo by Gustav Liersch & Co., Berlin.*

Swords of the German Army during the Imperial Era

Kaiser Wilhelm II in full-dress military uniform wearing an *IOD89* with portepee and Guard Star. Close examination reveals that this *Degen* has been artist enhanced for the studio portrait. *LTC (Ret.) Thomas M. Johnson Photo Collection. Photo by E. Bieber, Berlin.*

181

Pictured in color is a *"Grosser"* M89 Damascus Sword by the Clemen & Jung firm. The plain unadorned hilt is of *Grosser* proportions with a folding handguard and fish scale grip which features the crowned Imperial Eagle and Wilhelm II Cypher. The blade is a magnificent "band" pattern Damascus steel with a 10 inch gold engraved panel over a blued background, while the center of the obverse panel depicts an Imperial Eagle with shield and crown while the reverse panel shows flags, military equipment, and a floral background. Though a plain hilted sword, initial looks are sometimes deceiving…the blade is stunning! *Richard R. Williams Collection. Photo by Dick Scott Fine Photography, Houston.*

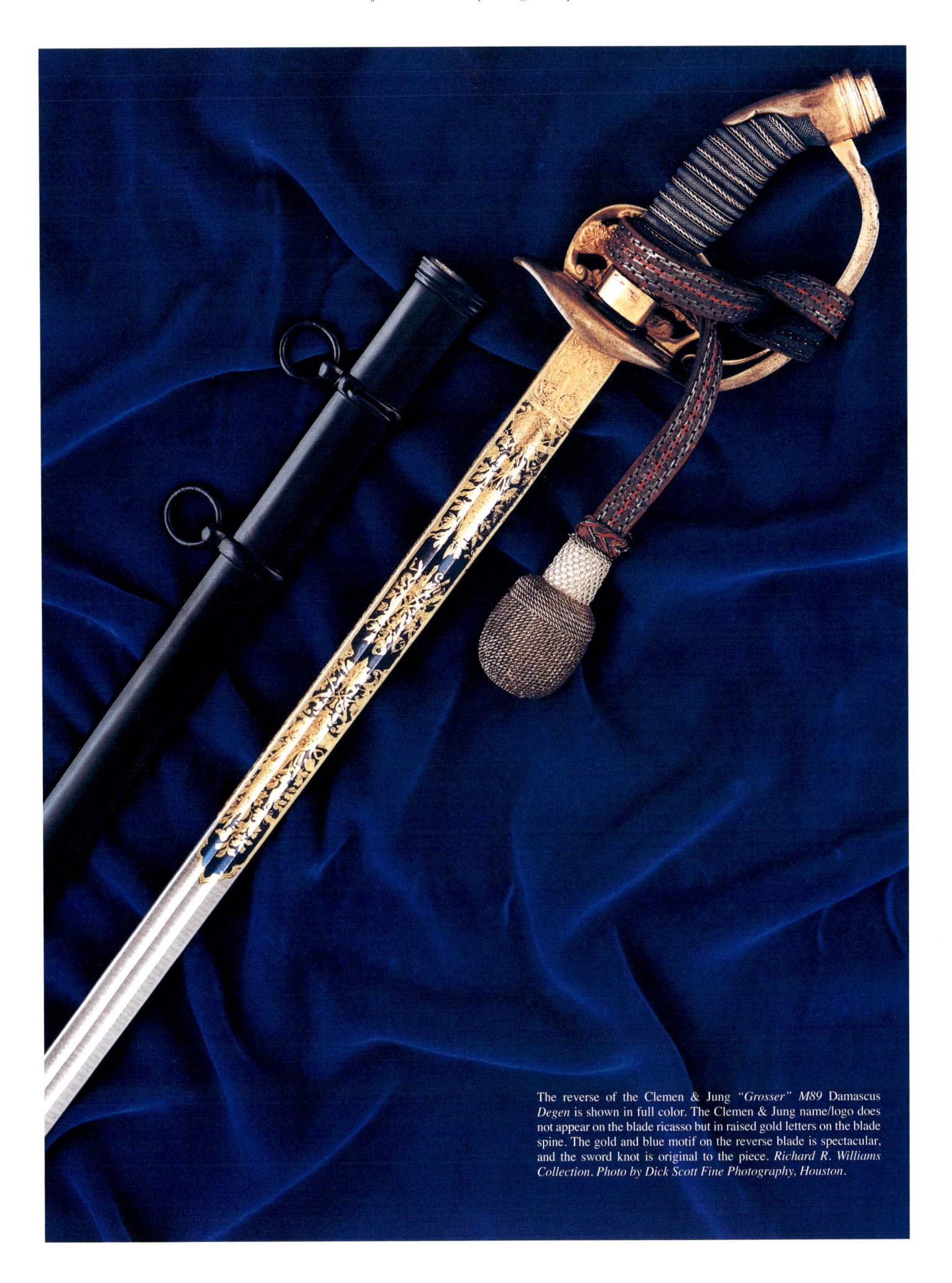

The reverse of the Clemen & Jung *"Grosser"* M89 Damascus *Degen* is shown in full color. The Clemen & Jung name/logo does not appear on the blade ricasso but in raised gold letters on the blade spine. The gold and blue motif on the reverse blade is spectacular, and the sword knot is original to the piece. *Richard R. Williams Collection. Photo by Dick Scott Fine Photography, Houston.*

Imperial German Edged Weaponry

General of the Infantry *von Bock und Polach* wearing his *"Garde du Corps"* Presentation *Degen*. The General is wearing among his array of orders, the "Star of the Order of the Black Eagle" (the Guard Star) below his parade medals. *Stephen Wolfe Photo Collection. Photo Courtesy of Stephen Wolfe.*

Blade detail showing the "small rose" pattern Damascus steel blade with gilded floral etchings. The gilded oval with the date "August 18, 1897" is the date the General assumed command of the Guard Corps. The blade also contains a second oval with the General's departure date of January 1, 1902. *Stephen Wolfe Photo Collection. Photo Courtesy of Stephen Wolfe.*

Close-up view of the *Bock und Polach* obverse blade dedication which reads: "Upon the departure of the commanding General. General of the Infantry *von Bock und Polach*. The Guard Corps". *Stephen Wolfe Photo Collection. Photo Courtesy of Stephen Wolfe.*

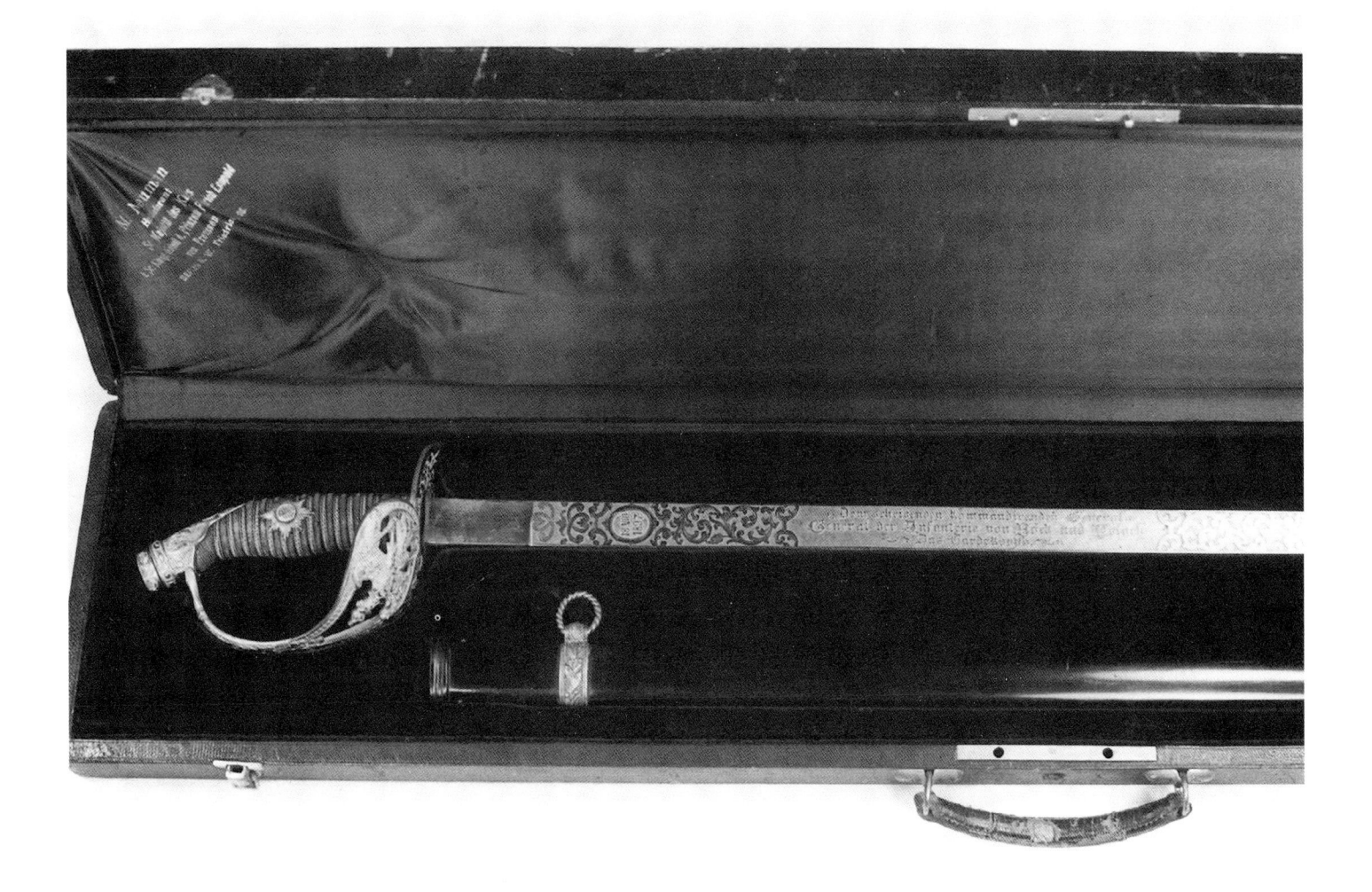

The cased *Bock und Polach Degen*. The brown leather covered case is lined with blue satin on the inside lid and blue velvet on the fitted sword encasement. The inner lid is stamped in gold with the retailer, *"M. Neumann Hoflieferant Berlin"*, the firm's Royal credentials and address. The Infantry Officer *Degen* features a Guard Star on the grip and a "small rose" pattern Damascus steel blade with the General's years of service and departure dedication. The scabbard is black metal with a single chiseled and gilded hanger band and ring. *Stephen Wolfe Photo Collection. Photo Courtesy of Stephen Wolfe.*

Outstanding Presentation *M89* Infantry *Degen* by WK&C with deluxe hilt, double-etched Damascus blade and original leather storage case. The gilded brass deluxe hilt features a heavily chiseled pommel, knucklebow, and non-folding handguard with the Imperial eagle and *"WRII"* cypher. Jeweler engraved on the oakleaf crossguard in a shield panel is the inscription *"IR144"* with the reverse crossguard jeweler engraved *"1893-1911"*. The recipient of the sword, Captain Schmidt, was assigned to Infantry Regiment 144 and served continuously in this unit until his reassignment to Infantry Regiment 159 during 1911 when he was presented this superb *Degen* as a departure gift from his fellow officers. The obverse blade features the translated inscription in raised gothic letters, "Upon the departure of comrade Captain Schmidt from the Officer Corps of Infantry Regiment Nr.144". The sword is complete with the original *Prussian* Officer's brown leather storage bag. *Richard R. Williams Collection. Photo by Dick Scott Fine Photography, Houston.*

Swords of the German Army during the Imperial Era

Reverse view of the superb Presentation *M89* Infantry *Degen* by WK&C presented to Captain Schmidt by his fellow officers in Infantry Regiment Nr.144. The outstanding Damascus steel blade contains a 14-inch panel on each side with the reverse blade being decorated with a gilt floral motif. The reverse crossguard is jeweler engraved, "1893-1911". The sword knot is original to the piece. *Richard R. Williams Collection. Photo by Dick Scott Fine Photography, Houston.*

INSET: Close-up view of the extraordinary heavily chiseled pommel and backstrap with raised eagle, crossed swords, flags, and cannons. The grip is black horn and is complete with a gilt *WRII* cypher and twisted wire. Note the detailed chiseling work on the top of the handguard. *Richard R. Williams Collection. Photo by Dick Scott Fine Photography, Houston.*

Imperial German Edged Weaponry

A pair of "*Kaiser* Prize" Model 89 swords shown side-by-side. Each year, the Army held shooting events within the various regiments. The winners were awarded these beautiful swords signifying the event, winner's name, regiment and date, all in raised lettering on the reverse of the Damascus blade. The obverse carried an elaborate raised etching with gold highlights and a blued panel bearing the *Kaiser's* cypher, *"W II"*. The sword's pommel also carried the *Kaiser* cypher deeply engraved. The left piece was awarded to an Infantry officer, and the right, a Guard officer. *Thomas T. Wittmann Collection. Photo by Charles H. Jenkins, III.*

OPPOSITE: Reverse view of the "*Kaiser* Prize" swords showing the raised and gilded inscription on Damascus, "maiden hair" pattern blade. Grip wrap was blue sharkskin and brass hilt fittings were gilded. *Thomas T. Wittmann Collection. Photo by Charles H. Jenkins, III.*

Swords of the German Army during the Imperial Era

Imperial German Edged Weaponry

LEFT: Honor Prize *Degen*. This *"Grosser"* size Infantry Officer *Degen* is fitted with a magnificent fullered Damascus blade. The obverse blued and gilded panel features military equipment and the Royal cypher. The scrolled *"EISENHAUER"* blade designation is also in gold. The blade is marked "WK&C" on the spine. *Stephen Wolfe Collection. Photo Courtesy of Stephen Wolfe.*

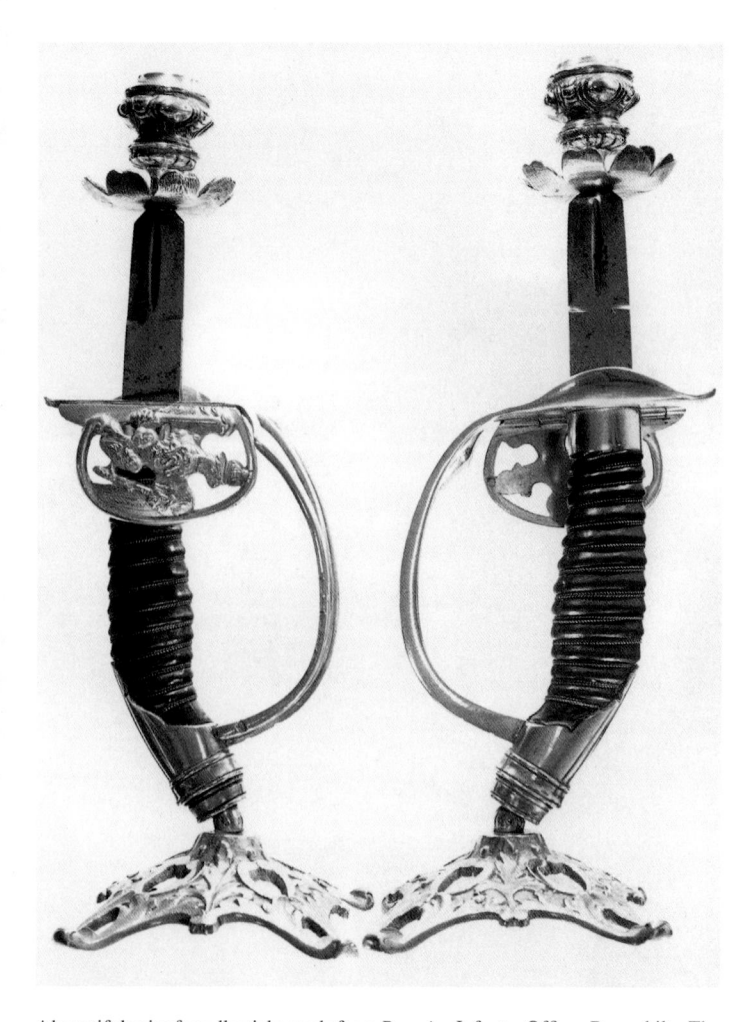

A beautiful pair of candlesticks made from *Prussian* Infantry Officer *Degen* hilts. The cast and gilded fittings produced an excellent decoration that graced a distinguished officer's mantel. These items were not "folk art", but regular production pieces used with a variety of brass hilted swords. The piece was assembled on a cut-down sword blade with an extended tang which was threaded to complete the assembly. It is interesting to note that the blades used were generally enlisted patterns rather than officer blades that usually matched the hilt. *Dave Rome Collection. Photo by LTC (Ret.) Thomas M. Johnson.*

A translation of the reverse blade dedication reads, "Honor prize for outstanding skill performance 1904. To Lieutenant Beesel from Grenadier Regiment King Frederick I (4th East *Prussian*) No.5". *Stephen Wolfe Collection. Photo Courtesy of Stephen Wolfe.*

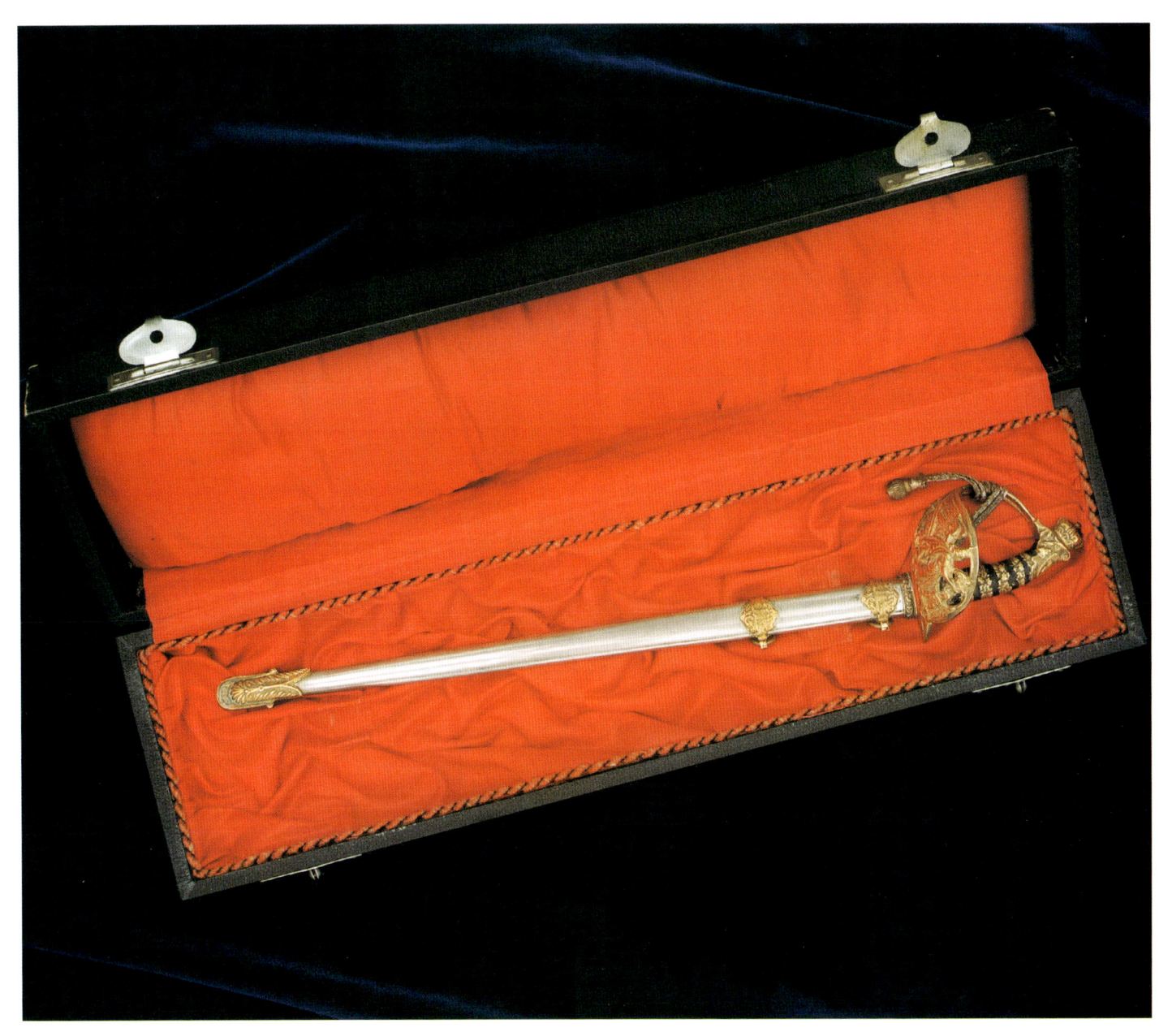

Cased Imperial Miniature Bismarck Honor Sword. Although this example is not marked, it was made by WK&C, as this company produced this popular Bismarck Honor Sword miniature. It was also this firm that made the large original counterpart for Otto von Bismarck. This most beautiful sword commemorated the elder German statesman's 80th birthday. It was presented to him on 1 April 1895, by the *Kaiser*, himself. Since the occasion was highly covered in the press throughout Germany, WK&C apparently saw a brisk market for a miniature. These miniatures were probably sold through expensive shops, catering to the wealthier aristocratic classes and money-laden, turn-of-the-century tourists on their Grand Tours of Europe. The hilt design is a magnificent classic basket, and the pommel features the *"Furst"* style crown, which was a title granted Bismarck by *Kaiser* Wilhelm I, the Grandfather of Wilhelm II. The stationary basket presents a spiked helmeted angel, bestowing an Imperial crown upon a *Prussian* eagle. The grip is wound with simulated, oak leafed wire. There is an original-to-the-piece, metallic portepee. The scabbard is a nickel plated variety having beautiful brass trim which has fine embellishment detail. The overall length of this miniature is about 12 inches. The black leatherette case is in excellent shape, showing only wear to the corners. There is a roped red border running around the top of the lower box portion. *Thomas T. Wittmann Collection. Photo by Charles H. Jenkins, III.*

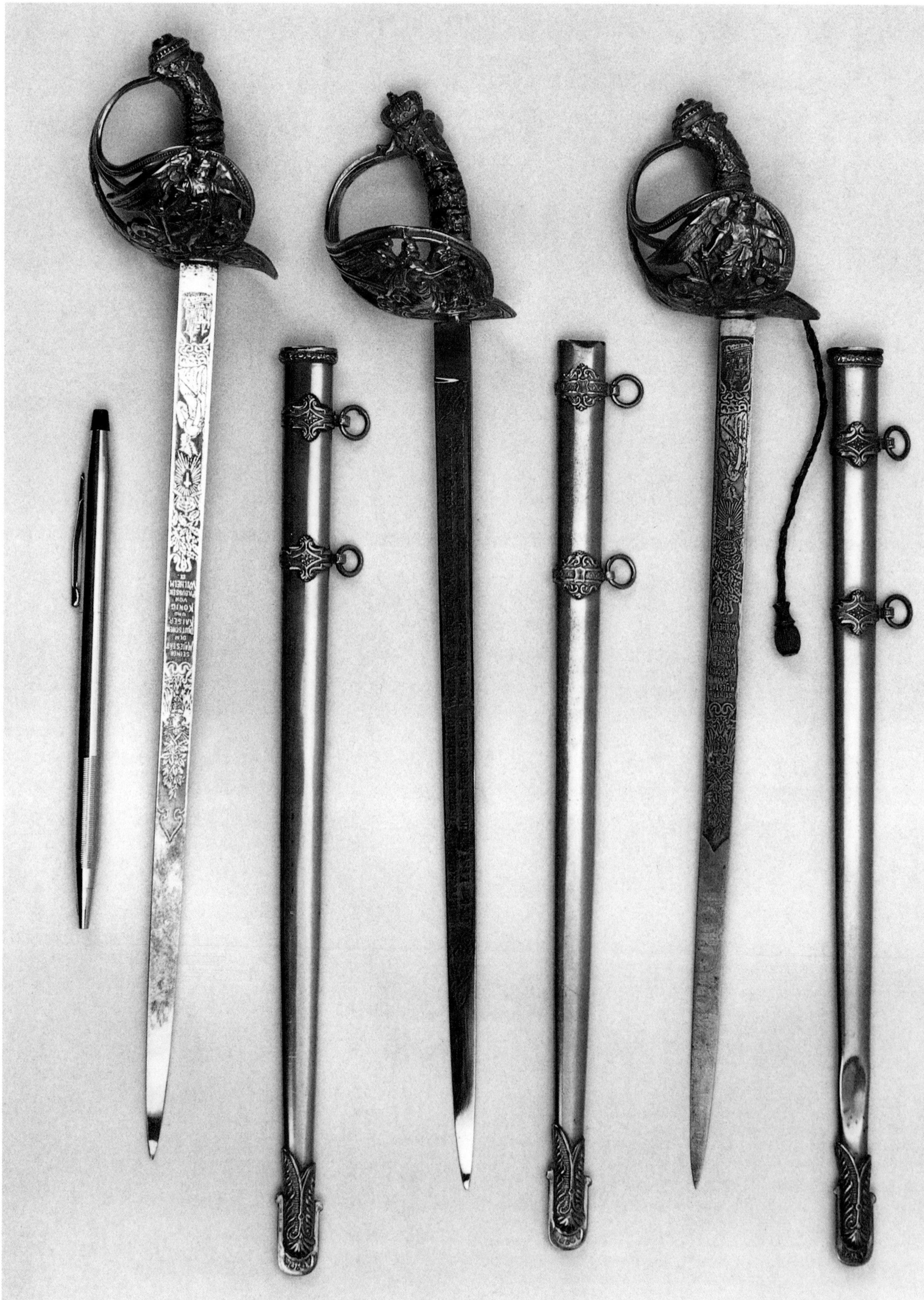

OPPOSITE: Letter openers resembling the Model 89 Infantry *Degen* were produced for sale to turn-of-the-century tourists and as gift items. The blade on the extreme right is genuine Damascus in the *"Grosser Rose"* pattern. It is decorated with blue panels with gold inlay. The etch commemorates a visit to Solingen by *Kaiser Wilhelm II* on 11 August 1899. The example on the far left cites the same event with statements proclaiming the merits of the smithy and the beauty of the German mountain country. *Jack Staehle and Thomas T. Wittmann Collection. Photo by Charles H. Jenkins, III.*

RIGHT: The 80th Birthday Honor *Degen* for *Kanzler* Bismarck. This custom ordered piece contains a "large rose" pattern Damascus steel blade that is etched, blued and gilded. The dedication on the obverse blade is in raised gold script letters and honors *Kanzler von Bismarck* on his 80th birthday on 1 April 1895. The manufacturer of this magnificent sidearm was the *Weyersberg, Kirschbaum & Cie* (WK&C) company in Solingen. The *Degen* is dated 1 April 1895. This exquisite sword currently is in the *Deutscheswaffenmuseum* collection in Solingen. *Johnson Reference Books & Militaria Archives.*

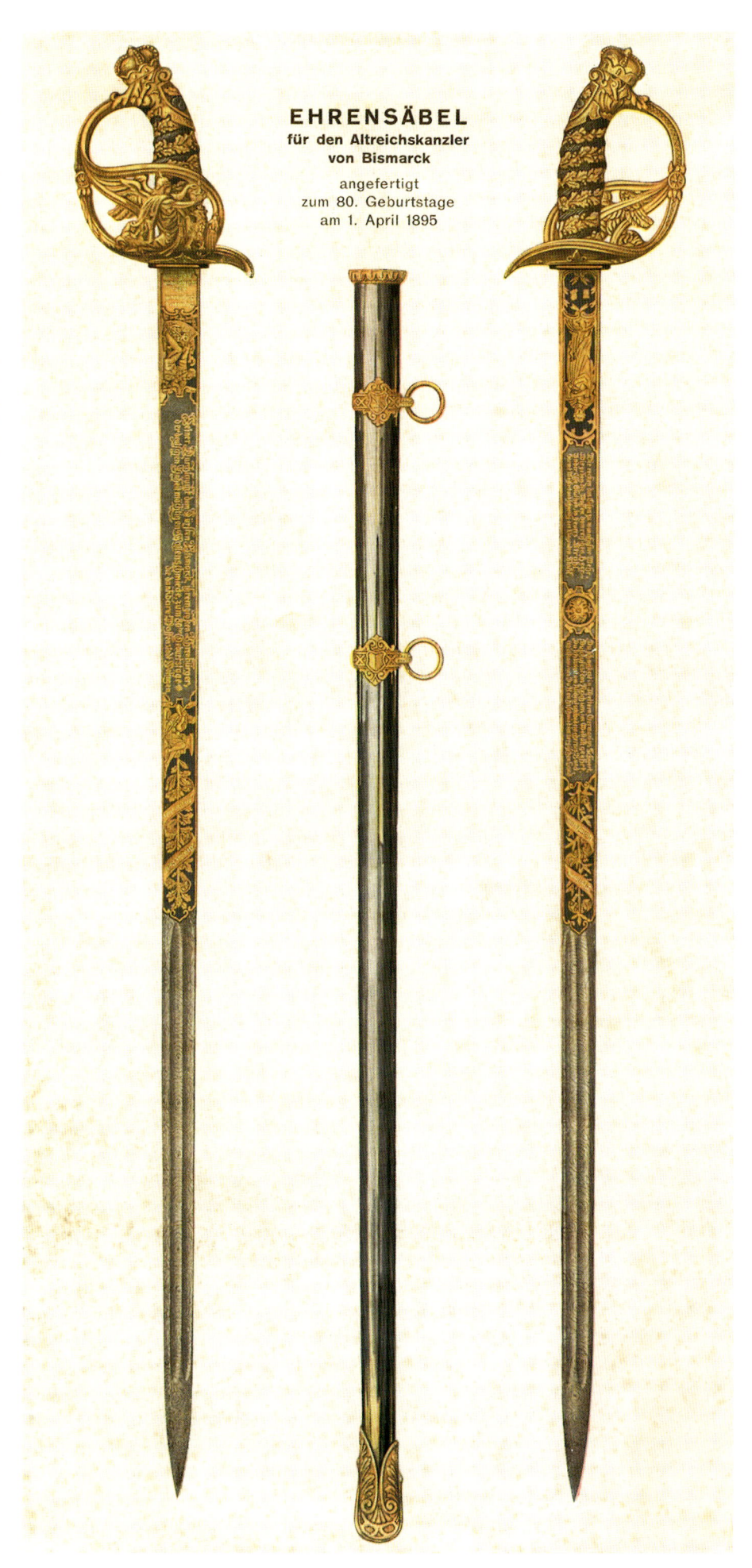

EHRENSÄBEL
für den Altreichskanzler
von Bismarck
angefertigt
zum 80. Geburtstage
am 1. April 1895

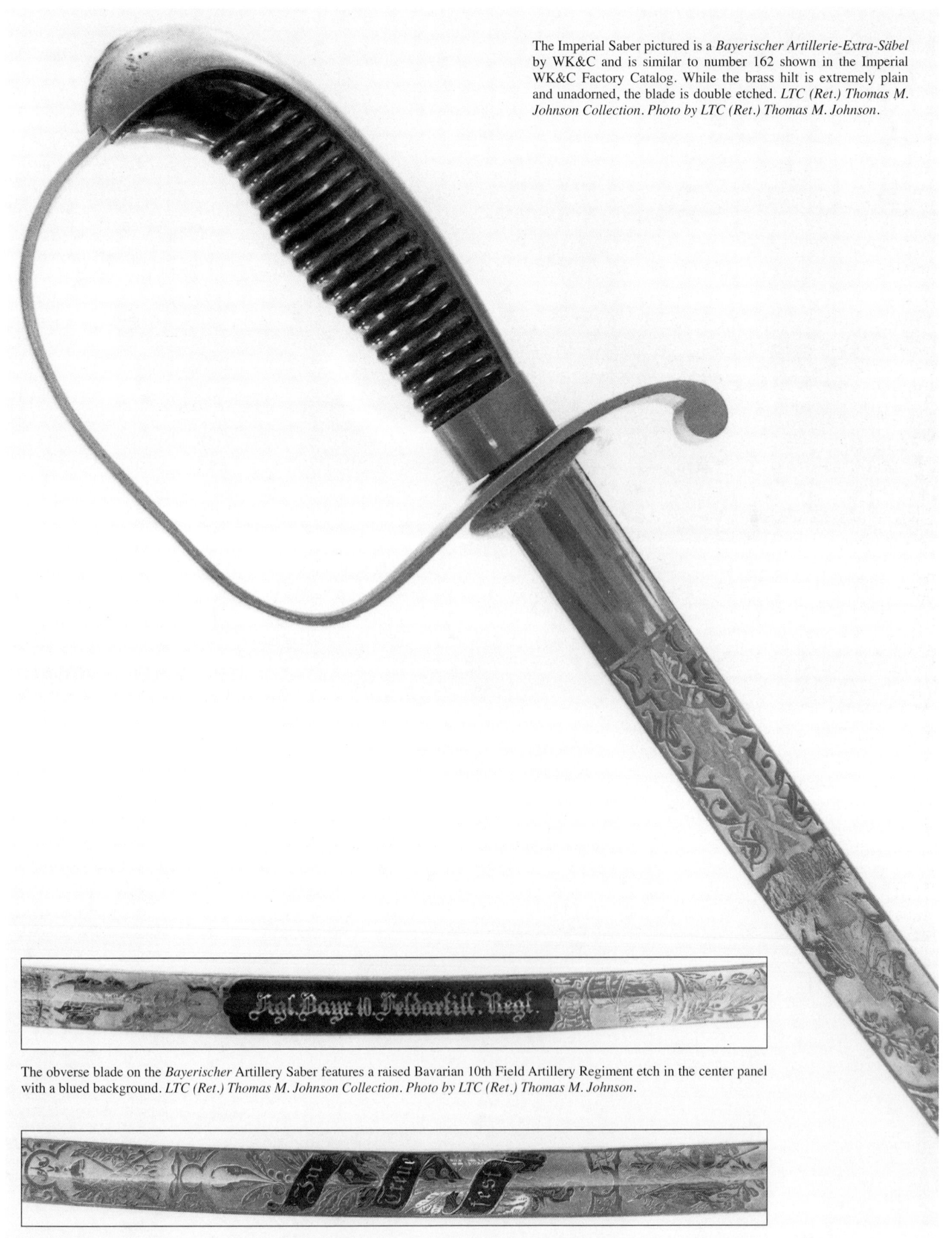

Imperial German Edged Weaponry

The Imperial Saber pictured is a *Bayerischer Artillerie-Extra-Säbel* by WK&C and is similar to number 162 shown in the Imperial WK&C Factory Catalog. While the brass hilt is extremely plain and unadorned, the blade is double etched. *LTC (Ret.) Thomas M. Johnson Collection. Photo by LTC (Ret.) Thomas M. Johnson.*

The obverse blade on the *Bayerischer* Artillery Saber features a raised Bavarian 10th Field Artillery Regiment etch in the center panel with a blued background. *LTC (Ret.) Thomas M. Johnson Collection. Photo by LTC (Ret.) Thomas M. Johnson.*

The reverse blade on the *Bayerischer* Artillery Saber by WK&C features the typical Imperial Bavarian *"In Treue fest"* motto raised on a blue ribbon panel. *LTC (Ret.) Thomas M. Johnson Collection. Photo by LTC (Ret.) Thomas M. Johnson.*

A one-year volunteer in the *Prussian* Infantry proudly displays his enlisted saber complete with *Faustriemen*. This volunteer is identified by the twisted black and white piping on the shoulder strap. One-year volunteers were usually highly educated, middle-class young men, who were privileged to serve only one year instead of the usual three year obligation. The one-year volunteers could choose their regiments, lived with other volunteers and usually messed in local restaurants. *LTC (Ret.) Thomas M. Johnson Photo Collection.*

On rare occasions, one can locate an original Imperial era photograph in color, as demonstrated by this formal studio portrait. *LTC (Ret.) Thomas M. Johnson Photo Collection. Photo by Gustav Fischer, Dresden.*

Imperial German Edged Weaponry

The importance that Imperial German military men placed on their edged weapons is evident in this studio portrait. Although the sword is merely a plain nickel-hilted Dove head model, it has been purposely moved to "center stage" to be readily visible in this photograph. *LTC (Ret.) Thomas M. Johnson Photo Collection. Photo by Atelier Tepper, Berlin.*

Imperial Telegraph One-year Volunteer who is wearing an enlisted nickel-plated saber with a typical leather strap *Faustriemen*. *LTC (Ret.) Thomas M. Johnson Photo Collection. Photo by Constantin Luck, Düsseldorf.*

Hessen Artillery officer with a variant pattern Lion head saber. *LTC (Ret.) Thomas M. Johnson Photo Collection. Copy Photo by Charles H. Jenkins, III.*

Imperial Infantry officer with his *Frau*. The Dove head pattern saber clearly shows the typical painted scabbard wear and the correct wrap of the officer sword knot. *LTC (Ret.) Thomas M. Johnson Photo Collection. Photo by Globus Atelier, Berlin.*

Prussian Lieutenant Kurt Poland in undress service uniform with Dove head officer saber adorned with officer knot. Many officers preferred the overcoat due to its great comfort. The back of the photo stated that Lt. Poland was killed in France in 1914. *LTC (Ret.) Thomas M. Johnson Photo Collection. Photo by Otto Wendt, Quedunburg.*

OPPOSITE: Another view of an Imperial sword sidearm complete with a sword knot mounted on a horseman's saddle utilizing a large leather hanging accouterment. The individual in the picture has scribbled across the top of the picture his last name and the date, "November 1914". *LTC (Ret.) Thomas M. Johnson Photo Collection.*

Prinz Georg of Bavaria is pictured wearing a Bavarian Infantry officer saber with a large *"Gala"* parade sword knot. *LTC (Ret.) Thomas M. Johnson Photo Collection.*

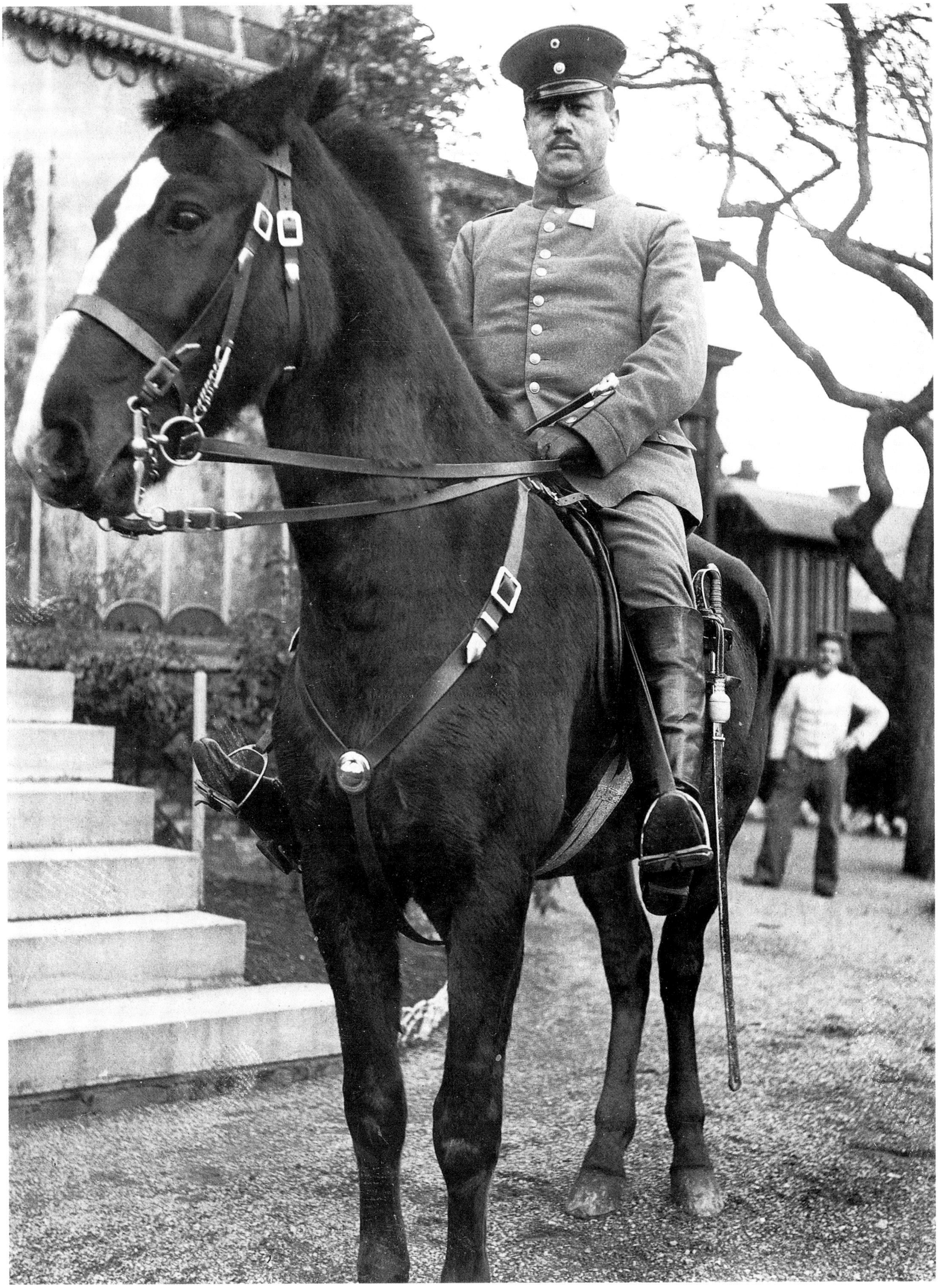

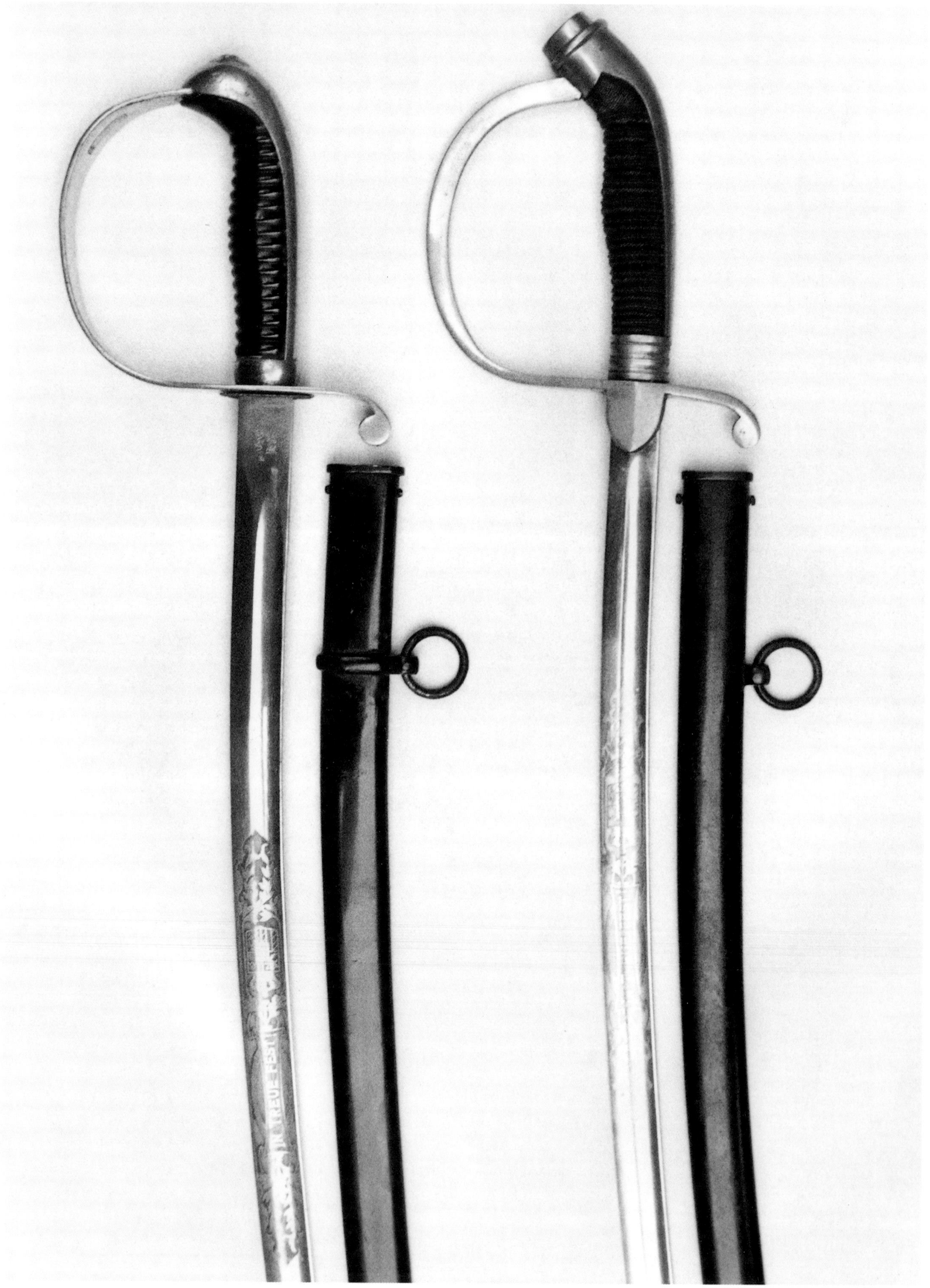

Swords of the German Army during the Imperial Era

OPPOSITE: Nickel-hilted Bavarian cavalry sabers. The enlisted pattern on the left has a nickel-plated steel hilt with slotted knucklebow. The grip is black celluloid over wood, without wire wrap. The single fullered blade is stamped with the king and knight heads logo of WK&C. The blade spine is marked with the retailer, *"JOS. VIERHEILIGS NACHF"*. The scabbard is black enamel. The Dragoon Officer pattern on the right has a solid German silver hilt with removable pommel. The handle is fishskin wrapped with silver wire. The blade is unmarked. The black enamel scabbard shows the single ring configuration without hanger band. Both blades are etched with the Bavarian coat-of-arms and the motto, *"In Treue Fest"*. *Rurik Diehl/Clarence Geier Collections. Photo by Victor Diehl.*

BELOW: Bavarian Infantry Officer sabers. The gilded B-shaped knucklebow of this saber is easily recognized. The two sabers shown are slightly different in hilt configuration and material. The left saber has a brass hilt, while the one on the right is gilded steel. Both sabers have slotted quillon ends. The left saber may be disassembled, while the pommel on the right model is peened over. The gilt grip wire is missing from the saber on the left. The blades of both sabers are identical with single fuller and false edge. The Bavarian motto, *"In Treue Fest"* is etched on each blade. *Dr. David L. Valuska Collection. Photo by Victor Diehl.*

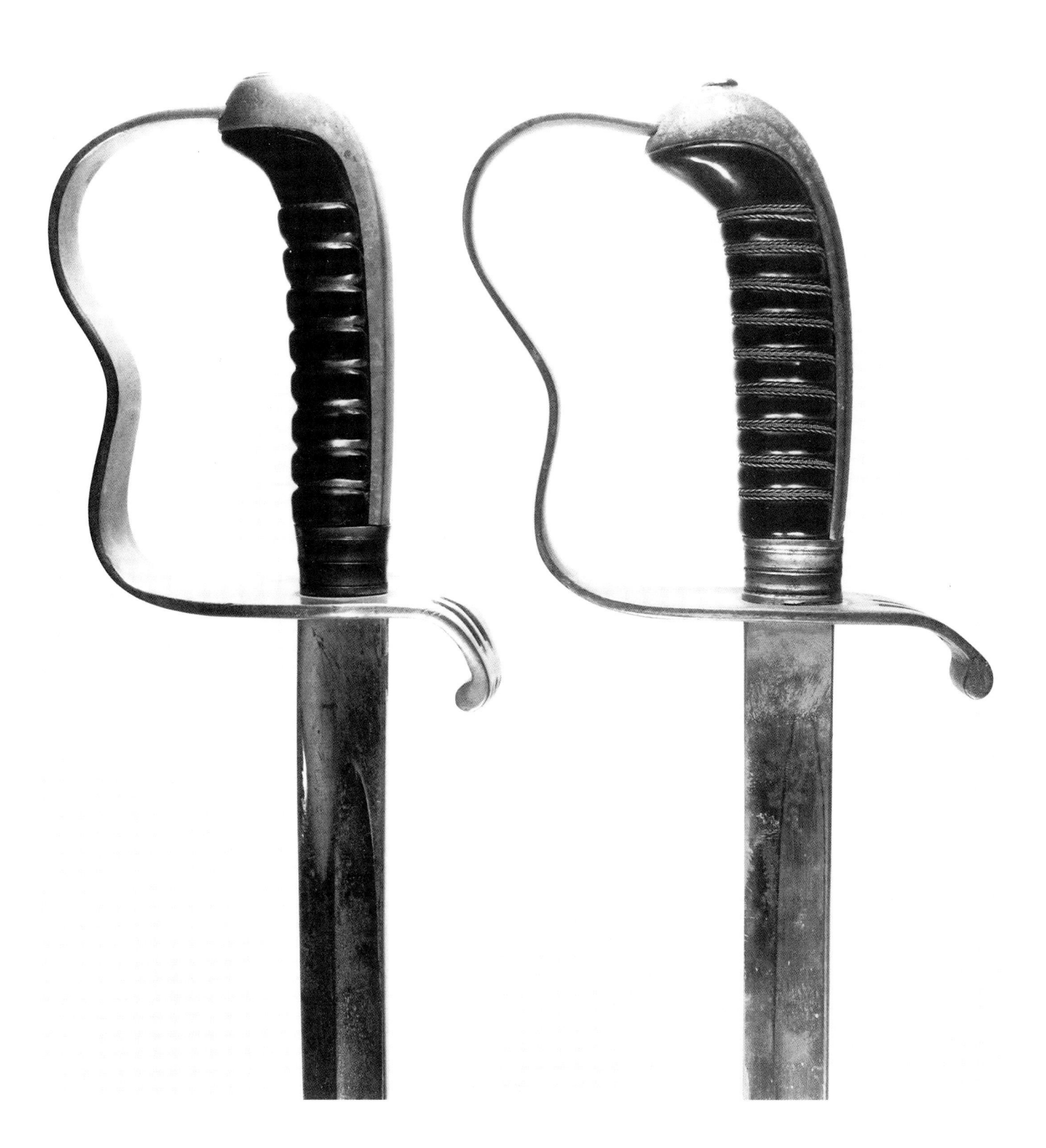

Pictured in color is a rare Imperial Damascus Bavarian Heavy Cavalry sword by J. A. Henckels, Solingen. This desirable sword was presented in commemoration of the 100-year founding of the *Reiter* (Rider) Regiment, 24 September 1915. The plain brass handguard features three brass "fingers". The unusual blade is "maiden hair" Damascus on the obverse side, and the reverse side is unfinished Damascus, i.e. appears as a normal, nickel-plated blade. *Richard R. Williams Collection. Photo by Dick Scott Fine Photography, Houston.*

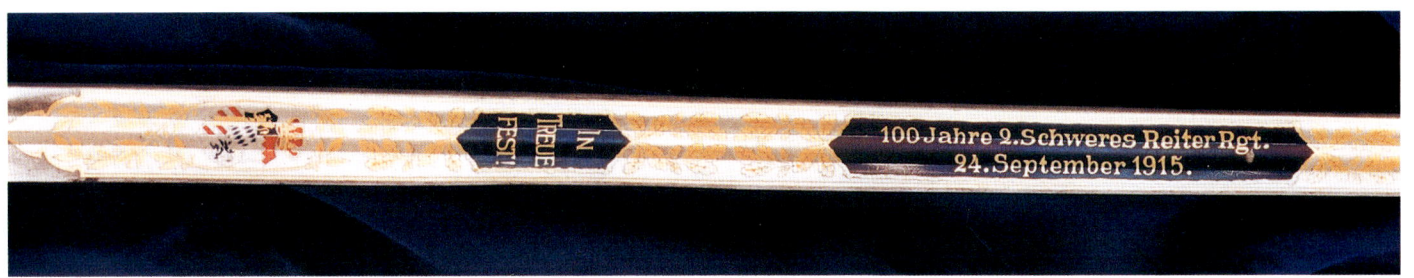

Swords of the German Army during the Imperial Era

Reverse view of the J. A. Henckels Imperial Damascus Bavarian Heavy Cavalry sword. The sharkskin grip is in perfect condition, and the backstrap is checkered brass at the bottom. Note that the reverse Damascus blade is unfinished. This was obtained by acid treating only one side of the blade and leaving the other side untreated. This was a difficult process, as one side had to be completely protected when dipped into the acid bath to bring out the pattern. *Richard R. Williams Collection. Photo by Dick Scott Fine Photography, Houston.*

On the obverse blade of the J. A. Henckels Imperial Bavarian Heavy Cavalry sword is a beautiful presentation panel which is bordered by raised gold oak leaves, acorns, and berries. Within this border is a dark blue panel with raised gold letters which state (translated), "This sword was given to commemorate the 100-year founding of the Rider Regiment". Beneath that inscription appears, "24 September 1915". Near the top of the panel is the Imperial motto, *"In Treue Fest!"* and a multi-colored red, blue, and black Royal Crest with a red background and two lions. The quality and uniqueness of this blade cannot be over-emphasized, as it is truly a work of art. *Richard R. Williams Collection. Photo by Dick Scott Fine Photography, Houston.*

Rare Imperial Bavarian Heavy Cavalry sword with colored panels by J. A. Henckels. The basket handguard features three brass "fingers", and the brass backstrap is checkered at the bottom. The grip is constructed of sharkskin over a wooden base. This interesting Imperial sword is genuine "maiden hair" Damascus steel on the obverse side and unfinished Damascus on the reverse. This result was obtained by acid-treating only one side of the Damascus blade and leaving the other side untreated. This was a difficult process, as the one side had to be completely protected. The J. A. Henckels "conjoined twins" trademark is visible stamped into the obverse ricasso. *LTC (Ret.) Thomas M. Johnson Collection. Photo by LTC (Ret.) Thomas M. Johnson.*

BELOW: Close-up view of the obverse blade of the rare Imperial Bavarian Heavy Cavalry sword by J. A. Henckels. The Damascus steel obverse blade features a beautiful presentation panel which is bordered by raised gold oak leaves, acorns, and berries. Within this border is a deep blue panel with a raised gold presentation which reads (translated), "This sword was given to commemorate the 100-year founding of the Riding Regiment. 24 September 1915". Approximately three inches above the presentation panel is another blue panel which features in raised gold letters the standard Imperial motto, *"In Treue Fest!"* Near the top of the Damascus blade is the multi-colored Royal Crest in red, blue, and black. *LTC (Ret.) Thomas M. Johnson Collection. Photo by LTC (Ret.) Thomas M. Johnson.*

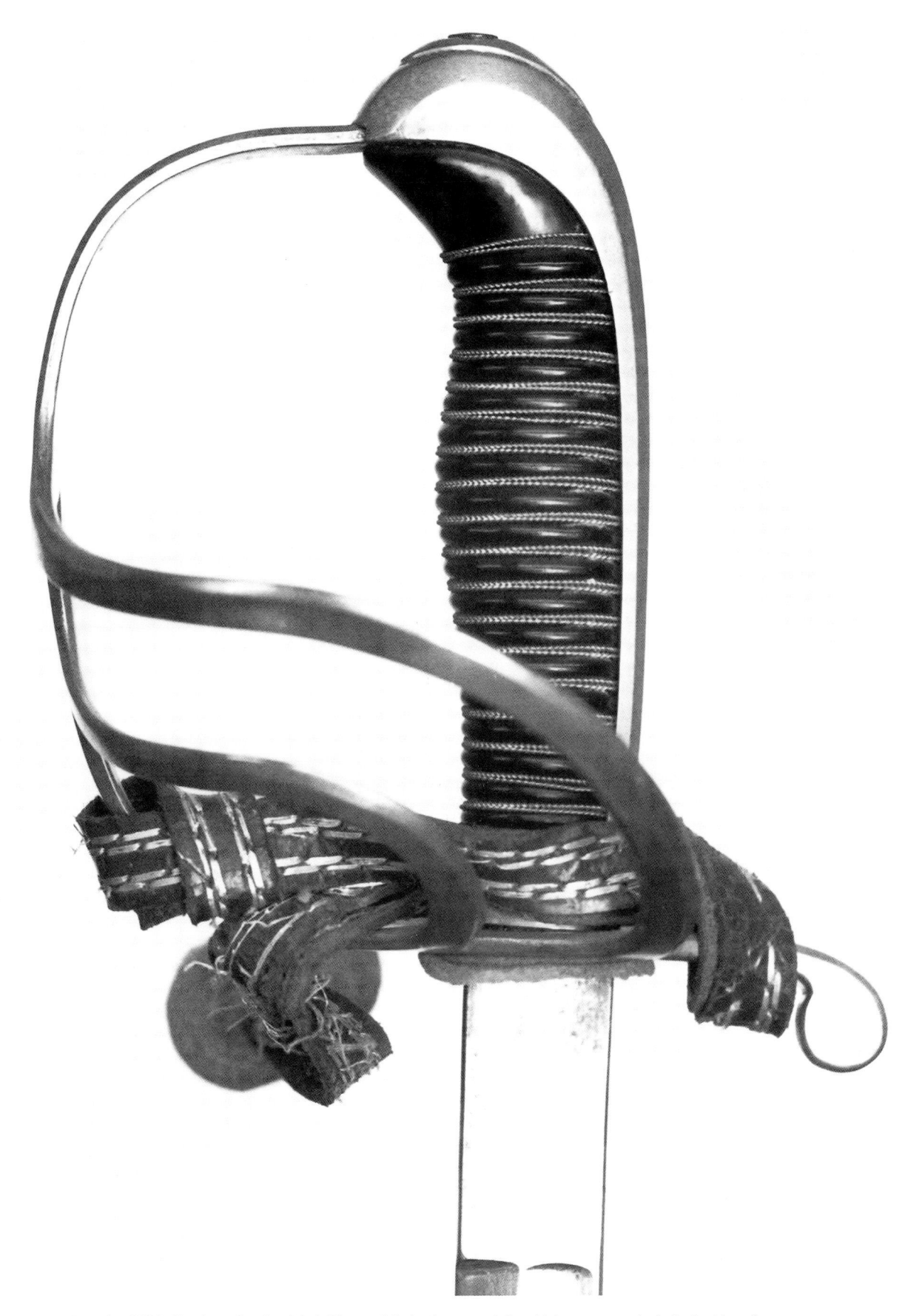

Bavarian NCO Cavalry saber in nickel. The straight backstrap and flat sidebars are standard. Both sides of the blade are etched with the Bavarian motto, *"In Treue Fest"* (Steadfast with Loyalty). *Edward M. Owen, Jr. Collection. Photo by Edward M. Owen, Jr.*

Imperial German Edged Weaponry

LEFT: An enlisted man in the *Hannover Train Batallion No.10* with his basket hilt saber model 1852, complete with *Faustriemen*. This saber was adopted by Imperial train units in 1900. *LTC (Ret.) Thomas M. Johnson Photo Collection. Photo by Fr. Walkenhorst, Hannover.*

BELOW: A Bavarian *Vizefeldwebel* named *Fischer* wearing the basket-hilt saber with silver and blue Bavarian officer portepee poses with his wife or girlfriend. The scabbard is painted black as directed by military regulations, and the photograph is dated 1916. *LTC (Ret.) Thomas M. Johnson Photo Collection.*

LEFT: This *Saxon Zahlmeister Aspirant* is wearing the beautiful *Saxon Garde Reiter* officer's sword complete with the distinctive *Saxon* sword knot. While not visible in this photo, the hilt of this saber features a highly detailed Lion head and the *Saxon* coat-of-arms at the union of the sidebars. This sword also features an integral metal thumb ring, rather than the usual leather *Fingerschlauf*. Metal thumb rings date to the 1600s. *LTC (Ret.) Thomas M. Johnson Photo Collection. Photo by Hugo Müller, Freiberg.*

ABOVE: Pictured is a Bavarian Cavalry officer wearing the distinctive basket hilt saber. The silver and blue Bavarian knot with split ring between strap and acorn is easily seen. *LTC (Ret.) Thomas M. Johnson Photo Collection. Photo by Ernst Marth, München.*

A great looking group of troops from the Royal Bavarian 2nd Train Detachment. They are all wearing the distinctive Bavarian Train Saber in nickel, complete with white leather hangers and Imperial "shaving brush" sword knots. Note the numerous "enhanced" mustaches provided by the photo studio. *LTC (Ret.) Thomas M. Johnson Photo Collection.*

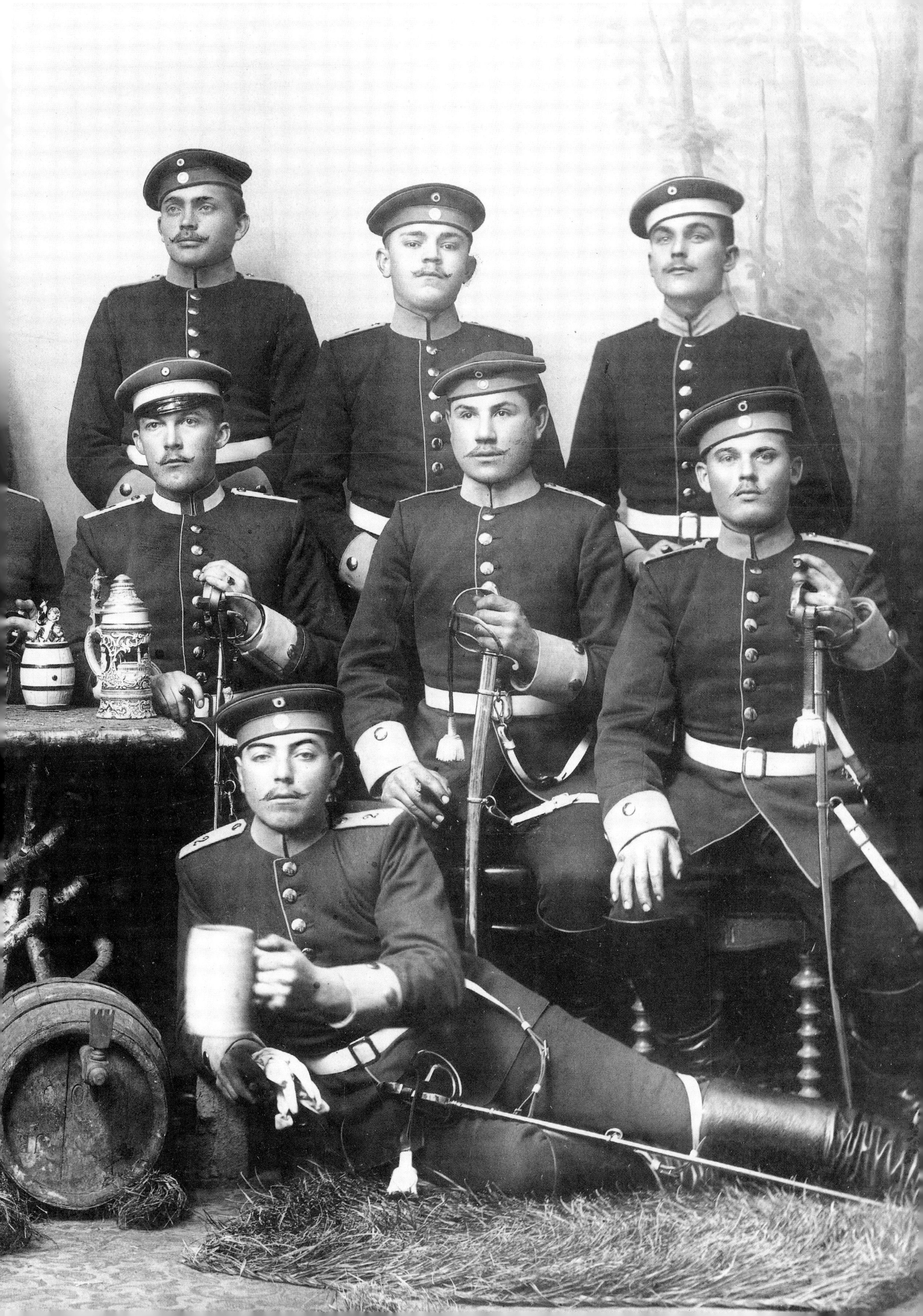

Bavarian Infantry *"Landsturmbrigade"* with sabers. The double sidebars are typical of this pattern. *LTC (Ret.) Thomas M. Johnson Photo Collection. Photo by Charles H. Jenkins, III.*

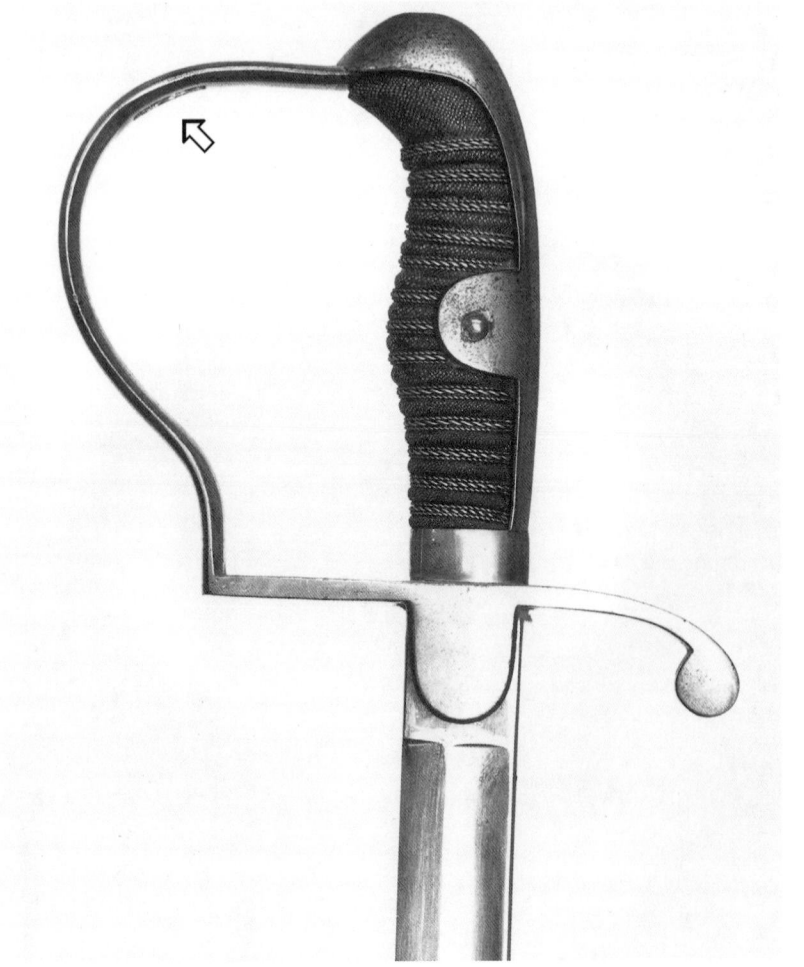

Nickel "Dove head" sword. Collectors should note the slot in the knucklebow for tying the portepee (see arrow). The single-fullered blade is marked to the firm WK&C. *Edward M. Owen, Jr. Collection. Photo by Edward M. Owen, Jr.*

210

Swords of the German Army during the Imperial Era

Two Imperial Noncommissioned Officers' swords with blue panel etched blades are pictured in color. At the left is a *"Grosser"* size sword with its original sword knot. The obverse blade inscription reads, *"1. Garde-Feld-Artill. Regt. Berlin"* next to a mounted Guard Officer, all in blued backgrounds. On the right is a standard size Noncommissioned Officer sword which bears an inscription of the famous *"Reiter Regt. 14"*. Richard R. Williams Collection. Photo by Dick Scott Fine Photography, Houston.

211

Imperial German Edged Weaponry

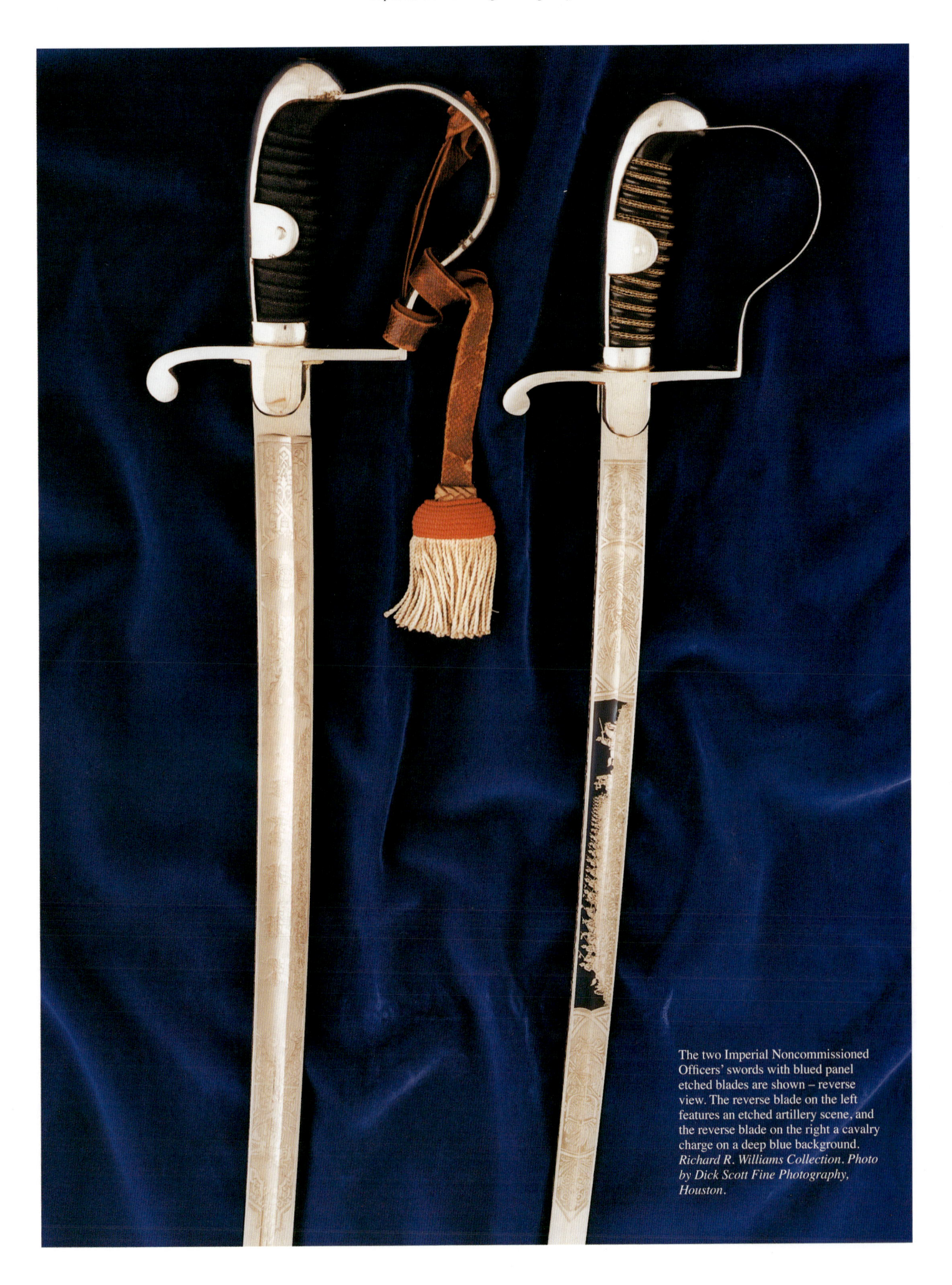

The two Imperial Noncommissioned Officers' swords with blued panel etched blades are shown – reverse view. The reverse blade on the left features an etched artillery scene, and the reverse blade on the right a cavalry charge on a deep blue background. *Richard R. Williams Collection. Photo by Dick Scott Fine Photography, Houston.*

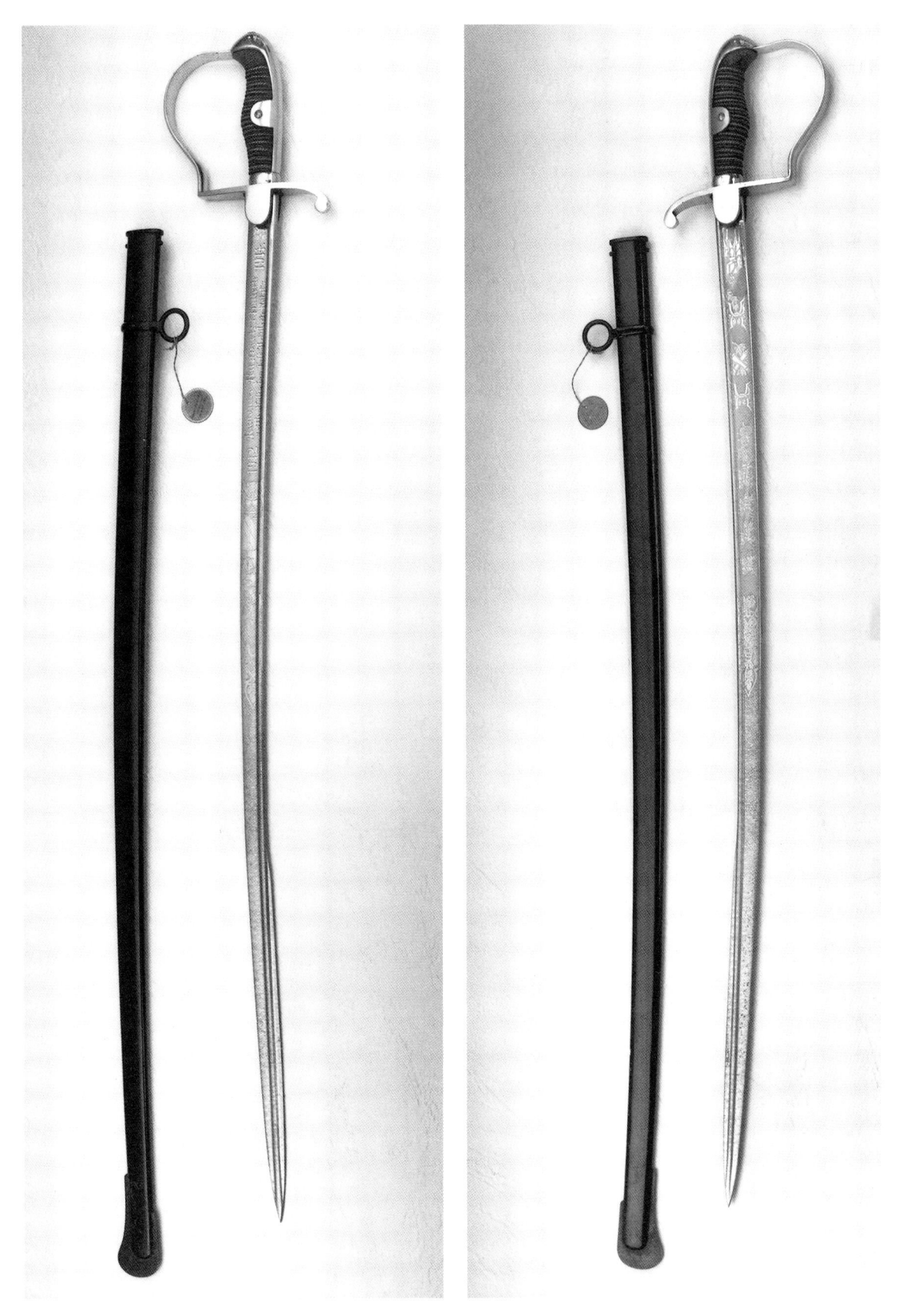

Imperial "Other Ranks" nickel plain hilt sword with Damascus steel blade. This very impressive Imperial nickel plain hilt sword for "Other Ranks" and "P"-shaped knucklebow is complete with Damascus blade and raised gold presentation (seldom encountered on an "Other Ranks" sword) but available at the purchaser's discretion. A translation of the blade inscription reads, "1912 Gunner Ruppertz, 1st Battery, 1st Westphalian Field Artillery Rgt. No.7, 1914". This sword was sent home in 1945 by U. S. Army PFC Chester Legenc, who picked it out of a pile of confiscated weapons. A unique feature of this piece is the tag still attached to the scabbard ring. It reads, "Bicycle Works, 'Bismarck', Inc., Bergerhof, Rhineland". This sword is now in the collection of Kevin Bourgeois of Manchester, New Hampshire who "purchased" it from his own Uncle, Chester. RIGHT: Reverse view of the Imperial nickel plain hilt sword for "Other Ranks", complete with Damascus blade and raised gold presentation. Note the detailed gold overlay design on the reverse Damascus blade. The design includes mounted German horsemen pulling artillery pieces, crossed artillery cannons, etc. *Kevin Bourgeois Collection. Photo by Raiche Photography.*

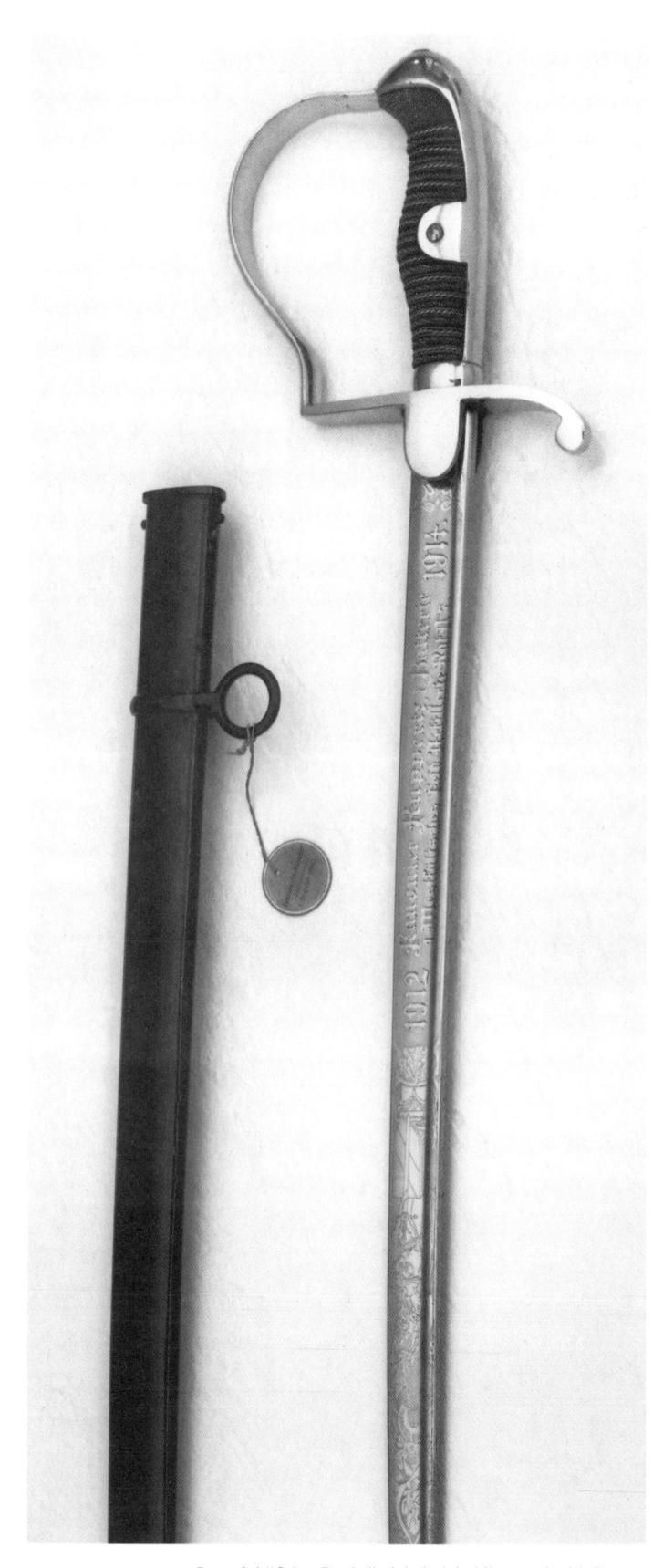

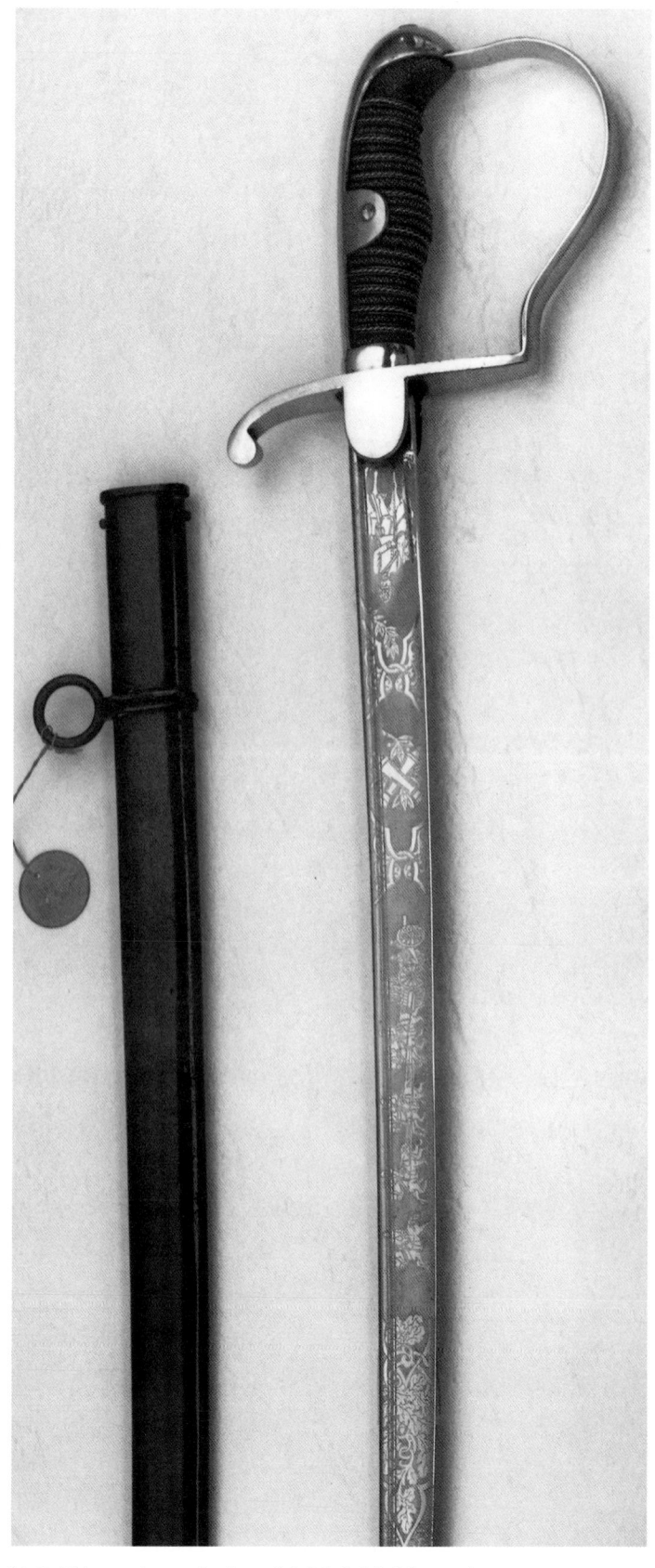

Imperial German Edged Weaponry

Imperial "Other Ranks" nickel plain hilt sword with Damascus blade. This very impressive Imperial nickel plain hilt sword for "Other Ranks" and "P"-shaped knucklebow is complete with Damascus blade and raised gold presentation (seldom encountered on an "Other Ranks" sword) but available at the purchaser's discretion. A translation of the blade inscription reads, "1912 Gunner Ruppertz, 1st Battery, 1st Westphalian Field Artillery Rgt. No.7, 1914". This sword was sent home in 1945 by U. S. Army PFC Chester Legenc, who picked it out of a pile of confiscated weapons. A unique feature of this piece is the tag still attached to the scabbard ring. It reads, "Bicycle Works 'Bismarck', Inc., Berghof, Rhineland". This sword is now in the collection of Kevin Bourgeois of Manchester, New Hampshire who "purchased" it from his own Uncle Chester. RIGHT: Reverse view of the Imperial nickel plain hilt sword for "Other Ranks", complete with Damascus blade and raised gold presentation. Note the detailed gold overlay design on the reverse Damascus blade. The design includes mounted German horsemen pulling artillery pieces, crossed artillery cannons, etc. *Kevin Bourgeois Collection. Photo by Raiche Photography.*

RIGHT: Pictured in color is the obverse hilt of a near mint condition Imperial Officer's Deluxe Saber with no manufacturer's trademark. An Imperial *Adler* (eagle) with a gold motif decorates both the obverse and the reverse upper blade. The grip is a brass wire wrapped black leather. *Major General (Ret.) Theodore W. Paulson Collection. Photo by Major General (Ret.) Theodore W. Paulson.*

BELOW: *Fusilier* gilt "Dove head" saber. The blade is marked, *"EISENHAUER"* and double-etched with floral and military motifs. The reverse blade is stamped, "Ewald Cleff, Solingen". *Edward M. Owen, Jr. Collection. Photo by Edward M. Owen, Jr.*

215

Imperial German Edged Weaponry

Personalized Army NCO sword distributed by M. Neumann, *Hoflieferant*, Berlin. This early presentation saber was presented from a soldier named "Frommel" to his close friend, "Ostmann". Note the early sharkskin-wrapped grip. *LTC (Ret.) Thomas M. Johnson Collection. Photo by LTC (Ret.) Thomas M. Johnson.*

Swords of the German Army during the Imperial Era

Extreme close-up of the early Ostmann personalized Army NCO sword. The panel behind the raised gold dedication is dark blue. *LTC (Ret.) Thomas M. Johnson Collection. Photo by LTC (Ret.) Thomas M. Johnson.*

The Imperial Bavarian portepee being properly worn with this scarce *Fusilier* sword. *Fusilier* scabbards were either 2-ring or with the upper scabbard fitting having a frog hook. *LTC (Ret.) Thomas M. Johnson Photo Collection. Photo by Carl Loos, Weidenau.*

Pictured is a Bavarian Senior NCO wearing his gold mounted Bavarian Infantry officer saber. This saber was offered with blades 20, 23, and 25 mm wide with corresponding hilt size. The silver and blue Bavarian Infantry sword knot is tied around the hilt. *LTC (Ret.) Thomas M. Johnson Photo Collection.*

Enlisted Artilleryman with "Dove head" issue saber. The tie of the *Faustriemen* is an important detail. *LTC (Ret.) Thomas M. Johnson Photo Collection. Photo by Charles H. Jenkins, III.*

A Junior NCO in the *1st Posen* Field Artillery Regiment No.20. The NCO lace around the uniform collar and cuffs, as well as the sword knot around his Artillery saber's hilt, denotes this proud young man's rank as *Unteroffizier*. *LTC (Ret.) Thomas M. Johnson Photo Collection.*

An enlisted member of the Field Artillery wears his "Other Ranks" saber with a distinctive *Faustriemen*. The *Faustriemen* is tied in the same manner as the officer sword knot. *LTC (Ret.) Thomas M. Johnson Photo Collection. Photo by C. Wachenfield, Halle.*

Three young *Cannoneers* serving with the *Field Artillery Regiment Field Marshal Count Waldersee (Schlesweg) No.9*. All three enlisted men are carrying the nickel hilted Dove head artillery saber complete with *Faustriemen*. The much favored overcoat and cap were the last model uniform items adopted in 1914. *LTC (Ret.) Thomas M. Johnson Photo Collection.*

A proud *Saxon* Artillery gunner wears his saber complete with *Faustriemen*. He is a member of the Royal *Saxon* 1st Field Artillery Regiment No.12 garrisoned in Dresden. *LTC (Ret.) Thomas M. Johnson Photo Collection. Photo by Franz Ehrlich Studio, Dresden.*

A Gunner in Field Artillery *Regiment von Scharnhorst* (1st Hannover) No.10, His enlisted Artillery saber is worn complete with *Faustriemen*. The regain chain is clearly visible on the leather hanging strap. *LTC (Ret.) Thomas M. Johnson Photo Collection. Photo by Paul Hassert Studio, Hannover.*

A Cavalry One-year Volunteer with his D-guard saber. The scabbard is pre-war nickel. Note the white leather sword hanger and "shaving-brush" sword knot. *LTC (Ret.) Thomas M. Johnson Photo Collection. Photo by Ludwig Giesecke, Erlangen.*

Three Imperial Army friends posing together for a photograph. Two of these *Cannoneers* are One-year Volunteers and the 3rd is an NCO who is on the right and displays an officer portepee on his sword. These *Cannoneers* are all members of the 9th Field Artillery Regiment founded in Itzehoe in 1866. *LTC (Ret.) Thomas M. Johnson Photo Collection. Photo by H. G. Mehlert, Itzehoe.*

Vizefeldwebel of the Field Artillery Regiment General Field Marshal Gr. Waldersee Nr.9. He is wearing a Lion head saber with nickel plated scabbard. The officer knot denotes his rank. This picture is dated June 1903. *LTC (Ret.) Thomas M. Johnson Photo Collection. Photo by A. Mocsigay, Hamburg.*

FAR LEFT: An NCO named Max Obenauf of the Royal *Saxon* 6th Field Artillery Regiment Nr.68. He is pictured wearing the nickel "P" guard Artillery saber with *Faustriemen* denoting his rank as a Junior NCO. *LTC (Ret.) Thomas M. Johnson Photo Collection. Photo by Donner, Riesa.*

LEFT: A Bavarian *"Unteroffizier mit Portepee"* in his dress uniform. The motto *"In Treue Fest"* is clearly seen on the belt buckle. The NCO is wearing the Bavarian "P" guard officer saber with blue and silver portepee. The double wrap of the saber knot around the backstrap is an alternate form for this model saber. *LTC (Ret.) Thomas M. Johnson Photo Collection. Photo by Carl Berne, München.*

Imperial German Edged Weaponry

This infantry sergeant is a member of the *Grenadier Regiment King Friedrich der Grosse (3rd East Prussian) No.4*. He is wearing a highly detailed Lion head saber with crossed sabers on the langet. The guard terminates in a beautiful Lion head. *LTC (Ret.) Thomas M. Johnson Photo Collection. Photo by Willy Koltre, Stendal.*

A One-year Volunteer in the *Vorpomm Feldart-Rgt. No.38*, garrisoned in Stettin, Germany. His Dove head artillery saber is complete with correctly tied sword knot. This young *cannoneer* is also wearing a non-regulation heavy gold bracelet for the portrait. *LTC (Ret.) Thomas M. Johnson Photo Collection. Photo by L. Klett, Stettin.*

Studio portrait of a Bavarian NCO and *Frau*. The tie of the silver and blue Bavarian knot on the hilt of the Infantry Officer saber is standard. *LTC (Ret.) Thomas M. Johnson Photo Collection. Photo by Georg Düll, München.*

Swords of the German Army during the Imperial Era

A group of senior NCO's in the *2nd Baden Grenadier Regiment Kaiser Wilhelm I No.110*. Their nickeled sabers are adorned with the new officer portepee for the occasion of this formal photograph. *LTC (Ret.) Thomas M. Johnson Photo Collection. Photo by Adolf Geiler, Rastatt.*

Imperial German Edged Weaponry

LEFT: A handsome One-year Volunteer in the Field Artillery Regiment Nr.10. He is wearing a pre-war "P" Guard saber with appropriate knot. *LTC (Ret.) Thomas M. Johnson Photo Collection. Photo by Emil Buch, Hannover.*

OPPOSITE: This original Imperial photograph is dated 1904 on the reverse. The officer is in the 9th Cavalry Brigade. He is wearing the rare "P" Guard saber with "tie down" ring on the top of the sword. When mounted on the side of the saddle this ring secured the saber in the scabbard. Note the white leather Lion head hangers. *LTC (Ret.) Thomas M. Johnson Photo Collection. Photo by Atelier Hülsen, Berlin.*

BELOW: A group of Bavarian Infantry Officers relaxing behind the front, circa 1916. The photograph may be dated by close examination of the uniforms being worn. The tunic with covered buttons on the *Bluse* (or blouse) was introduced in September 1915. At least four "B" Guard Infantry Officer sabers are visible. *SSGT (Ret.) T. Wayne Cunningham (USAF) Photo Collection. Copy Photo by Charles H. Jenkins, III.*

Swords of the German Army during the Imperial Era

This Bavarian Government Official is wearing his wartime "B-guard" infantry officer saber, complete with Bavarian knot on the occasion of his wedding in 1926. *LTC (Ret.) Thomas M. Johnson Photo Collection.*

An Imperial Bavarian officer named Ludwig Kast poses for a formal studio portrait wearing his "B-guard" officer saber with split-ring type Bavarian officer portepee. *LTC (Ret.) Thomas M. Johnson Photo Collection. Photo by Ant. Hillenbrand Schwabmünchen, Bobingen.*

A Bavarian infantry officer in his pre-World War I uniform. He is wearing an Infantry officer saber with silver and blue Bavarian portepee. *LTC (Ret.) Thomas M. Johnson Photo Collection. Photo by Adolf Koestler, München.*

Infantry *Leutnant* wearing his nickel hilted Dove head saber with portepee and beautiful nickeled scabbard. This officer obviously had little affinity for edged weapons or he would have chosen either a Lion head or chiseled and fire gilded *IOD89*. *LTC (Ret.) Thomas M. Johnson Photo Collection. Photo by Ferd. Bauer, Würzburg.*

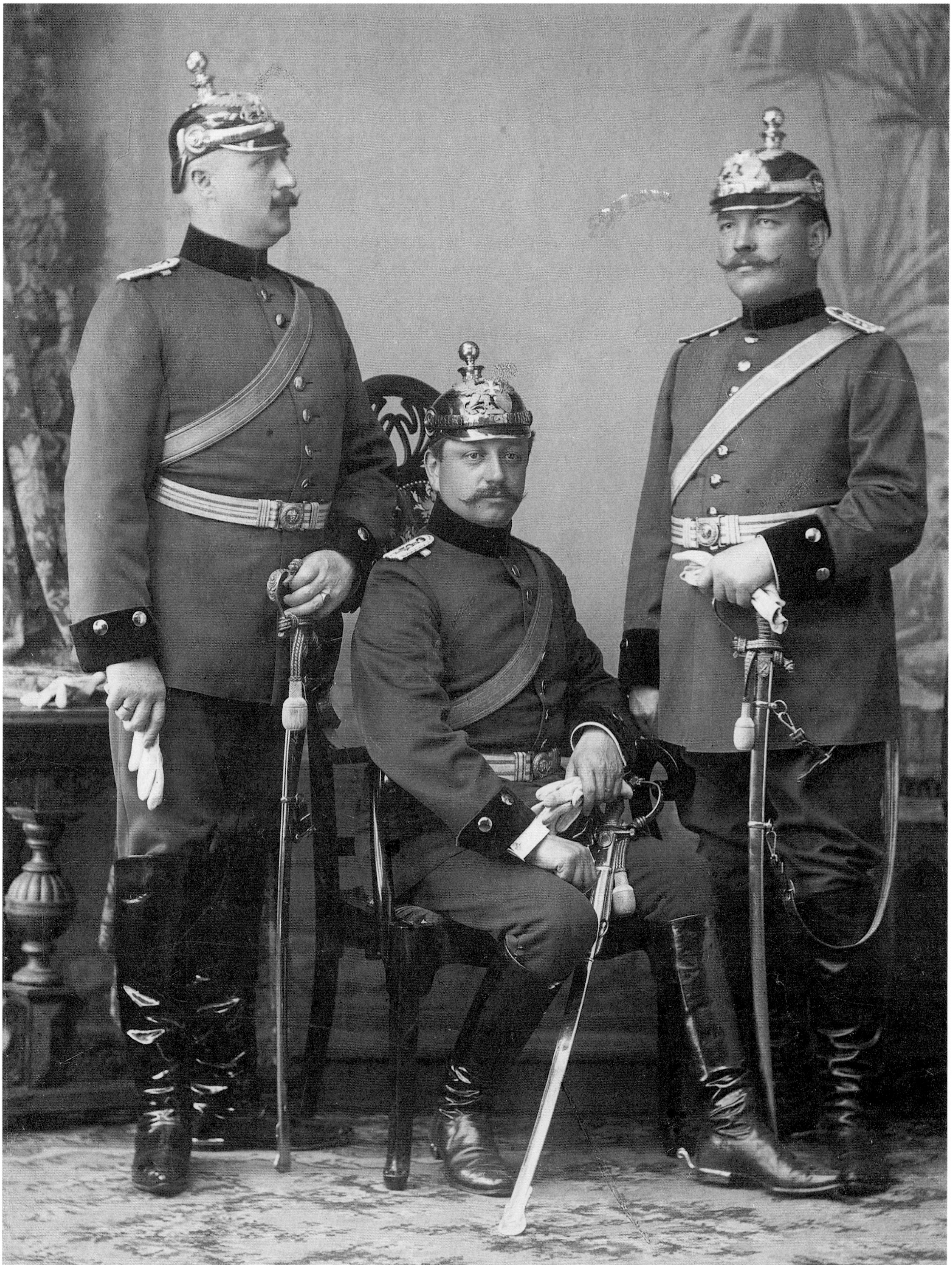

ABOVE: A Bavarian infantry officer wearing a nickel hilted officer's saber with "B-guard". This sword was modeled after the Austrian Infantry Officer's sword. *LTC (Ret.) Thomas M. Johnson Photo Collection. Photo by Karl F. Wunder, Hannover.*

OPPOSITE: Three *Baden* Artillery officers in dress uniforms pose for this studio portrait. They all selected the pre-war presentation grade Lion head sabers. The crossed cannons are seen on the langet of the sword being held by the officer on the right. *LTC (Ret.) Thomas M. Johnson Photo Collection. G. H. Hase & Sohn, Hofphotograph.*

RIGHT: This Infantry Lieutenant Colonel has selected a distinctive wrapping for his sword knot. The infantry *Degen* is of the pre-1906 configuration with nickeled scabbard and two hanger rings. *LTC (Ret.) Thomas M. Johnson Photo Collection.*

LEFT: Prince Arnuf of Bavaria and his wife. The distinctive Bavarian portepee with its blue and silver stemmed acorn is tied around a standard Bavarian Infantry Officer saber. *LTC (Ret.) Thomas M. Johnson Photo Collection. Photo by Anton Grainer, Traunstein.*

OPPOSITE
TOP: A grouping of One-year Volunteers with the Imperial Field Artillery Regiment 15 from Straasburg. The three NCOs in front are wearing their nickel Artillery sabers with *Faustriemen*. *LTC (Ret.) Thomas M. Johnson Photo Collection.*

BOTTOM: This 1897 portrait of the Cadre Detachment from the Military School in Lechfeld (South of Augsburg) illustrates both the Imperial "Dove head" and the *IOD M89* swords being worn. *LTC (Ret.) Thomas M. Johnson Photo Collection.*

Swords of the German Army during the Imperial Era

The famous "Hitler-Ludendorff" photo taken in 1923. Kriebel, Ludendorff and Röhm are all wearing Infantry officer *Degens*. The officers on the right and left sides are wearing Imperial "P-guard" sabers. *Photo Courtesy of Adam J. Portugal*.

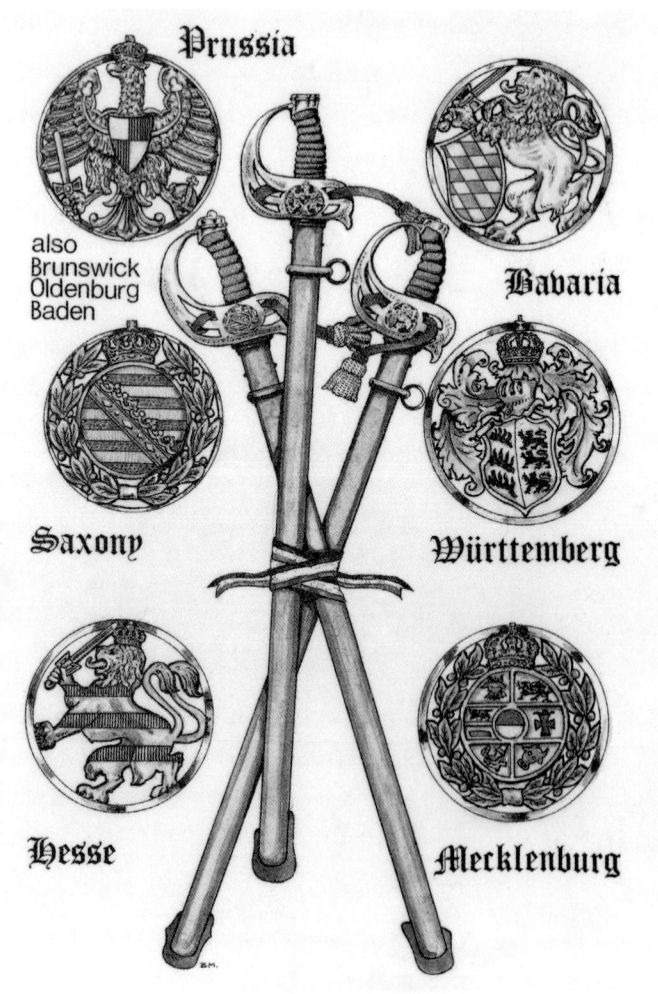

Cavalry *Degen* Model 1889 with Heraldic Arms of the Sovereign German State. These seals also adorned the guards of other models such as the *Infanterie Offizier's Degen* Model 89. *Artwork by Brian Molloy, United Kingdom*.

A good view of the Bavarian crest in the guard of a Model 1891 Bavarian Cavalry sword. The folding guard is indicative of privately purchased swords. The grip is a black colored material and is ribbed. A rotating nut secures the blade tang at the pommel. *LTC (Ret.) Thomas M. Johnson Photo Collection. Photo by LTC (Ret.) Thomas M. Johnson.*

The double etched blade is 32 3/4 inches long and has the regimental name on one side. The inscription reads, *"Kgl. Baÿr. 3. Chevaul. Herzog Carl Theodor"*. Duke Carl Theodor (1839-1909) was a General of Cavalry in the Bavarian Army. Raised in 1724, the regiment was named in honor of Carl Theodor in 1894 and at the same time he was appointed Chief of the Regiment. The bright steel scabbard has two fixed carrying rings. *LTC (Ret.) Thomas M. Johnson Photo Collection. Photo by LTC (Ret.) Thomas M. Johnson.*

Prussian Cavalry *Degen 89* with Damascus blade by Carl Eickhorn. The *Prussian* eagle dominates the folding guard. *LTC (Ret.) Thomas M. Johnson Photo Collection. Photo by LTC (Ret.) Thomas M. Johnson.*

Swords of the German Army during the Imperial Era

Reverse hilt of the *Prussian* Cavalry *Degen 89* with Damascus blade by Carl Eickhorn. The reverse blade bears scroll-work containing, "*Eisenhauer, Damast Stahl*". *LTC (Ret.) Thomas M. Johnson Photo Collection. Photo by LTC (Ret.) Thomas M. Johnson.*

Bavarian *Chevauleger* (Light Horse) NCO with Cavalry *Degen* Model 89. The *Degen* contains the Bavarian shield on the guard, and correct sword knot for *Unteroffizier*. The swallows nest on the shoulders signifies band membership, perhaps Regimental Trumpeter. The hanger strap is clearly visible. *LTC (Ret.) Thomas M. Johnson Photo Collection. Copy Photo by Charles H. Jenkins, III.*

Cavalry *Degen* Model 1889. The obverse folding basket contains the *Saxon* coat-of-arms. The knuckebow is slotted to facilitate tying the portepee. *Edward M. Owen, Jr. Collection. Photo by Edward M. Owen, Jr.*

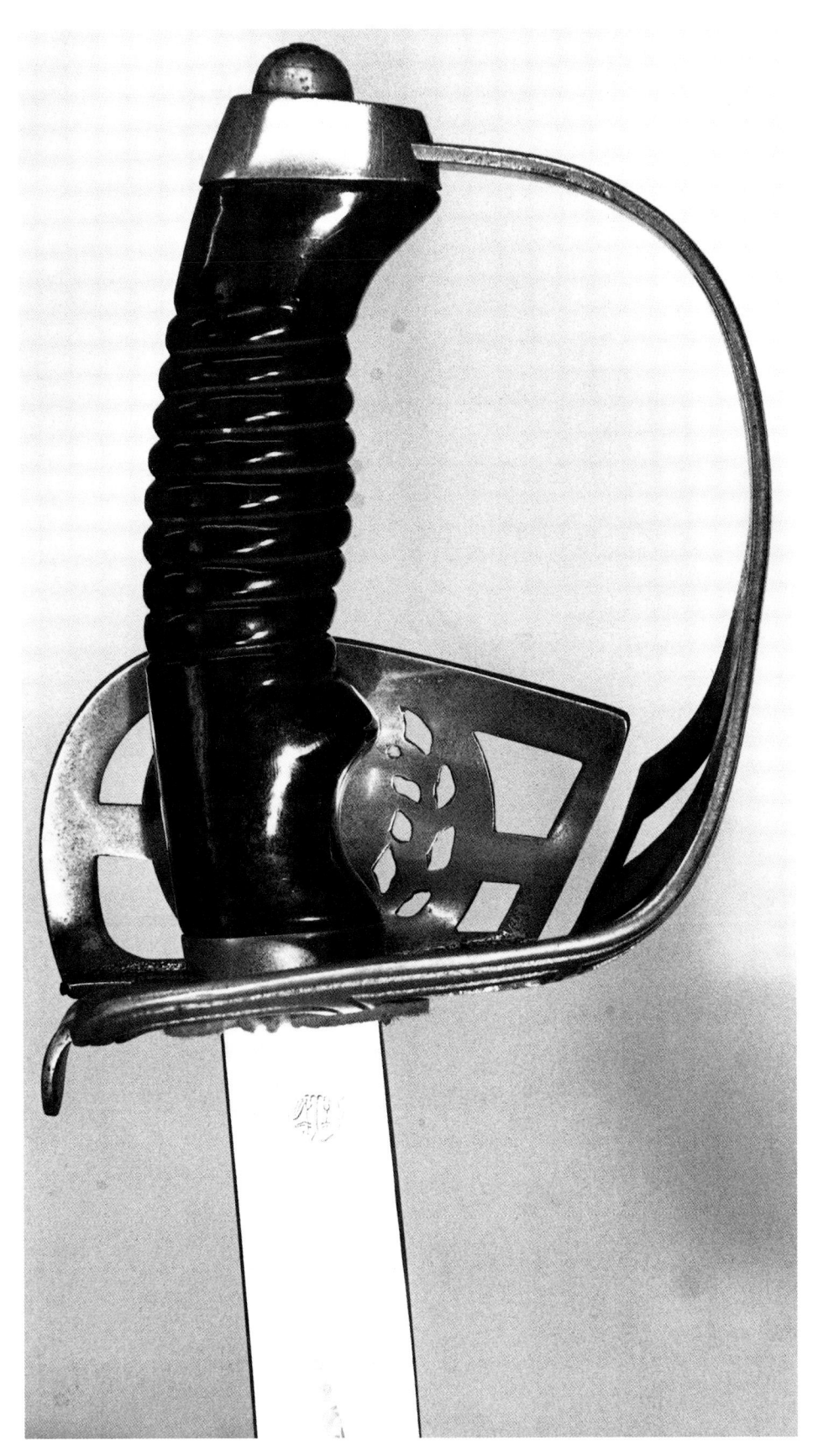

Saxon Cavalry enlisted man with his *KD89 Degen*. The black and white twist on the shoulder strap signifies his status as a One-year Volunteer. *LTC (Ret.) Thomas M. Johnson Photo Collection.*

KD89 reverse. The horn grip was issued without grip wrap. The blade bears the back-to-back squirrels logo of the Carl Eickhorn Company. *Edward M. Owen, Jr. Collection. Photo by Edward M. Owen, Jr.*

Imperial German Edged Weaponry

Saxon Cavalry Officer's Saber in gold with double folding basket guards. The quill back blade is etched with the Royal cypher *"AR"* for Albrecht King of *Saxony* from 1873-1902. *Edward M. Owen, Jr. Collection. Photo by Charles H. Jenkins, III.*

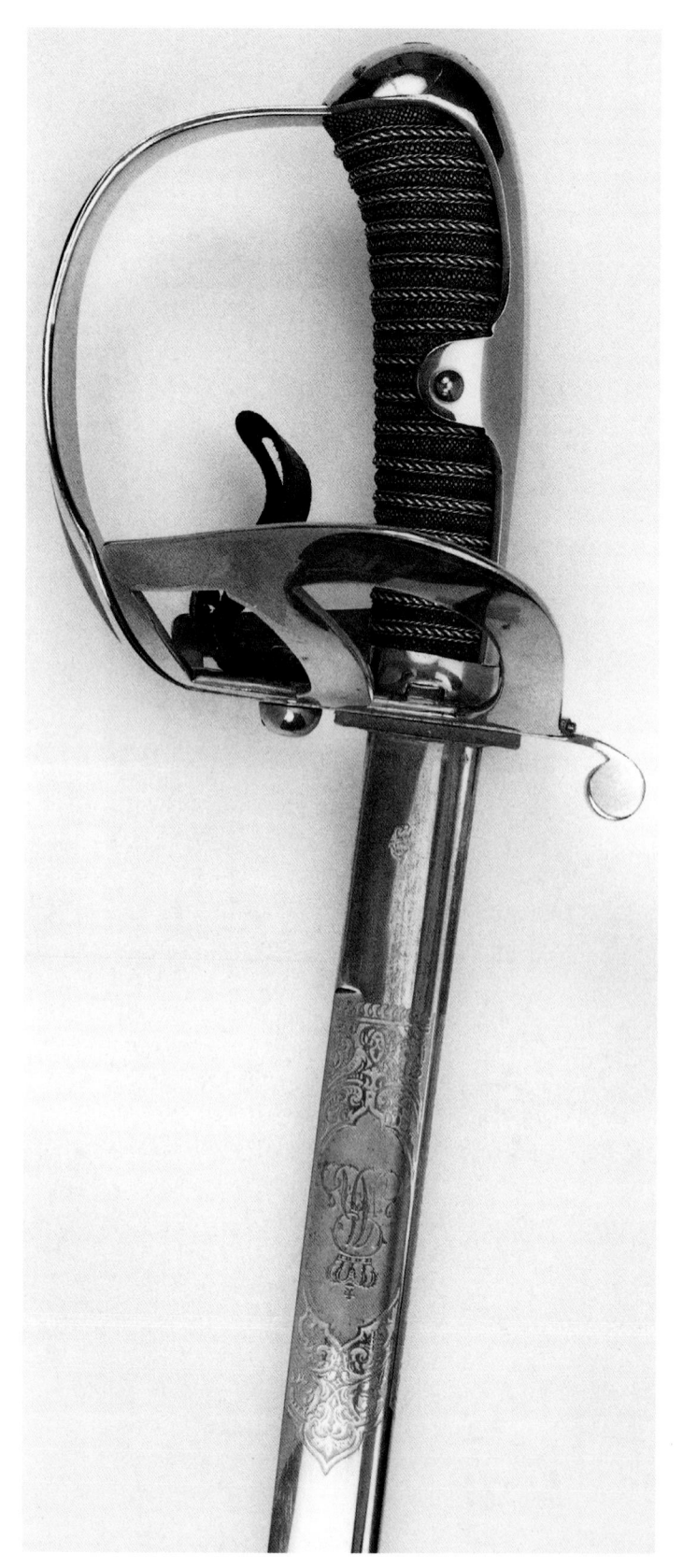

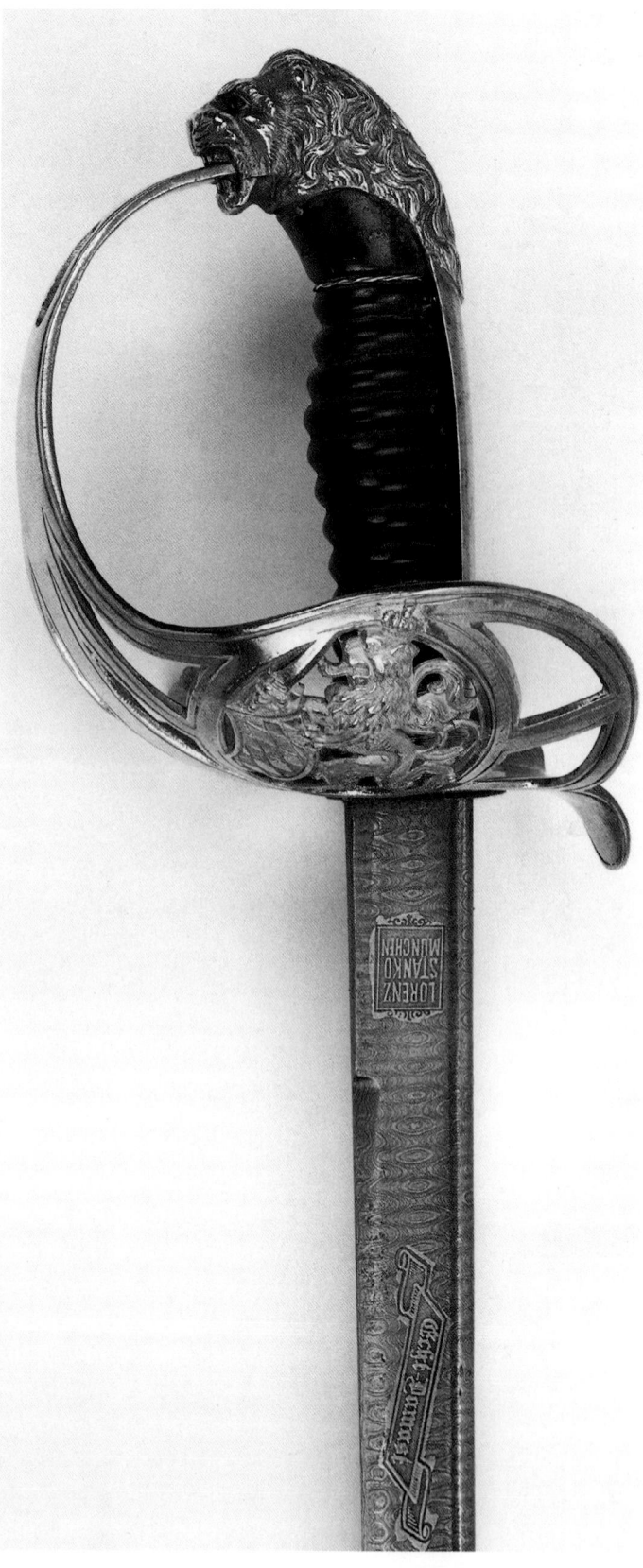

Bavarian Lion head Officer's basket hilt saber. The basket design incorporates the Bavarian lion motif. Hilt design is of gilded brass with wood grip. Only one layer of brass grip wire wrap remains intact. Blade is of "band" pattern Damascus, made by the firm of Lorenz Stanko, of the Bavarian capital city, München. Also featured on the obverse blade is the ribboned slogan, *"Echt Damast"* (genuine Damascus steel). *Thomas T. Wittmann Collection. Photo by Charles H. Jenkins, III.*

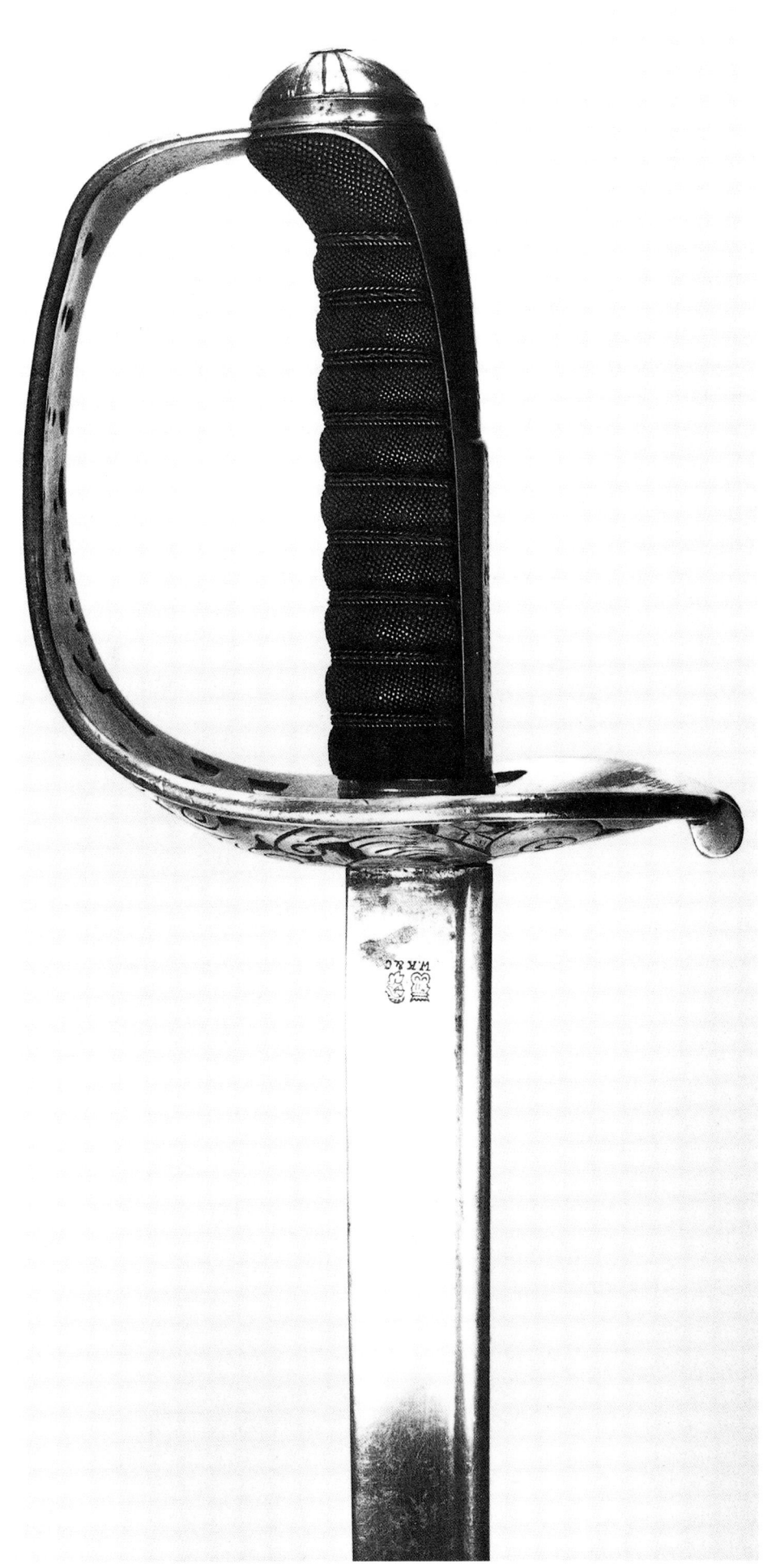

LEFT: *Württemberg* Officer Saber. The hilt of this saber is nickeled steel. The fishskin grip is triple gold wire-wrapped. The *"Fingerschlauf"* leather loop has been removed. The "pipe backed" blade is marked to the firm of WK&C. *Dr. David L. Valuska Collection. Photo by Victor Diehl.*

BELOW: Decorative knucklebow of the *Württemberg* saber. The pierced, scrolled design is identified as a "Honeysuckle" pattern. The state seal is worked into the motif. A close examination reveals a portion of the presentation found on the quillon end. The engraved presentation reads, *"A. Wilker s./l. E. Oppenlander"*. *Dr. David L. Valuska Collection. Photo by Victor Diehl.*

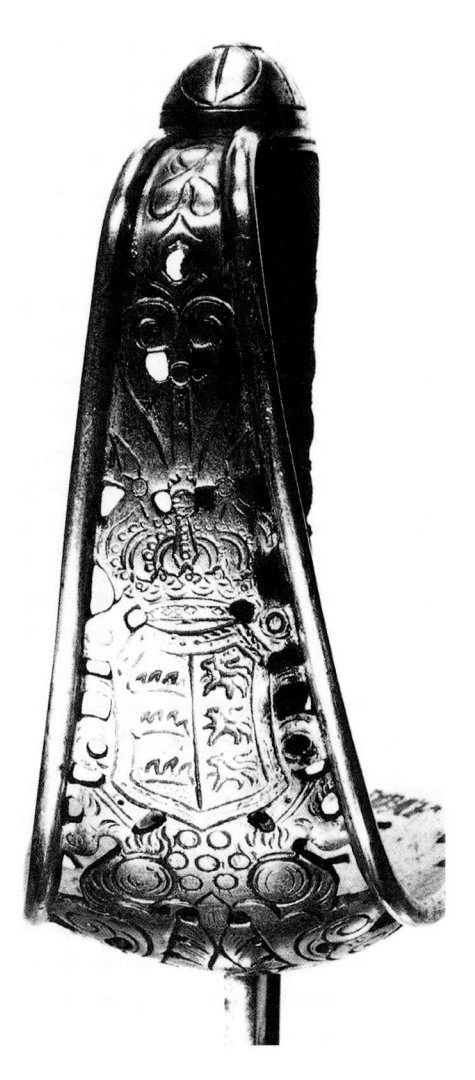

Two friends posing for their war-time photograph. The private on the left is a member of the Bavarian 2nd Light Cavalry Regiment *"Taxis"*. He is wearing the *KD90 Degen* with Bavarian Lion on the guard complete with *Faustriemen*. His friend is in the 28th Infantry Regiment. *LTC (Ret.) Thomas M. Johnson Photo Collection.*

Obverse view of a Deluxe Bavarian *Degen*, complete with its original Bavarian silver sword knot with blue stripes. Note the unusual construction of the Bavarian knots i.e. the acorn, crown, and stem are a separate entity attached to the strap via a circular metal connector. The Bavarian Lion is highlighted on the obverse langet. *LTC (Ret.) Thomas M. Johnson Collection. Photo by LTC (Ret.) Thomas M. Johnson.*

Imperial German Edged Weaponry

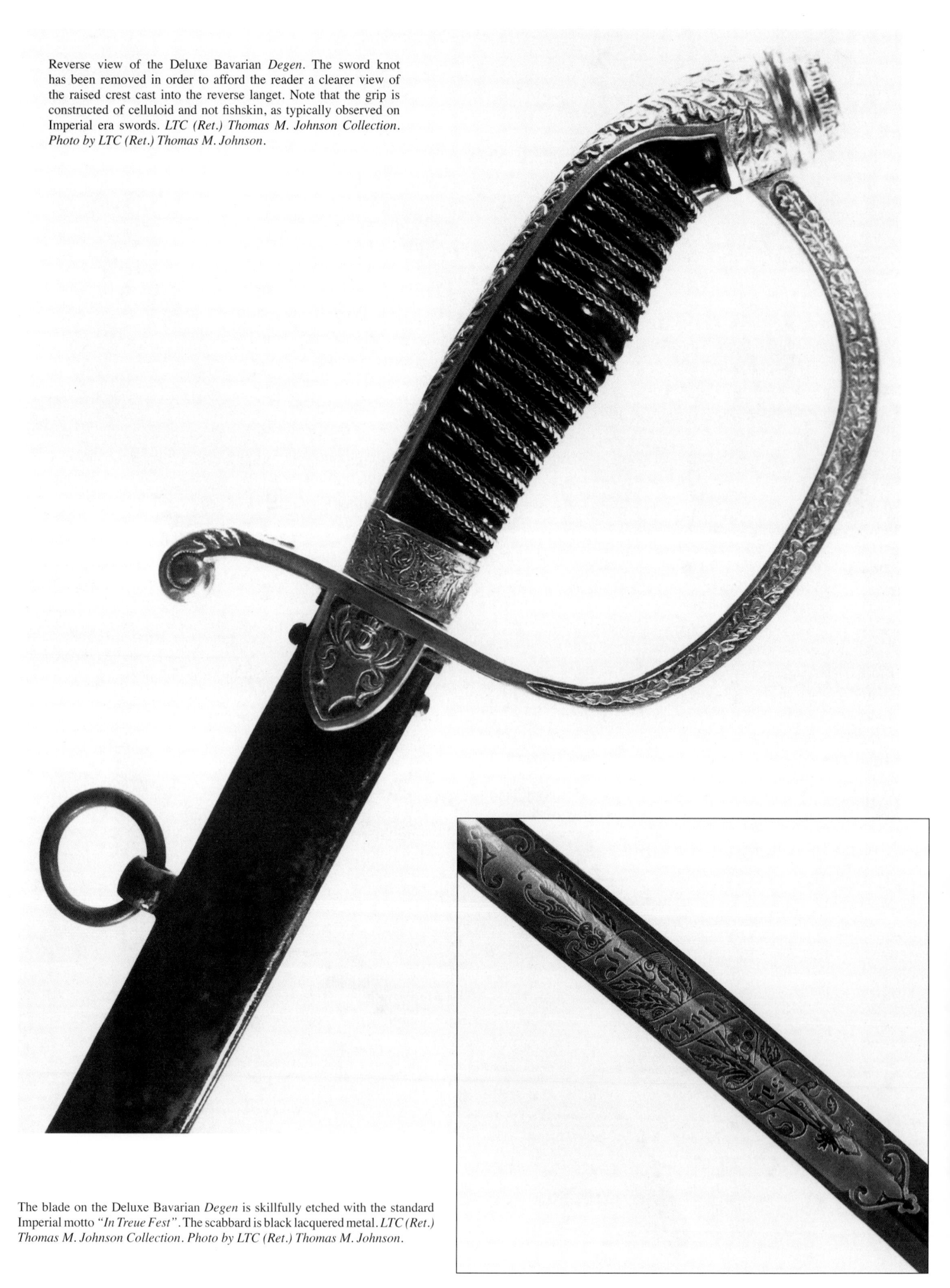

Reverse view of the Deluxe Bavarian *Degen*. The sword knot has been removed in order to afford the reader a clearer view of the raised crest cast into the reverse langet. Note that the grip is constructed of celluloid and not fishskin, as typically observed on Imperial era swords. *LTC (Ret.) Thomas M. Johnson Collection. Photo by LTC (Ret.) Thomas M. Johnson.*

The blade on the Deluxe Bavarian *Degen* is skillfully etched with the standard Imperial motto *"In Treue Fest"*. The scabbard is black lacquered metal. *LTC (Ret.) Thomas M. Johnson Collection. Photo by LTC (Ret.) Thomas M. Johnson.*

Swords of the German Army during the Imperial Era

A scarce Deluxe Imperial *Württemberg Degen* obverse hilt is pictured. The *Württemberg* royal crest dominates the hilt. Also, of note is the outstanding oak leaves and acorns motif applied to the pommel area. Unfortunately, the grip wire appears to have been lost to time. *LTC (Ret.) Thomas M. Johnson Collection. Photo by LTC (Ret.) Thomas M. Johnson.*

Close-up view of a portion of the obverse blade inscription and the sword knot on the scarce Imperial Deluxe *Württemberg Degen*. Note that both the blade and the accompanying sword knot are in mint condition. *LTC (Ret.) Thomas M. Johnson Collection. Photo by LTC (Ret.) Thomas M. Johnson.*

Imperial German Edged Weaponry

Pictured is a high-quality Imperial *Württemberg* Infantry *Degen* by WK&C. This model sword is shown in the WK&C 1905 Sales Catalog. Note the heavily chiseled pommel, backstrap, knucklebow, and folding handguard with the *Württemberg* coat-of-arms with royal crown. The pommel cap on this specimen is engraved with the monogram of the original owner in ornate script. The grip is black horn with twisted silver wire wrap. *LTC (Ret.) Thomas M. Johnson Collection. Photo by LTC (Ret.) Thomas M. Johnson.*

A December 1910 photo of an Infantry officer wearing his saber under his overcoat. While this manner of wear seems ungainly, it was the traditional manner of wear. *LTC (Ret.) Thomas M. Johnson Photo Collection. Photo by Ateliergerdom, Thorn.*

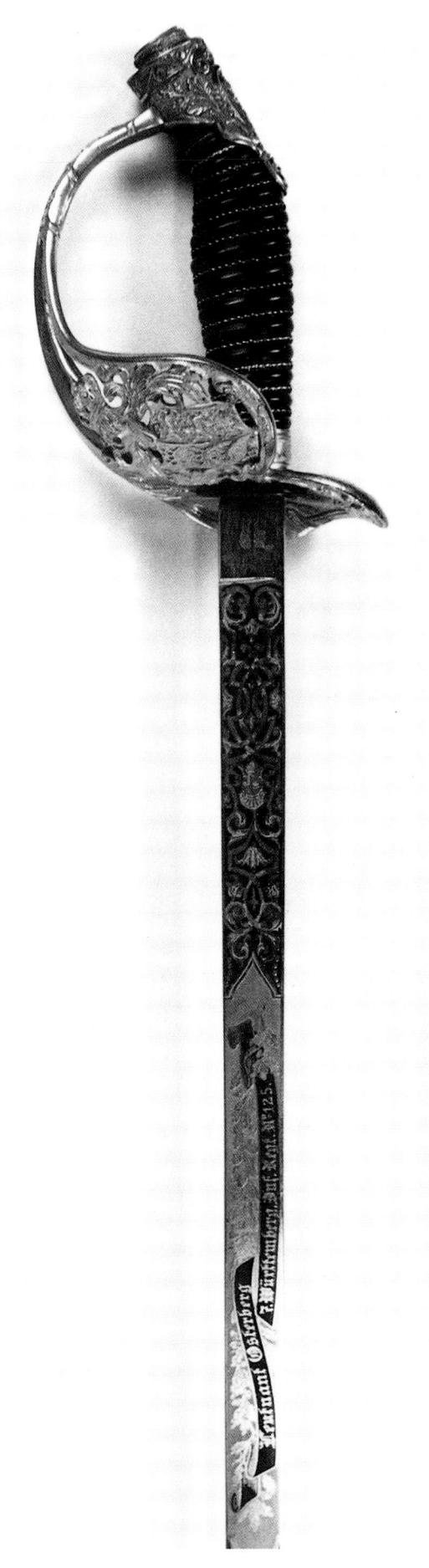

Württemberg Damascus Presentation *Degen*. The unfullered Damascus blade features blued and gilded floral patterns and presentations along nearly its entire length. The blade has both the trademark of WK&C and the retailer's name, "*M. Richter, Berlin*". *Stephen Wolfe Collection. Photo Courtesy of Stephen Wolfe.*

Württemberg Damascus Presentation *Degen*. The unfullered Damascus blade features blued and gilded floral patterns and presentations along nearly its entire length. A translation of the obverse presentation reads, "Lieutenant Osterberg 7th *Württemberg* Infantry Regiment No.125". *Stephen Wolfe Collection. Photo Courtesy of Stephen Wolfe.*

Württemberg Damascus Presentation *Degen*. The unfullered Damascus blade features blued and gilded floral patterns and presentations along nearly its entire length. A translation of the obverse presentation reads, "Lieutenant Osterberg 7th *Württemberg* Infantry Regiment No.125". The blade has both the trademark of WK&C and the retailer's name, "M. Richter, Berlin." *Stephen Wolfe Collection. Photo Courtesy of Stephen Wolfe.*

A translation of the reverse blade presentation on the *Württemberg* Damascus Presentation *Degen* by WK&C reads, "For Outstanding Accomplishments in the Military Gymnastics Institute 1913". *Stephen Wolfe Collection. Photo Courtesy of Stephen Wolfe.*

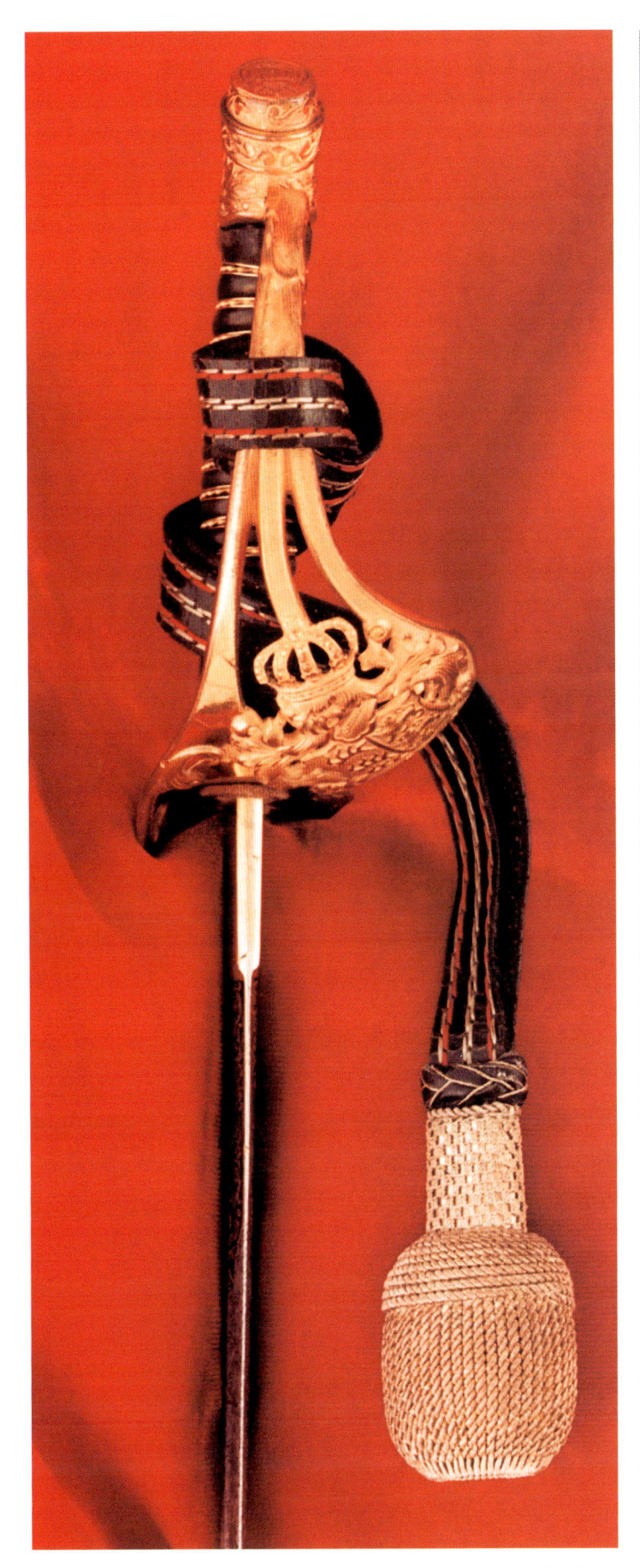

Swords of the German Army during the Imperial Era

The knucklebow on the impressive *M89 Württemberg* Infantry *Degen* distributed by *Hans Romer, Hoflieferant, München* features a deeply and intricately sculptured Royal *Württemberg* crest. The *Degen* is complete with the original *Württemberg* officer sword knot. *Richard R. Williams Collection. Photo by Dick Scott Fine Photography, Houston.*

A *Württemberg* officer is pictured with his saber. The early scabbard is nickel plated and the clamshell is the folding variety. The national symbol is seen on both the helmet and saber. This officer is in the Infantry Regiment 126 *Gross Herzog von Baden*. LTC (Ret.) Thomas M. Johnson Photo Collection. Photo by Fred Gollas & Co., Straasburg.

Presentation *IOD89* with *Württemberg* crest on fixed guard. The *Degen* is the large *"Grosser"* pattern produced by WK&C. The blade obverse was etched, "To Captain Cramer of the 10th *Württemberg* Infantry Regiment Number 180". The reverse was inscribed, *"Als Bestem Schutzen 1901"* (the best shot for the year 1901). The *Degen* was originally carried in a nickeled two-ring scabbard, but this was replaced with a black enameled, single-ring scabbard to meet the regulation of 1910. *LTC (Ret.) Thomas M. Johnson Collection. Photo by LTC (Ret.) Thomas M. Johnson.*

Extreme close-up of the ornate *Württemberg* shooting presentation *Degen* knucklebow. Note the gilded *Württemberg* crest. *LTC (Ret.) Thomas M. Johnson Collection. Photo by LTC (Ret.) Thomas M. Johnson.*

Extreme close-up of the Weyersberg, Kirschbaum & Cie, Solingen trademark on the reverse ricasso of the *Württemberg* shooting presentation *Degen*. *LTC (Ret.) Thomas M. Johnson Collection. Photo by LTC (Ret.) Thomas M. Johnson.*

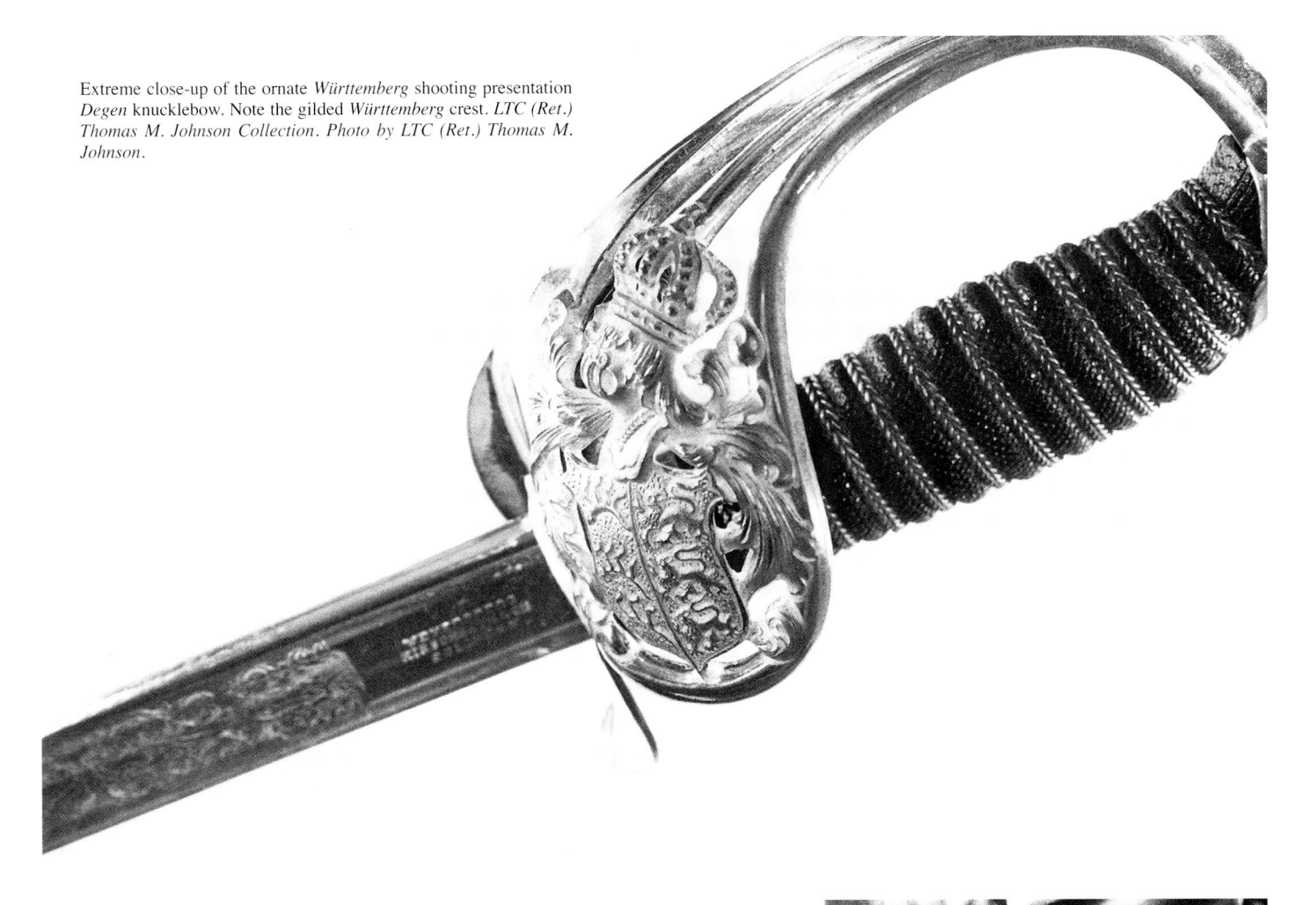

ABOVE: Obverse blade of the *Württemberg* shooting presentation *Degen*. The dedication and floral design were etched and nickel-plated. A translation of the obverse blade presentation reads, "To Captain Cramer of the 10th *Württemberg* Infantry Regiment Number 180". *LTC (Ret.) Thomas M. Johnson Collection. Photo by LTC (Ret.) Thomas M. Johnson.*

BELOW: *Württemberg* shooting presentation *Degen* blade. The dedication and floral design were etched and nickel-plated. The reverse of this blade carries the etched crowned "W" of Wilhelm II, in addition to the presentation inscription, *"Als Bestem Schutzen 1901"* (the best shot for the year 1901). *LTC (Ret.) Thomas M. Johnson Collection. Photo by LTC (Ret.) Thomas M. Johnson.*

Backstrap of the presentation *IOD89* shooting presentation *Degen* by WK&C. Note that the leather *Fingerschlauf* is still present and intact. *LTC (Ret.) Thomas M. Johnson Collection. Photo by LTC (Ret.) Thomas M. Johnson.*

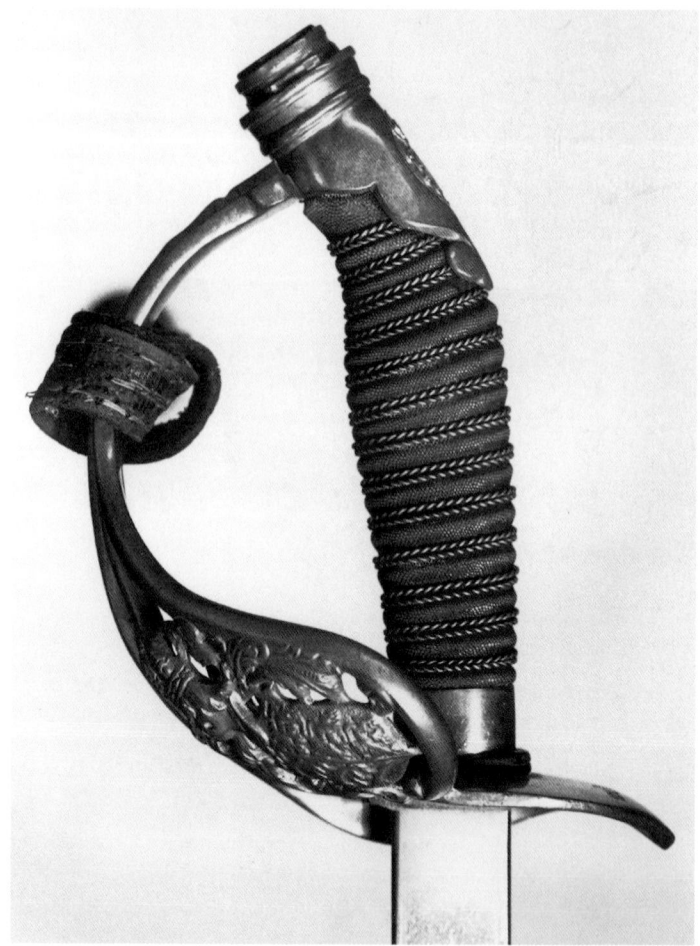

IOD89 NCO sword with *Württemberg* crest on the fixed guard. The hilt and scabbard are marked to Infantry Regiment 121. The unit crest is applied to the short backstrap. The blade spine is marked with the cypher "W". The blade is marked "WK&C". *Edward M. Owen, Jr. Collection. Photo by Edward M. Owen, Jr.*

Highly decorated officer of the 10th *Württemberg* Infantry Regiment No.180. This officer is carrying a Dove head saber with properly tied portepee. For this studio portrait, he is wearing both the Iron Cross 1st and 2nd Class decorations. *LTC (Ret.) Thomas M. Johnson Photo Collection. Photo by Eugen Rühle, Tübingen.*

This Junior NCO is a member of the *Saxon* Infantry and is pictured on his wedding day. He is holding a *Saxon* Infantry Officer sword with folding guard. The scabbard has been blackened and the lower ring removed as per regulations of 14 December 1910. Note that he has opted to wear his spiked helmet for this studio photograph. *LTC (Ret.) Thomas M. Johnson Photo Collection. Photo by Fiedler Hofphotograph, Dresden.*

Highly decorated *Saxon Obergefreiter* with both the Imperial Iron Cross and Wound Badge. He is wearing the *Saxon* Infantry Officer *Degen*. The sword knot contains a center green stripe. *LTC (Ret.) Thomas M. Johnson Photo Collection. Photo by Atelier Straub, Leipzig.*

The brass mounted *Saxon* Infantry officer saber is pictured in wear. This officer has selected the model with a folding clamshell (WK&C model #191, *Sächsischer Infanterie-Offizier-Säbel mit Charmier*). His officer portepee completes the hilt. *LTC (Ret.) Thomas M. Johnson Photo Collection. Photo by Alfred Fritzsching, Löbau.*

Pictured is a *Saxon* officer wearing his folding clamshell Infantry officer saber. The *Saxon* officer portepee contains a light green center stripe on the dark leather strap and a uniquely shaped acorn. The officer is a member of the Royal *Saxon* Infantry Regiment. *LTC (Ret.) Thomas M. Johnson Photo Collection.*

A decorated *Saxon* Infantry officer. He is holding the nickel mounted *Saxon* sword with knot and folding clamshell. *LTC (Ret.) Thomas M. Johnson Photo Collection. Photo by Martin Herzfeld, Leipzig.*

An Imperial *Saxon* infantry officer's sword with folding guard is seen in wear. The suspension straps and *Saxon* portepee are clearly visible and available for study. *LTC (Ret.) Thomas M. Johnson Photo Collection.*

The King of Sweden is pictured wearing the *Prussian* Infantry Officer *Degen* for the *Queen Augusta Garde Grenadier Regiment No.4*. The unusual folding clamshell contains the dates "1861-1886". The *Degen* is in gold with a black enamel steel scabbard. *LTC (Ret.) Thomas M. Johnson Photo Collection. Photo by Ernst Sandau Hofphotograph, Berlin.*

CHAPTER TWO

THE EDGED WEAPONS OF THE GERMAN CAVALRY

by Victor Diehl

"Every day is lost to a cavalryman, on which he does not drill or exercise with horse and weapon."
— Field Marshal F.H.E. von Wrangel

INTRODUCTION

Flashing saber blades, blood curdling yells, and the earth shattering pounding of hundreds of horse hooves during a cavalry charge have sent terror through the hearts of soldiers on battlefields throughout history. The German cavalry has added a significant chapter to the history of these legendary horsemen.

The German Cavalry of the twentieth Century had its beginning in the reorganization and expansion of the cavalry during the reign of Frederick the Great from 1740 to 1786. Frederick developed three types of cavalry: the *Kürassier,* the *Dragoons,* and the *Hussars.*

This cavalry reorganization took place because of the poor showing of the Prussians against the Austrian cavalry during the First Silesian War. During the next twenty years, Frederick, with the help of a number of superior cavalry officers including Hans Joachim Zieten, "The *Hussar* King" and Frederich Wilhelm von Seydlitz, worked to teach a cavalry charge that combined speed and weight. The cavalry charge as defined by Frederick began at 2,000 yards. At 200 yards flags were unfurled, swords were drawn, trumpets blared, and the charge was completed with as much yelling and screaming as possible. The charge combined the three elements of cavalry. First were three ranks of *Kürassiers,* who with their powerful horses and iron breast plates were to crush the enemy cavalry and the flanks of the Infantry. Then came three ranks of *Dragoons,* who combined massive fire power and mobility operating as medium cavalry on the attack and as infantry on the defense, followed by three ranks of *Hussars* that protected the rear and flanks.

Frederick was a legendary equestrian and widely respected by his men. One incident in Frederick's life as a horseman provided continued inspiration for his cavalry. During the Seven Years War 1756-1763 after the battle of Leuthen, Frederick, who had outridden his troops after the day's victory, stopped at the Castle of Lissa to rest for the night. Upon his arrival within the estate, Frederick realized that the castle was a hospital and officer's quarters for his enemy Austrians. The calm, poised King of Prussia simply asked, "Can a tired, victorious General find a room here for the night?" The awed Austrians offered Frederick food for the evening, and he retired after sending out victory dispatches.

During the next century the cavalry branch of the German army was assigned a wider variety of tasks. These tasks included reconnoitering the enemies' position, protecting quartered troops against surprise attack, and maintaining communications among all branches of the military. On the field of battle, cavalry is used in force depending upon the circumstances. By the time of the Franco-Prussian War, cavalry charges against well-entrenched Infantry provided little chance of victory. More success was garnered with flanking actions or against Artillery and Infantry formations that were in disarray or retreat. By 1914, cavalries continued most of their historical roles, but many times, were armed and used as Mounted Infantry.

The legends surrounding the German cavalry at times far exceeded its real capabilities. Military history is replete with many real instances which attest to the riding skill, resoluteness, coolness, and courage bordering on rashness of the German cavalryman.

An extreme example of this defiance of danger occurred during the Franco-Prussian War. One of the many roles of the cavalry was to assist the Army in determining troop strength of the enemy. The strength of troops garrisoned at Bitsch was cause for concern, so a Prussian Lieutenant von Munchhausen of the *Schleswig-Holstein Dragoons* was dispatched to make a determination for the staff.

The young lieutenant led a patrol under the cover of darkness and stealthily broached the French lines. As he approached the garrison, Munchhausen positioned a cavalryman on a hill that would enable the private to see the entire garrison and its primary entrances. Munchhausen then cloaked himself in tarred clothing and, with his mount, stole his way past the sleeping French sentries into the garrison. Once he made his way to the center of the camp, he threw off his camouflage, adorned himself with his *Dragoon* Eagle festooned *Pickelhaube,* raised his cavalry saber in defiance, and screamed at the top of his voice, "Long live His Majesty, the King of Prussia". The lieutenant then wheeled about, mounted his glistening black steed, and with a defiant saber salute charged through the developing crowd of dazed soldiers. He then galloped out of the garrison under a hail of bullets. The rifle fire caused the entire garrison to rush out of their barracks. Thus, the private stationed on the hill with field glasses was able to estimate the troop strength of the garrison which he reported to Munchhausen upon his return to the Prussian lines.

Other examples of cavalry derring-do during the Franco-Prussian War involved the *2nd Leib Hussars* at Worth, the *1st Hannoverian Uhlans* at Le Mans, and the *7th Magdeburg Kürassiers* along with the *16th Altmarkische Uhlans* and their *"Todesritt"* at *Vionville-Mars-la-Tour*. The latter was an engagement during which they lost half of their men and mounts, while charging two lines of French Artillery and two French cavalry brigades.

During World War I, modern weaponry such as the machine gun and motor vehicles severely limited the traditional roles of mounted troops. An early war example of this improved weaponry versus cavalry occurred at the Belgian town of *Haelen*. An entire platoon of advancing *Uhlans* was mowed down by the deadly fire of portable Hotchkiss machine guns carried by Belgian cyclists. A similar calamity involved the German Cavalry at the battle of Marne.

The cavalry did participate in numerous successful campaigns, and following each success, they provided a spectacle unmatched in splendor. Such an event was reported by correspondent Alexander Powell after the fall of Antwerp:

> "For five hours the mighty host poured through the streets of the deserted city. Company after company, regiment after regiment, brigade after brigade swept past, until the eye grew weary of watching. As they marched they sang and the canyon formed by the high buildings along the *Place de Meir* echoed with voices roaring out, *"Die Wacht am Rhein"* and, "A Mighty Fortress Is Our God". Hard on the heels of the Infantry, rumbled the Artillery. And then, heralded by a blare of trumpets and a crash of kettle-drums, came the cavalry: *Kürassiers* in helmets and breastplates of burnished steel; *Hussars* in parade jackets and fur *Busbies;* and finally the *Uhlans* riding amid forests of lances under a cloud of fluttering pennons."

ORGANIZATION OF THE GERMAN CAVALRY

The German Cavalry of the Kaiser era consisted of those numbered regiments incorporated into the Prussian Army by military accord or annexation and the Bavarian Army Corps which used its own regimental markings and uniform distinctions. It should be noted that *Saxony, Württemberg,* and *Baden* retained their own trim and emblems even though they were incorporated into the Prussian Army.

In terms of training and equipment, the cavalry was divided into heavy and light cavalry. The *Kürassiers, Garde Reiter,* and *Schwere Reiter* Regiments were considered heavy cavalry; while the *Uhlans, Hussars, Dragoons,* and *Bavarian Chevauleger* were considered light cavalry.

The heavy cavalry contained the Prussian *Kürassiers* (Cuirassier) which consisted of the *Garde du Corps*, named after a French regiment which served under Louis XIV, and the *Garde Kürassier* Regiment, along with eight numbered regiments. The Saxon Heavy Cavalry had two regiments. The Bavarian heavy cavalry contained two *Schwere Reiter* Regiments.

The Prussian *Kürassier*

The heavy cavalrymen and their preferred Holstein horses were the direct descendants of the 15th Century German knights who, with their *Kürasses, Gorgets,* distinctive *Sallets,* and *Pallasches* or broadswords had played a major role in early German history. By the time of Frederick the Great, however, only the breastplate and broadsword were retained. The famed *Kürassier* helmet was reintroduced in 1843. The 21st Century reader will find it interesting to note that Frederick established height regulations for *Kürassiers* in 1755 in order to have soldiers large enough to handle the breastplate and broadsword. This minimum height requirement was 5 feet, 3 inches.

The *Pallasch* continued to be the standard edged weapon of the heavy cavalry until the end of World War I. The 19th Century *Kürassier* broadsword was based on the French Empire *Cuirassier* sword model 1802-1803. A new *Pallasch* for troopers was based on the pattern model 1854 and was carried beginning in 1876. These weapons had a knuckle-bow and three side-bars which joined together to become one bar that ended in the rounded *Phrygian* helmet-style grip cap. The heavy grip did not have a backstrap and was wrapped in black leather and bound in brass wire with a *Fingerschlauf* placed between the ferrule and guard. A straight, double-fullered, single-edged blade with center point, and an iron scabbard with one or two hanger rings depending on unit regulation completed the sword as worn by troopers. The straight, single-edged blade which originally was 38 inches long by 1 inch wide was reduced in 1896, to 32 ½ inches long.

The broadsword for officers had the same configuration with the exceptions of a flat, tiered grip cap, a fishskin wrapped grip, and more rounded decorative sidebars. Private purchase options for officers were many, including folding guards and highly detailed, chiseled hilts in either Tombac or brass with a variety of gilt treatments. Blades could also be ordered in etched, blued, gilted, or a combination of treatments including genuine Damascus. By the turn of the century, a variety of blade widths and lengths were offered based on the size and preference of the individual placing the order. National emblems are not found on the Prussian broadsword; however, officers of the guard had the Guard Star affixed to the grip.

A slightly different pattern Prussian *Pallasch* was based on the Russian broadsword of 1808. The pattern was favored by the *Garde du Corps* and was distinguished in the standard form by two instead of three sidebars and a narrow-waisted grip cap. The grip cap was rounded on top for troopers and flat for officers. The side-bars attached plainly to the flat, angular guard which had a flat, square quillon end. The trooper grip was straight with a leather wrap bound in brass wire. The officer grip had the more characteristic curve and was wrapped in sharkskin and bound with a gold three-wire wrap. The blades for all ranks were straight and double fullered, with a center point. The scabbard had two hanger bands and rings.

Kürassier officers could choose from two other swords for "interim" or undress occasions when a sword was to be worn. These choices were either the cavalry lionhead saber or the *Stichdegen*.

The extremely popular lionhead saber is highly detailed in this volume of the series, and the reader is directed to that section.

The *Kürassier* officer *Stichdegen*, like the 1796 British pattern officer sword, was based on the 17th Century "small-sword". Regulations of 1876 allowed the *Kürassier* officer to carry the *Stichdegen*, whereas, before, he had to wear the heavy broadsword or lionhead.

The *Stichdegen* was a gold-mounted straight-bladed sword with a D-guard carried in a leather scabbard with gold fittings. The large, round pommel with its baluster-shaped top extension was characteristic of this piece. The curved knuckle-bow terminated into either a single or double cruciform "Russian type" quillon. The grip with center swell was wrapped with contrasting silver wire. Below the quillons were double clamshell guards. The rear guard generally folded down to facilitate both wear and storage. The obverse clamshell was tear-drop shaped with the left side of the clamshell tapering into the knuckle-bow. The fittings were available in either Tombac or brass with fire gilt. A wide range of ornamentation was available from heavily chiseled to polished fittings.

The *Stichdegen* blade was nickel-plated, double-edged, and single-fullered. The blade ended in a center point. The forte of most blades were etched with a military or floral motif. Blade widths ranged from 16 to 23 mm wide with length based on the height of the wearer.

The scabbard was black leather with a center back stitch and contained two decorative grooves down each side of the front. The gilted brass scabbard fittings were stapled onto the back of the leather scabbard. The top fitting contained the scabbard throat as well as a long carrying hook. The chape was straight with a rounded end.

The sword knots for the officer *Pallasch* were made in silver braid. The silver straps and slide had black silk stripe work throughout. For the lionhead and *Stichdegen* the Infantry pattern sword knot with silver strap was carried.

Troopers carried the traditional *Faustriemen* of red-brown leather with a plaited leather slide. The tassels in all cases were white. In order to distinguish squadrons, the crown was colored as follows; 1st squadron wore white, 2nd red, 3rd yellow, 4th light blue, and 5th green.

The *Pallasch*, *Stichdegen*, and lionhead were worn on sword belts when the *Kürassier* was dismounted. When mounted, the *Pallasch* was affixed to the left rear of the saddle with a specially designed leather hanger.

Saxon Heavy Cavalry

The steel lobster tail helmet with the magnificent silver *Saxon* lion attached to the crown, the traditional sheepskin saddle, covers and the awesome lionhead *Pallasch* are visual reminders of the tradition-rich *Saxon* Heavy Cavalry.

These regiments were composed of the *Garde Reiter Regiment* (1. *Schweres Regiment*) formed in 1680, and the *Karabiner Regiment* (2. *Schweres Regiment*) raised in 1849.

Four sword patterns were allowed by regulation for the *Saxon* Heavy Cavalry. These included the *Kavallerie Degen* model 1891 for troopers, the Lionhead "interim" saber, the *Saxon* Officer Saber model 1879 for the *Karabiner Regiment*, and the Lionhead *Saxon Garde Reiter* saber.

The cavalry *Degen* adopted in Prussia in 1889 was not adopted in *Saxony* until 1891, for enlisted cavalrymen. The straight-bladed sword had the standard sheet-metal sidebars with or without the *Saxon* coat of arms placed horizontally on the front of the guard. This guard may be folding or stationary. This *Degen* was carried in a single ring scabbard. The hilt of this sword was in polished steel for *Karabiner* troopers while *Garde Reiter* enlisted men carried the same model in brass.

The Lionhead "interim" saber was offered in the typical wide range of options. One distinguishing feature of many *Saxon* lionhead sabers was the gilt panel on the blade below the crossguard. The reverse panel contained the *Saxon* coat of arms while the obverse panel from 1904-1918 contained the crowned FA cypher of King Friedrich August III. This crowned cypher was found many times on the obverse langet.

The two most distinctive *Saxon* heavy cavalry swords were the model 1879, designated as *Saxon* pattern 67, and the Lionhead *Garde Reiter Pallasch*.

The model 1879 was reminiscent of the *Prussian* basket hilt model 1852. Although its hilt was more refined, it remained a massive weapon over 40 inches long. The nickeled hilt was of dove head configuration with three fixed or folding sheet-metal sidebars terminating in a single knuckle-bow. At the point of juncture of the sidebars and the knuckle-bow was a cast seal of the state of *Saxony*. The backstrap was polished and extended to the quillon which ended in a polished scrolled disc. The fishskin grip bound in triple silver wire swelled toward the top and was pinned in place using the lobes of the backstrap. A variation of this sword for enlisted men had a grip in celluloid with a forefinger groove above the ferrule much like the KD 91.

The blade was a curved quillback with a false edge measuring over 34 inches in standard length. Many examples contained the gilt panel below the hilt with the royal cypher. The iron scabbard was either double- or single-ringed depending on date of manufacture.

The *Saxon Garde Reiter* officer *Pallasch* was a gold lionhead broadsword with a two-sidebar guard. The deeply-cast lionhead extended into a decorative backstrap. The crossguard of the sword was heart-shaped and extended into the single knuckle guard where it was joined by the two round sidebars. At this junction the *Saxon* coat of arms was cast. Inside the front of the hilt was a distinctive brass forefinger ring which extended up from the crossguard. The grip was covered with fishskin and bound with triple, gold wire wrap.

The 32-inch quill back blade was straight with a false edge. These blades frequently had gilded panels. This sword was also fitted many times with a genuine Damascus blade with a variety of gilt treatments. The steel scabbard was found in both single- and double-ring formats.

The sword knots for the heavy cavalry follow the *Prussian* pattern, except *Saxon* green was used as a substitute for *Prussian* black, where appropriate. The officer sword knot had a black and silver strap with a crown and ball of silver and green. The core of the ball was green.

The Bavarian Heavy Cavalry

The Bavarian Heavy Cavalry had a major reorganization in 1879 under Ludwig II. Until that time, the heavy cavalry was composed of a *Garde du Corps* and two *Kürassier Regiments*. The reorganization resulted in two heavy cavalry or *Schwere Reiter Regiments*. The first regiment was identified as the *Schwere Reiter Regiment Prinz Carl von Bayern*, and the second was the *Schwere Reiter Regiment Erzherzog Ferdinand von Osterreich-Este*.

In terms of edged weapons, the sword pattern for troopers was a straight bladed, brass hilt *Pallasch* very similar to the *Prussian* pattern with the exceptions of two, instead of three, sidebars, and a flat, tiered grip cap rather than the *Phrygian* helmet variety. Most Bavarian blades are etched with the Bavarian motto, "*In Treue Fest*".

There also existed an extremely heavy model of this *Pallasch* officially designated as the *Reiter Extrasabel mit Ordonnanz Gefass* (French Pattern). The grip of this piece differed in that it had a distinct center swell and was leather bound with very closely wrapped brass wire. The brass hilt had two sidebars which angled sharply to the front where they joined the knuckle-bow rather than raising high in a basket form. A massive, single-edged, double-fullered blade with centerpoint completed the sword. The iron scabbard had a single hanger ring.

The officer pattern *Pallasch* displayed the characteristic Bavarian curved grip. The brass or nickeled hilt contained a flat, tiered pommel and a backstrap that joined the crossguard. The crossguard had a downward-turned quillon end. The hilt was completed by three round sidebars which joined the knuckle-bow half way to the pommel. Where the sidebars joined the crossguard, each contained a round attachment like the *Prussian* variety. The fishskin grip had a distinct center swell and was bound in either silver or gold wire. The hilt did not contain a langet. The straight, double-fullered blade contained the Bavarian motto. The iron scabbard had two hanger rings and may or may not have had hanger bands.

A second example of this officer *Pallasch* had a hilt which contained interchangeable knuckle-bows. The officer could switch from a simple D-guard to a basket hilt with two sidebars by removing the pommel cap and grip and changing the single-cast knuckle-bow and crossguard. This model contained a langet with the D-guard model but none with the basket hilt. Both officer patterns could be ordered in an endless combination of finishes and decorations.

The sword knot for officers had a silver strap with two light blue stripes on red Moroccan leather. The slide and the stem were light blue worked with silver cord. The crown and ball were also light blue and silver.

The Light Cavalry – *Dragoons*

As noted earlier, the light cavalry contained the *Dragoons*, *Hussars*, *Uhlans*, and *Bavarian Chevauleger Regiments*.

The *Dragoons* are the descendants of the 16th Century *Arkebusiers*, named after their muskets, who fought on foot and also acted as mounted Infantry. The *Dragoons* gained much fame under the Great Elector Frederick Wilhelm when Field Marshal von Derfflinger, "the old Derfflinger", at the age of 70 years, surprised and defeated the invading Swedish Army at Fehrbellin in 1675. This victory became the first battle honor of the Prussian Army. It was the reorganization under Frederick the Great that developed *Dragoons* into cavalrymen.

The *Dragoons* contained two *Garde* units; The *1. Garde Dragoon Regiment Konigin Viktoria v. Grossbritannien u. Irland* formed in 1815, and the *2. Garde Dragoon Regiment Kaiserin Alexandra von Russland* formed in 1860. In addition to the Garde units, the *Dragoons* had 26 numbered regiments. The *Prussian* regiments were the 1st to 16th, *Mecklenburg* the 17th and 18th, *Oldenburg* the 19th, *Baden* the 20th, 21st, and 22nd, *Hessen* the 23rd and 24th, and *Württemberg* the 25th and 26th regiments. Saxony had no *Dragoons*.

Bavaria had six regiments of *Chevaulegers* which fought as *Dragoons*. The name *Chevaulegers* is French from the time of Henry IV, designating light cavalry equipped with firearms. In Germany this term was introduced by the princes of the Rhenish Confederation during the time of Napoleon.

In order to get some understanding of the long *Dragoon* tradition, the reader should know that the *1. Brandenburg Dragoon Regiment Nr. 2* was formed at *Schwedt an der Oder* in 1689. The *Dragoon* Eagle of these "*Schwedter Dragoons*" became a "Tradition Badge" whose wear extended into the Third Reich. The *Dragoon* Eagle cap badge was worn by the Regimental Staff and 2nd Squadron of the *6. Reiter-Regiment* in 1921, the 4th squadron of the same regiment in 1926, and the 3rd Motorcycle Battalion and all units of the 3rd Cavalry Division in 1944.

The edged weapons of the *Dragoons* were many and varied. The enlisted troopers by 1914 were usually carrying KD 89's. On some occasions, the polished D- or P-guard dovehead saber was carried.

Prussian Dragoon officers could choose from a variety of "interim" sabers. These included both the popular lionhead and dovehead models with their numerous options. Officers of the *Brandenburg Dragoons* many times had a silver *Dragoon* Eagle attached to the langet of their "interim" saber.

The preferred sword for wear by officers of the *Brandenburg Dragoons* was their famed eaglehead saber. This sword had a highly detailed full eaglehead pommel and chiseled backstrap. The single D-guard knuckle-bow extended downward from the open mouth of the eagle to join two round sidebars which raised in a low semi-basket form over the lower grip before joining the crossguard. The crossguard ended in a downward scrolled disc. The fishskin-wrapped grip had a center swell and was bound with silver triple-wire wrap. The grip was pinned to the hilt through the lobes of the backstrap. The langet was very distinctive being a somewhat rounded lozenge shape. This langet was affixed vertically to the crossguard.

The curved, single-edged blade had a flat back and false edge. Blades could be ordered in widths from 23 to 30 mm. The forte may or may not have been etched with a floral motif. The steel scabbard with hanger bands had one or two rings. The nickeled basket hilt saber model of 1852, with 1879 quillback, was used by a number of *Dragoon* officers.

A special version of this saber was carried by the *Dragoon Regiment Prinz Albrecht von Prussian No. 1*. This saber featured a large, silver *Dragoon* Eagle which entirely covered the sidebars of the basket hilt. The *Dragoon* Eagle has wide, upswung wings. The eagle grasps a straight sword in its right taloned foot. The sword guard is cruciform. The left talon holds a scepter. The eagle looks to the right as with infantry eagles. The sword eagle differs from the spiked helmet variety in that the ribbon containing the words, "*mit Gott für Koenig und Vaterland*" was not incorporated into the design.

The 28-mm wide blade for this saber was curved with a flat back and false edge. Many times, the forte was etched with a floral motif. The scabbard was steel with hanger bands and rings.

The *Dragoon* Regiments from Mecklenburg, Oldenburg, Baden, Hessen, and Württemberg adopted saber patterns similar to the Prussians. These included the *KD 89*, model 1852, and the lionhead "interim" saber.

The states of Württemberg, Baden, and Hessen adopted a saber based on the Austrian pattern, even though they were part of the Prussian Army after 1871. These patterns contained a nickeled dovehead hilt which contained a graduated 3- or 4-tiered pommel. The Württemberg pommel was slightly different, being rounded and covered with a downward sloping, raised flower petal design. The gold basket D-guard was of medium width and extended into a crossguard which folded slightly over the hand. The knucklebow and continuous crossguard were pierced and etched in a design commonly called "Honeysuckle". The D-guard many times incorporated the state coat of arms in its pierced design. The quillon end was a downward scroll. The fishskin-wrapped grip swelled at the pommel and was bound with silver, triple-wire wrap.

The blades of these sabers were curved, single-edged, and flat backed, with a false edge. The forte in many cases was etched and blued and contained the state seal. The scabbard was standard steel.

The saber carried by the *Mecklenburg Dragoon Regiments 17 and 18* was distinctive. The silver hilt was a dovehead pattern with raised petal-design pommel like the Württemberg pattern. The single bar D-guard extended downward into round, double sidebars which formed the basket hilt. The quillon end was a downward-sloping, rounded point.

The grip with center and pommel swells was pinned to the backstrap. The fishskin grip was bound with triple silver wire and ended in a ferrule. A *Fingerschlauf* completed the grip. The straight quillback blade was fitted to a steel scabbard.

The *Bavarian Chevauleger* troopers, as with other *Dragoon Regiments*, carried the KD 89 version adopted in 1891. *Chevauleger* officers could choose from a number of swords. These included a nickel-hilted *Pallasch* identical to the heavy cavalry model, an "interim" lionhead saber, and a deeply cast and engraved dovehead model with a D-guard and straight *Pallasch* blade. The sword of choice, however, was the magnificent Lionhead version of the KD 1891. This gilt sword featured the full-maned Bavarian Lionhead as the pommel. The lionhead extended into a backstrap which was straight. The flat, metal D-guard extended from the lion's roaring mouth downward to the sheet-metal sidebars which rounded into a downward sloping quillon end. The basket contained the rampant lion and shield of Bavaria. This basket could be ordered in the folding variety. The grip with center swell was wrapped in fishskin or celluloid with triple gold wire. This sword could be ordered in either standard or large, "*Grosser*" size.

The blade was a straight quillback with false edge usually containing the Bavarian motto. A steel scabbard completed the weapon.

The *Hussars*

The *Hussar* was easily recognized by his distinctive fur-covered *Busby*, looped jacket or *Atilla*, and basket hilt saber with *Sabertache*. The *Hussar* was the native cavalry of Hungary, and they were famous throughout Europe. The first Prussian *Hussars* appeared under Frederick the Great in 1721. At that time, they were cavalry attached to *Uhlan* Regiments. Frederick was so impressed with them that they were reorganized as separate *Hussar* Regiments. The *Zietenhussars*, named for Hans Joachim Zieten, participated in nearly every major battle throughout both the Silesian and Seven Years Wars. Their bold attacks at the battles of Mollwitz, Prague (where they rounded up fleeing Prussian Infantry and made an heroic counter-attack), Hochkirch, and Liegnitz (where Zieten was promoted to General) surrounded their name with glory. The tales of these battles were told and retold around a thousand campfires engulfed the *Zietenhussars* in a legendary mystique.

By the 1900s, the Prussian *Hussars* consisted of the *Leib Garde Hussars*, the 1st to 16th Regiments, and 17th Regiment of *Brunswick Hussars*. The 18th, 19th, and 20th Regiments were *Saxon*. The 3rd Regiment carried the famed *Zieten* designation. Bavaria had no *Hussars*.

The *1st Leib Hussar Regiment No. 1*, the *2nd Leib Hussar Regiment Konigin Viktoria No. 2*, and the *Braunschweig Hussar Regiment No. 17*, were known as the Black *Hussars*. They all wore black jackets and a *Totenkopf* or death's head insignia on the *Busby*. The death's head was the traditional insignia of a unit that "gave no quarter" in battle. The Black *Hussars* were called by the French, who dreaded their great boldness, "*Hussards de la mort*". This skull and bones insignia became both famous and infamous throughout the Third Reich.

Hussar swords were generally numerous variations of a few standard patterns. Troopers, as did other cavalry enlisted, carried the late pattern 1852, or the KD 89, based on regimental requirements. There were some units like the *2 Leib Garde Hussar Regiment No. 2* where the non-commissioned officers also carried the KD 89 with officer knot.

Prussian officers carried either the Model 52/79 basket hilt saber or the much preferred, low profile, ½ lionhead saber. *Braunschweiger Hussar* officers carried their own distinctive pattern. *Saxon* officers usually carried the *Saxon* model 1879 basket hilt sword discussed earlier.

The *Hussar* model 52/79, when carried by any of the Garde regiments, many times had a *Garde* Star affixed to the point where the sidebars joined the broad knuckle-bow. There were some examples noted where both the "*Totenkopf*" and the guard were affixed to the knuckle guard.

The lionhead saber carried by the *Prussian 1st* and *2nd Leib Garde* and as "interim" saber by the *Braunschweig Hussars* is one of the most sought-after edged weapons of the period.

The gold 1/2 lionhead saber for these "Death's Head *Hussars*" many times were seen in the favored "*Grosser*" size. The low profile lionhead was deeply chiseled and the mane extended down the backstrap to a ferrule. The fishskin-wrapped grip with gilt triple wire wrap was secured by the backstrap. The P-shaped guard extended from the lions' mouth and ended in a straight crossguard, usually ending in a smaller lionhead quillon end. The knuckle-bow, crossguard, and quillon end were also deeply cast with a variety of patterns. The front of the knuckle-bow on many of these sabers contained a silver applied death's head. The guard star was usually placed on the langet. Officers not in *Garde* units generally had the Royal Cypher of Wilhelm II placed on the langet.

The blade for most *Hussar* lionhead sabers was a curved quill back with false edge. A large number of these pieces were exquisitely etched or made of genuine Damascus. A steel scabbard was used.

The Duchy of *Braunschweig*, while using mainly Prussian sword patterns due to their long established association with Prussia, produced a distinctive cavalry saber adopted by the *Hussar* Regiment No. 17.

The gilt, basket hilt saber was based on the "Gothic Pattern" British saber model 1822. The 4-tiered pommel was somewhat flattened with a protruding knob covering the peened tang of the blade. The backstrap was deeply cast with a floral design. The grip with pommel and center swells was fishskin-wrapped and bound with a gold, 3-wire wrap. The D-guard knuckle-bow extended from the pommel downward into a basket of three pierced sidebars. This pierced basket was decorated with the crowned "W" of Duke Wilhelm of the Royal House of *Braunschweig*. These sidebars extended into a scrolled quillon end.

The blade was produced with a single-edge blade with a flat back. The forte of the blade was etched with a floral design surrounding the coat of arms of *Braunschweig*.

The steel scabbard pattern for *Hussars* was very distinctive. Instead of the usual narrow hanger bands, the *Hussar* pattern had large, flat, round bands securing the hanger rings.

The *Uhlans*

The *Uhlans* were the traditional cavalry of Poland just as the *Hussars* were of Hungary. The *Uhlan's* distinctive mortar-board shaped helmet or *Chapka* provides for easy recognition of this light cavalry arm. They were the traditional lancers of the cavalry and, when mounted, carried this weapon vertically around their shoulder with the butt end affixed in the socket on the side of the stirrup.

The *Uhlans* were light and swiftly-moving cavalry. Besides battle maneuvers, they were responsible for destroying communication lines, surprising enemy outposts, blowing up viaducts and bridges, and foraging. When they were not destroying enemy communications, they were establishing communication lines for their own troops. The *Uhlans* could do this very quickly. Riders were sent out with coils of wire rapidly being unwound. With them were riders carrying insulators and other equipment. On open ground they would thrust their lances in the ground ever so often and affix the wire to it. In wooded and settled areas, they would use trees and posts as available. In this manner communication was established very quickly and efficiently.

The *Uhlans* were composed of three *Garde* units: the 1st, 2nd, and 3rd *Uhlanen Garde Regiments* and 21 numbered regiments. Prussian Regiments were the 1st to 16th, *Saxony* the 17th, 18th, and 21st Regiments, and Württemberg the 18th and 19th Regiments. Bavaria offered two Regiments, the *Koniglich Bayern 1. Uhlanen Regiment Kaiser Wilhelm II, Konig Von Prussen*, and the *Koniglich Bayern 2. Uhlanen Regiment Konig*.

The sword patterns for *Uhlan* troopers were generally the same as other cavalry regiments, i.e. the KD 89 and the model 1852. A P-guard dovehead model designated the *Uhlan* model 1873 was also worn. Saxon and Württemberg carried models discussed earlier.

Uhlan officers carried the "interim" lionhead with crossed lances on the langet. The model 52/79 was preferred by many officers.

The *Uhlan Regiment Kaiser Alexander III von Russland* No. 1 did wear a different saber than all other units. This saber with the eaglehead pommel was the same as worn by the *Brandenburg Dragoons*, except the *Uhlan* model was in gold instead of silver.

Bavarian Uhlan troopers carried the KD 91. *Uhlan* officers generally preferred the lionhead KD as did *Chevauleger* officers. The "interim" lionhead saber was also worn.

When we think of *Uhlans*, we generally think of lances. However, in 1889, Wilhelm II ordered the entire cavalry force to be equipped with the lance, as he considered it to be the "Queen" of weapons. The lance then became the standard weapon of the entire German cavalry. The basic lance remained unchanged for nearly a thousand years. The model of 1889 was 10 feet, five inches long and weighed 3 pounds 9 ounces. The lance head was a four-edged point, 12.9 inches long, and made of well-tempered steel. The butt end also contained a much shorter steel point so that a close range thrust could be made to the rear. The lance shaft was made of rolled-steel plate instead of the traditional wood. Below the lance head, the weapon carried a small flag, showing the provincial colors. Even though the *Kaiser* established the lance as the uniform cavalry weapon, its usefulness in modern warfare was debated by many officers. By early World War I the weapon generally was relegated to ceremonial use much like the *Kuirasse*.

Special Units

The *Jager zu Pferde* and *Leib-Gendarmerie* were two small units with officers and men who shared uniforms and accouterments with the cavalry.

The *Jager zu Pferde* was the youngest branch of the German Army. The 13 units were raised between 1905 and 1913. The primary mission of these regiments which had been established by an AKO directive of 1895 was to serve as couriers or mounted dispatch riders (*Meldereiter*). The title was changed to *Jager zu Pferde* in 1897. Initially, these troops came from the *Garde Corps* and the 1st and 15th Army Corps. During this period of initial organization, edged weapons worn varied with the individual unit. After 1905, the detachments were formed into regiments.

Troopers wore the *KD 89* as did other cavalry branches. Officers wore the *Kürassier Pallasch*, "interim" lionhead, and *Stichdegen*. The *Stichdegen* was identical to the *Kürassier* model with the exception that it was worn in a brown leather instead of black leather scabbard.

Leib-Gendarmerie

This elite corps was composed of officers and enlisted men from Prussian cavalry regiments whose duty it was to protect the royal family. The *Leib-Gendarmerie* was the personal escort of the *Kaiser*, while the *Kaiserin* was protected by the *Leibgarde der Kaiserin*. These mounted troops were also responsible for carrying the Royal Standards.

The edged weapons of both units were the same with the notable exception of the officer of the *Kaiser's* bodyguard. The officer for this troop was rotated on a yearly basis from different cavalry units. All branches could be represented as well as their particular swords. Many of these specially selected officers wore presentation swords attesting to their elevated status, and these swords are especially sought out by collectors.

Cavalry Schools

Occasionally, the collector will find a cavalry saber with a rider's school presentation. These schools included the Military Riding Institute in Hannover, and the Officers' Riding Schools in Paderborn and Soltan.

This concludes the description of edged weapons of the German Cavalry. It is hoped this overview will provide the reader with a general knowledge with which to conduct an even more detailed study of this interesting and specialized area.

The Edged Weapons of the German Cavalry

Pictured above in color is an outstanding Imperial *Prussian Pallasch* as carried by the Guard *Cuirassier* Regiment (the *Kaiser's* personal guard). The hilt is brass with a fishskin wrapped grip. The massive 37 inch blade is unmarked and made of a rare modified "band" Damascus steel. *Richard R. Williams Collection. Photo by Dick Scott Fine Photography, Houston.*

Imperial German Edged Weaponry

Lion head saber in *"Grosser"* size, as preferred by many *Kürassier* officers for "interim" wear. This saber is highly detailed; including a pierced knucklebow, red ruby eyes, and an etched blade. *LTC (Ret.) Thomas M. Johnson Photo Collection. Photo by LTC (Ret.) Thomas M. Johnson.*

OPPOSITE: The massive *Prussian Kürassier Pallasch* with a 37 inch "band" Damascus steel blade (center) is shown in color bordered by two other Imperial *Cuirassier* swords which also feature Damascus steel blades. A fantastic "threesome" for any Imperial edged weapons collection! *Richard R. Williams Collection. Photo by Dick Scott Fine Photography, Houston.*

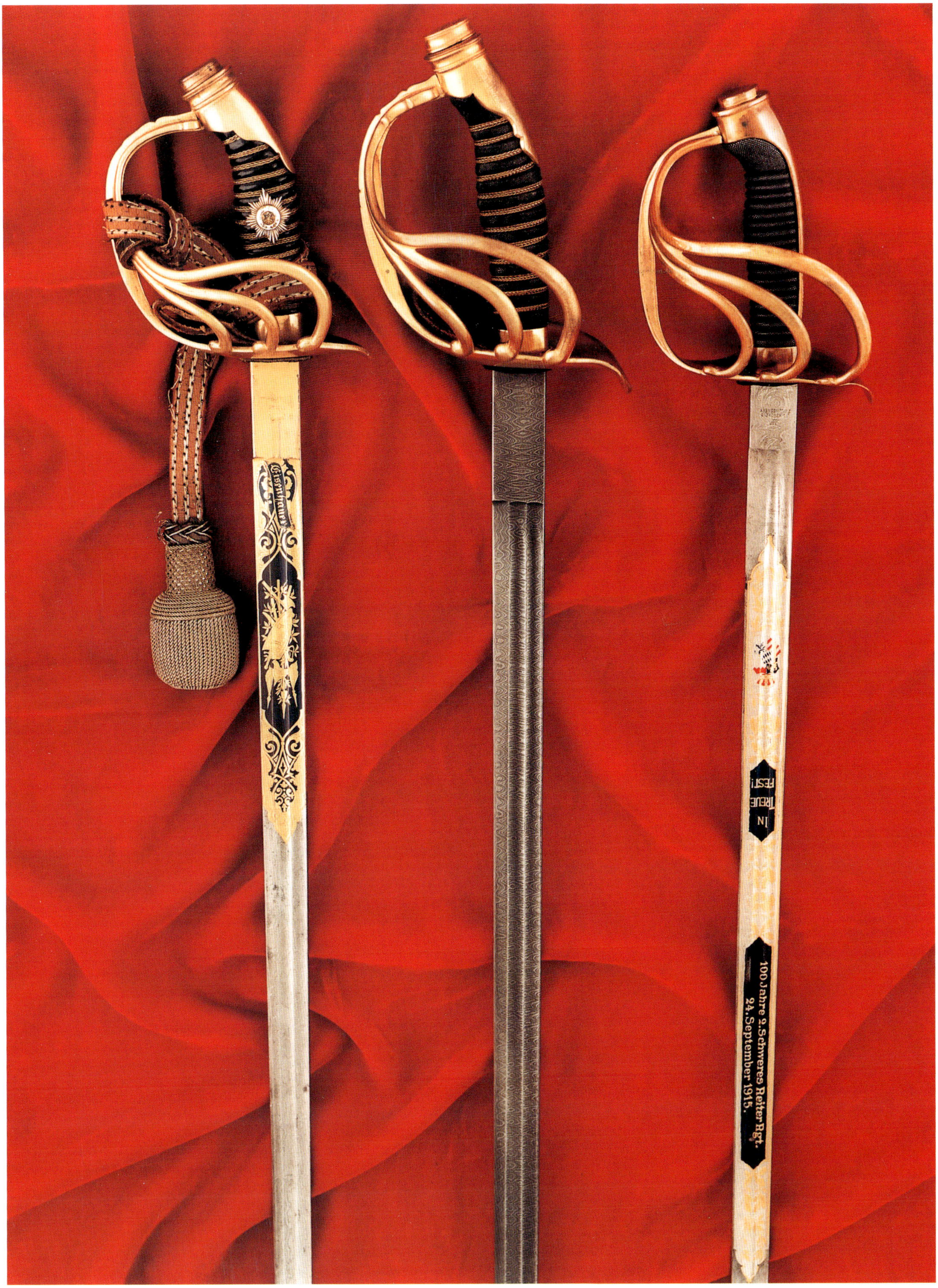
In Treue fest!
100 Jahre 2.Schweres Reiter Rgt.
24.September 1915.

Imperial German Edged Weaponry

OPPOSITE
LEFT: NCO of the *Garde du Corps*, the personal escort of the *Kaiser*. Tall men were preferred for this Corps, and most individuals were over 6 feet and at least one as tall as 6 feet 7 inches. The NCO pictured is wearing the officer pattern *Cuirass* and wearing the parade eagle on his helmet instead of the spike. *LTC (Ret.) Thomas M. Johnson Photo Collection. Photo by Achill de Veer, Berlin.*

RIGHT: *Kaiser* Wilhelm poses for a formal portrait wearing his personal *Cuirassier* officer *Degen*. Note the unusually small portepee for this size sidearm. This studio portrait is dated 1905. *LTC (Ret.) Thomas M. Johnson Photo Collection. Photo by Reichard & Linder, Berlin.*

Prussian Cuirassier Pallasch as carried by the Guard *Cuirassier* Regiment. The hilt is brass, with fishskin covered grip. The grip is triple brass wire wrapped. The knot is tied in an approved variation. *MAJ (Ret.) John L. Harrell Collection. Photo by LTC (Ret.) Thomas M. Johnson.*

ORIGINALAUFNAHME DER
OFPHOTOG. REICHARD & LINDNER
BERLIN 1905.
20
VERLAG VON
GUSTAV LIERSCH &
BERLIN.

Imperial German Edged Weaponry

Close-up detail of the massive hilt and scabbard of a French 1st Empire *Cuirassier* sword, Model AN. XI (1802-1803). The hilt fittings are brass. The grip is leather covered with twisted brass wire wrap, and the blade is double-fullered. These captured French broadswords were carried by various *Prussian Cuirassier* Regiments until 1874. The *Garde du Corps* Regiment carried this sword until 1850, and 1st and 2nd Bavarian *Cuirassier* Regiments carried this sword until 1879. *MAJ (Ret.) John L. Harrell Collection. Photo by LTC (Ret.) Thomas M. Johnson.*

INSET: Close-up detail of the *Prussian* unit markings stamped on the upper reverse scabbard of the massive French *Cuirassier* sword. The marking, "1.L.R.4.10" is also stamped on the brass hilt guard and indicates that this sword was issued to the 1st *Landwehr* (Cavalry) Regiment, 4th Squadron, sword number 10. *MAJ (Ret.) John L. Harrell Collection. Photo by LTC (Ret.) Thomas M. Johnson.*

Ultra rare presentation Guard *Cuirassier* Officer *Pallasch*. The single-fullered blade obverse is etched with a military motif and stamped with the retailer's name of Carl Grasser, Vienna. *Thomas T. Wittmann Collection. Photo by Charles H. Jenkins, III.*

Kürassier Officer *Pallasch*, reverse view. The *ricasso* is marked to the blade firm of Weyersberg and Stamm, Solingen, circa 1870. The *Eisenhauer* blade is etched with the names of the unit officers. *Thomas T. Wittmann Collection. Photo by Charles H. Jenkins, III.*

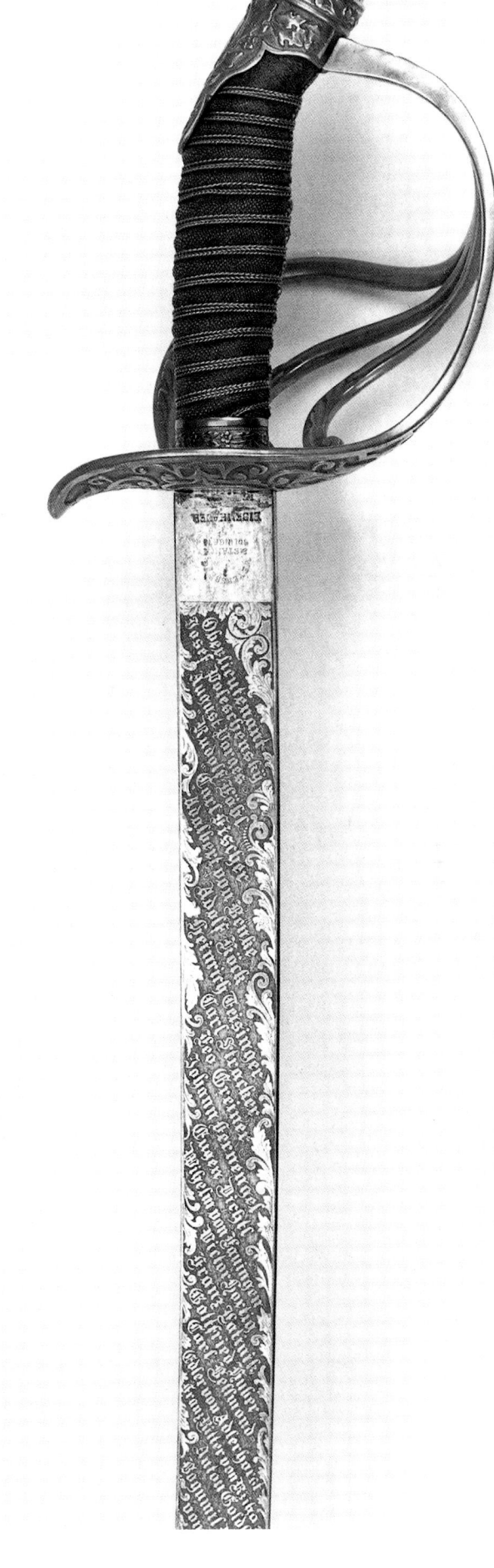

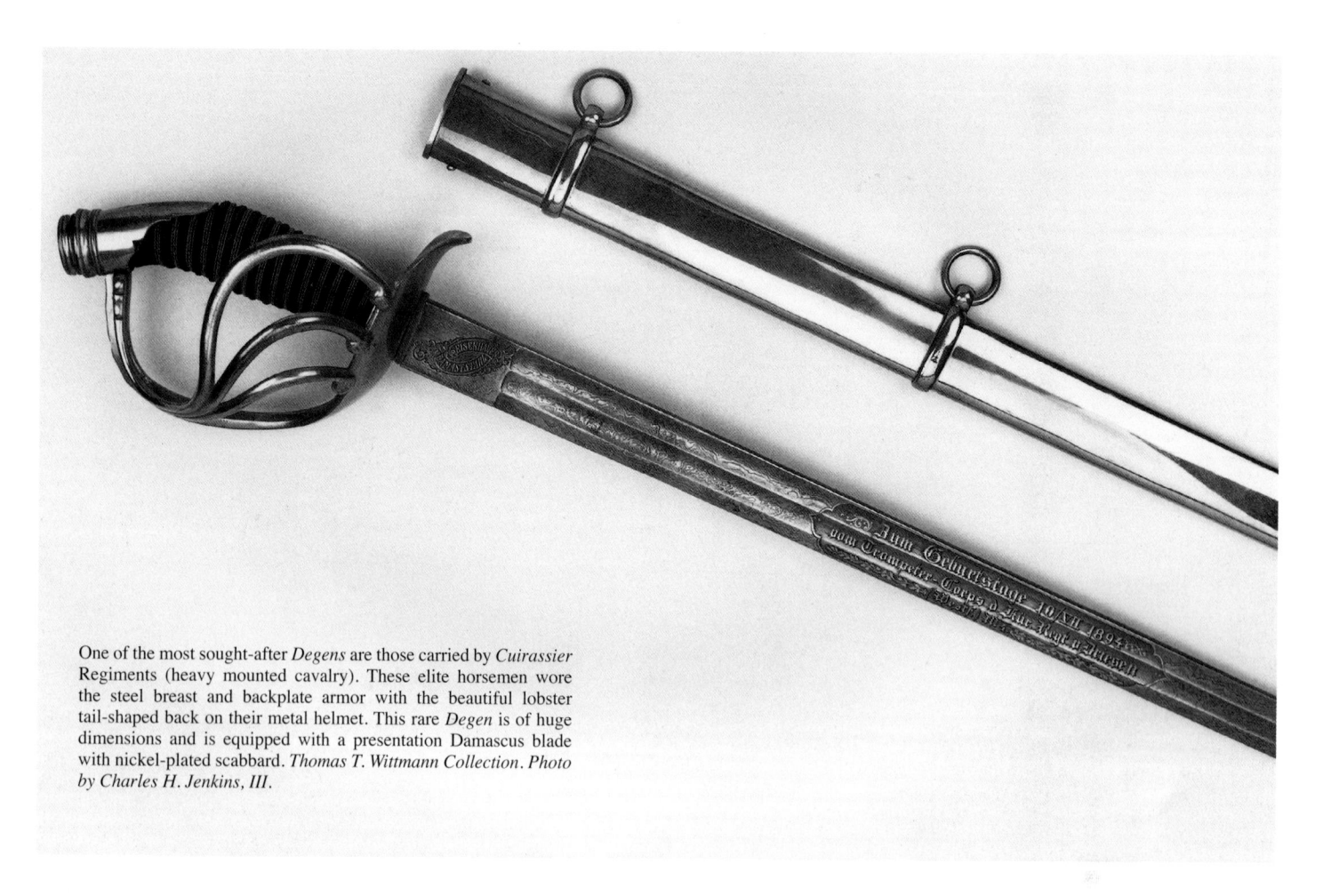

One of the most sought-after *Degens* are those carried by *Cuirassier* Regiments (heavy mounted cavalry). These elite horsemen wore the steel breast and backplate armor with the beautiful lobster tail-shaped back on their metal helmet. This rare *Degen* is of huge dimensions and is equipped with a presentation Damascus blade with nickel-plated scabbard. *Thomas T. Wittmann Collection. Photo by Charles H. Jenkins, III.*

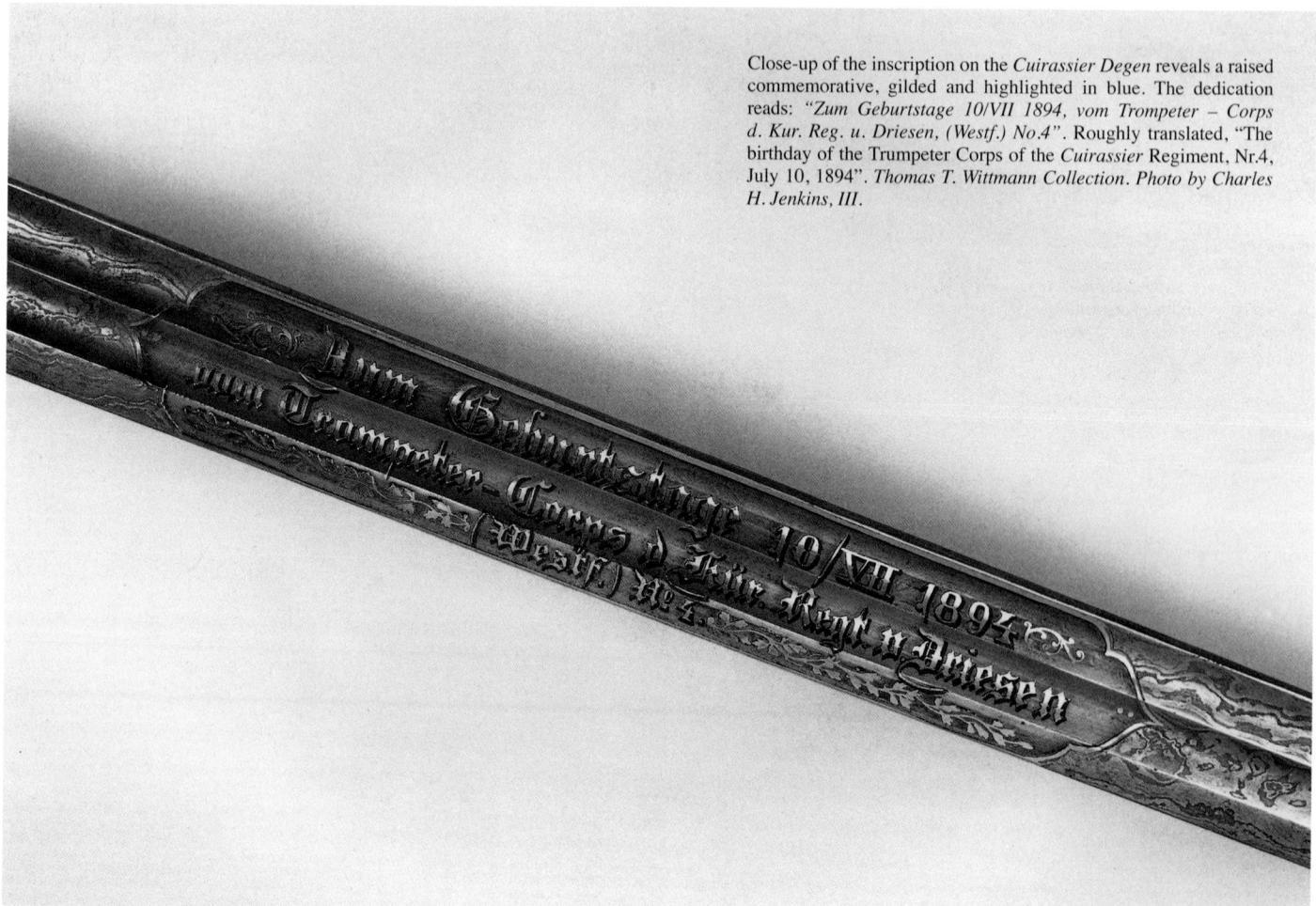

Close-up of the inscription on the *Cuirassier Degen* reveals a raised commemorative, gilded and highlighted in blue. The dedication reads: *"Zum Geburtstage 10/VII 1894, vom Trompeter – Corps d. Kur. Reg. u. Driesen, (Westf.) No.4"*. Roughly translated, "The birthday of the Trumpeter Corps of the *Cuirassier* Regiment, Nr.4, July 10, 1894". *Thomas T. Wittmann Collection. Photo by Charles H. Jenkins, III.*

The Edged Weapons of the German Cavalry

Kürassier officer with Pallasch. The broadsword pictured is the "Extra" pattern with plain brass hilt and leather instead of fishskin wrapped grip. The knot is tied in the standard manner for the Pallasch, knotted around the grip, slipped through the second sidebar, and wrapped around the knucklebow. LTC (Ret.) Thomas M. Johnson Photo Collection.

Three generations of Wilhelms. Both the *Kaiser* and the Crown Prince are dressed in *Kürassier* (Heavy Cavalry) uniforms. The Crown Prince wears the Parade *Cuirasses* (body armor) which was not worn in the field after the 1880s. The Crown Prince also wears the distinctive *Pallasch*. *LTC (Ret.) Thomas M. Johnson Photo Collection.*

271

Imperial German Edged Weaponry

Lion head saber with rare ribbon pattern Damascus steel blade which has the raised name of owner, Otto Beck, *Wachmeister* in gold with blue highlights. The high quality hilt is deeply cast and chiseled. Cavalry rank designations differ slightly from the Army. The Cavalry *Wachmeister* is the same as the Army Sergeant Major, and the Cavalry *Rittmeister* is the same as the Army Captain. *Robert P. Zill Collection. Photo by Mark Harper.*

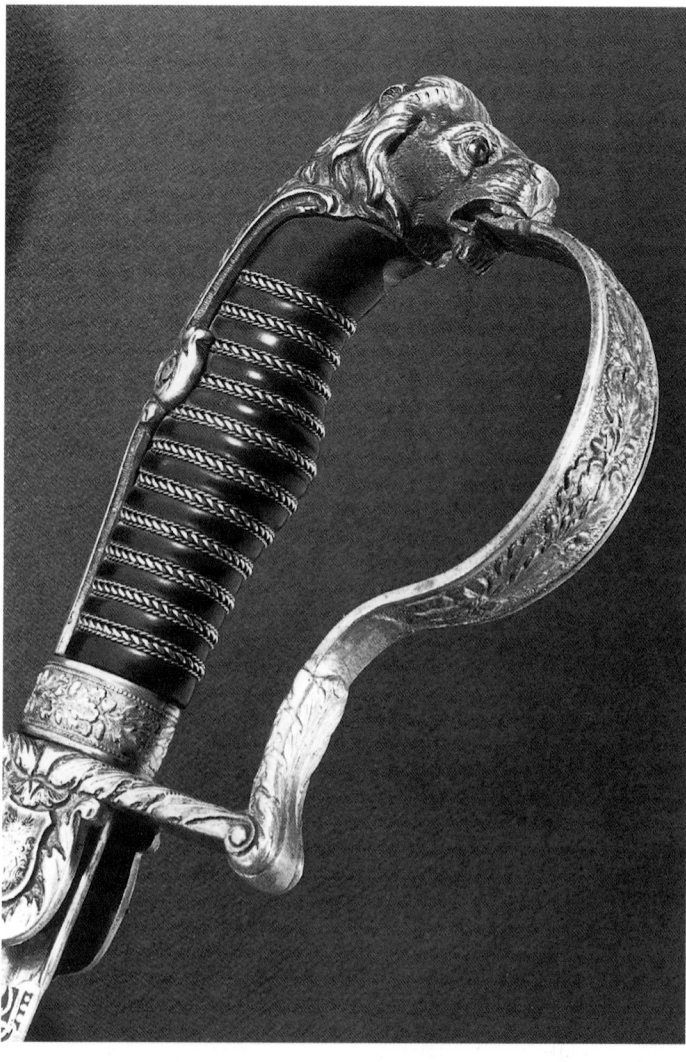

Highly detailed Lion head cavalry saber. The grip is celluloid rather than the usual sharkskin. The personal coat-of-arms of the owner is seen on the reverse langet. The obverse langet of this saber contains a *Garde Star*. The etching on the blade of this saber contains a *Kürassier Pallasch* leading the writer to think this Lion head was worn as an "interim" saber by a member of a *Garde Kürassier* unit. *Bonnie Hameister Collection. Photo by Richard Hansen.*

Close-up of the engraving on the *Garde Kürassier* Lion head saber. The *Kürassier Pallasch* in the center of the etching is very distinct. *Bonnie Hameister Collection. Photo by Richard Hansen.*

272

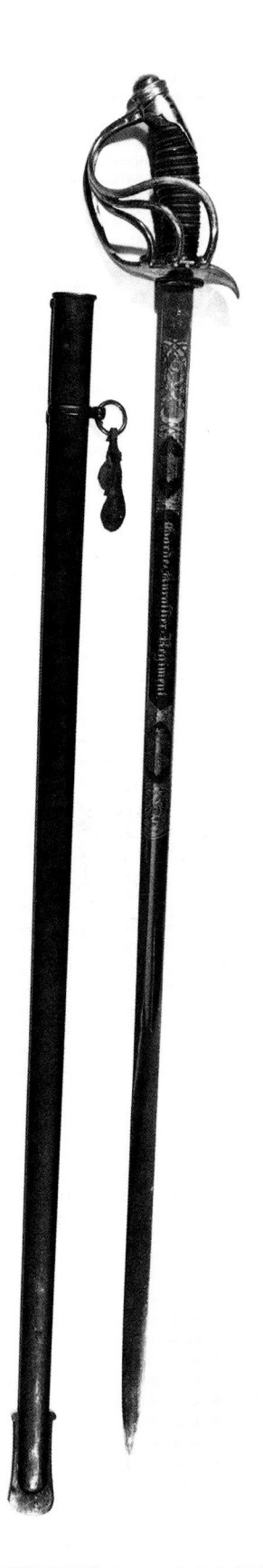

The Edged Weapons of the German Cavalry

LEFT: Pictured is a Carl Eickhorn factory Model #834, *Preussischer Kürassier-Extrasäbel* (Prussian Kürassier Deluxe Saber) – full length obverse view. This model sword is shown on page 70 of the Carl Eickhorn *Müsterbuch* (Sample Book). *Larry Braun Collection. Photo by Andy Southard.*

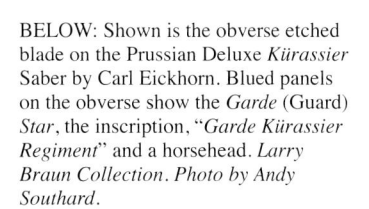

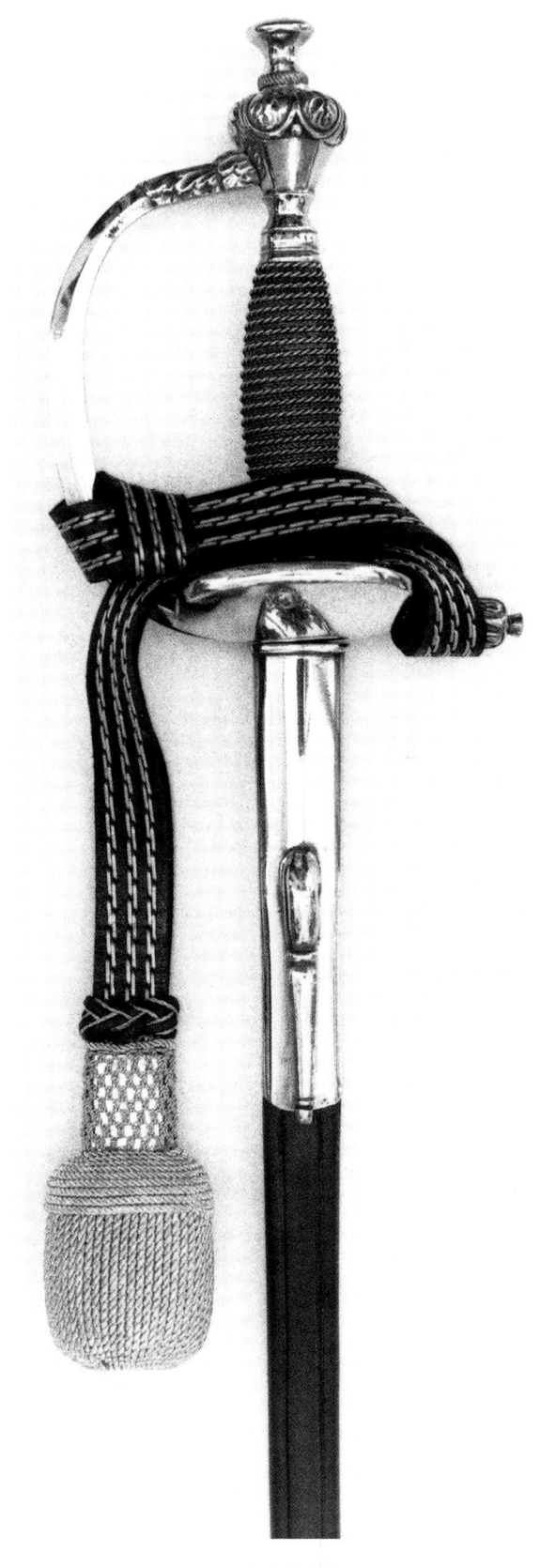

RIGHT: Exquisite *Kürassier* officer *Stichdegen* or "Interim" sword. This particular sword has no maker's mark. The components of the hilt are marked with an inspector's mark #10. The etched blade is 34 1/4 inches long. The scabbard is black leather with brass fittings. *Joseph Viotto Collection. Photo by Joseph Viotto.*

BELOW: Shown is the obverse etched blade on the Prussian Deluxe *Kürassier* Saber by Carl Eickhorn. Blued panels on the obverse show the *Garde* (Guard) Star, the inscription, "*Garde Kürassier Regiment*" and a horsehead. *Larry Braun Collection. Photo by Andy Southard.*

BOTTOM: The reverse etched blade on the Prussian *Kürassier* Saber by Carl Eickhorn depicts a *Kürassier* engagement scene on a blued panel. *Larry Braun Collection. Photo by Andy Southard.*

273

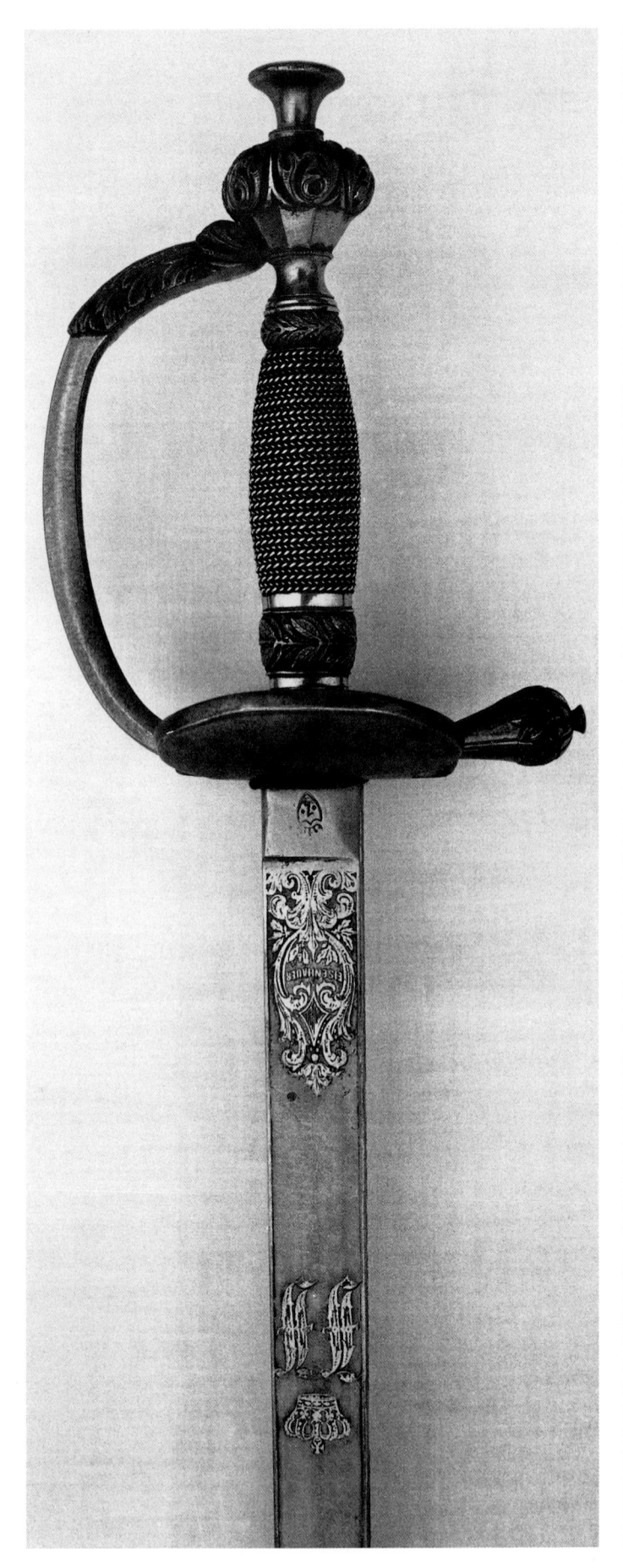

Presentation grade *Kürassier Stichdegen* with owner's initials on the blade. The highly detailed chiseling and maker's mark are easily observed. *Robert Meistrell Collection. Photo by David Delich.*

Kürassier Stichdegen as viewed from the back of the blade. This photo provides an excellent view of the folding clamshells, the deep castings of the hilt components and the etching of the blade spine. *Robert Meistrell Collection. Photo by David Delich.*

The magnificent *Prussian* "Interim" sword is worn by a *Cüirassier* officer. The portepee is properly wrapped around the hilt. *LTC (Ret.) Thomas M. Johnson Photo Collection. Photo by Fritz Leyde & Co., Berlin.*

Prussian Kürassier officer circa 1899 carrying his broadsword complete with sword knot. *Artwork by Brian Molloy, United Kingdom.*

ABOVE: *Garde du Corps* troopers in full dress at their *Kaserne* in Berlin. Each trooper wears the "Extra Pattern" *Pallasch* and distinctive *Garde du Corps* eagle-top helmet. *LTC (Ret.) Thomas M. Johnson Photo Collection. Photo by Charles H. Jenkins, III.*

Cuirassier Pallasch obverse blade detail showing the blued panels with Guard Star and regimental inscription. The Guard *Kürassier* Regiment was raised in 1815 and garrisoned at Berlin. *MAJ (Ret.) John L. Harrell Collection. Photo by LTC (Ret.) Thomas M. Johnson.*

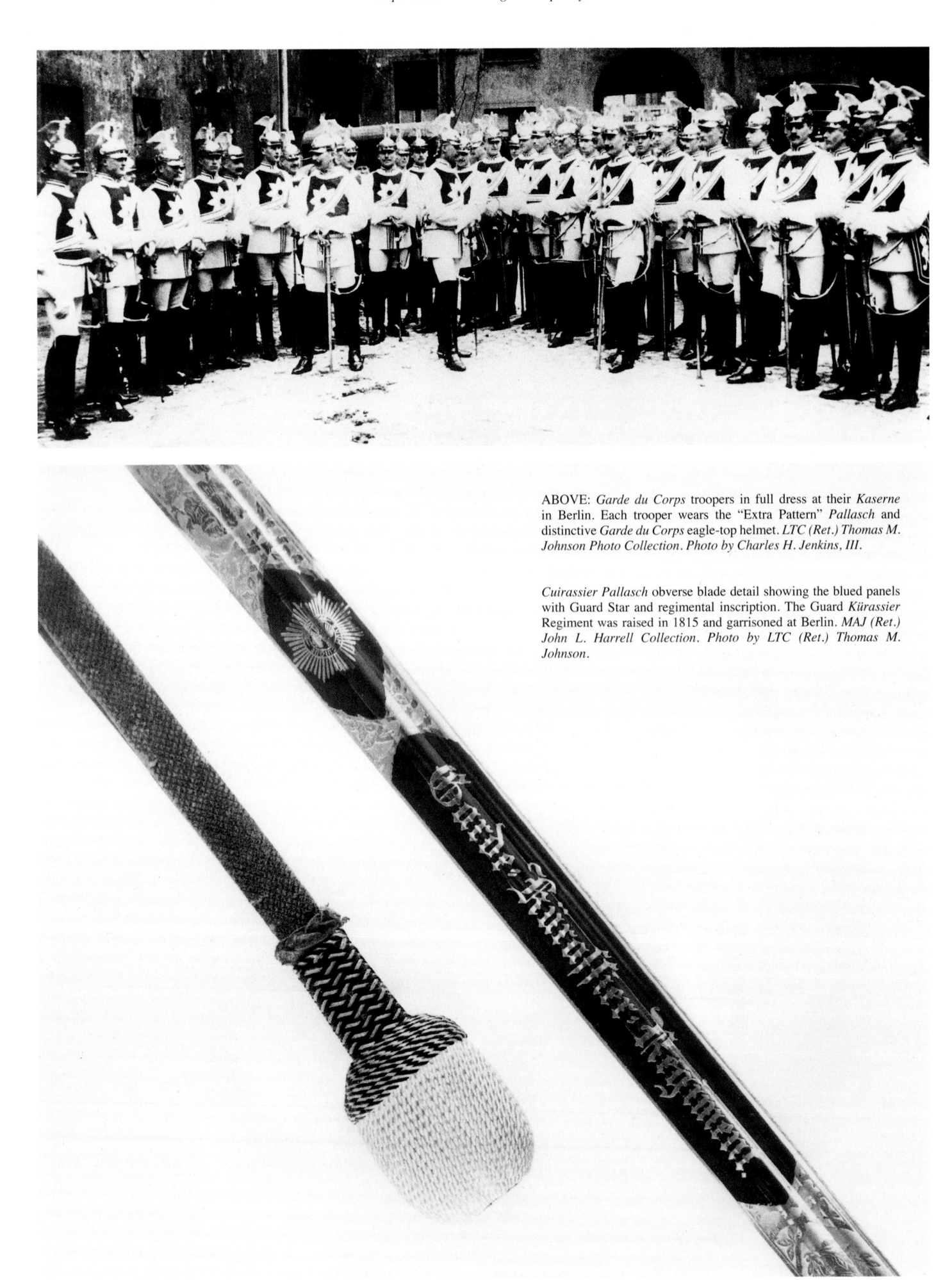

The Edged Weapons of the German Cavalry

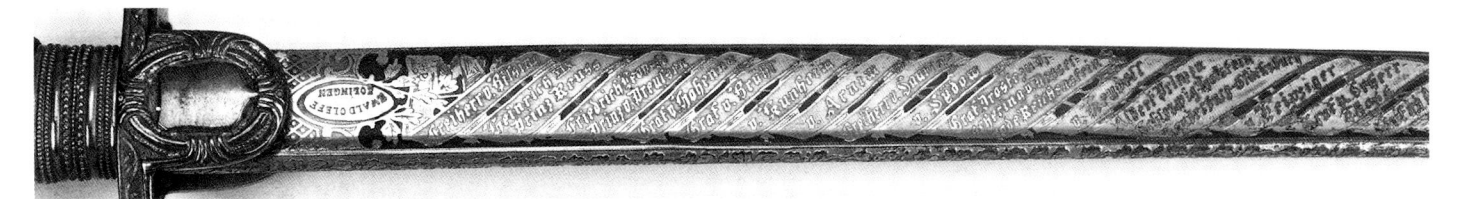

The reverse blade of this *Garde du Corps* Presentation features the names of the presenters – almost without exception, all are of Royalty! *Robert A. Johnston Collection. Photo by Charles H. Jenkins, III.*

Reverse of the Guard Cuirassier Regiment broadsword showing highly detailed etching of charging Cuirassiers attacking a similar group of heavy cavalry. The etching is interesting, in that it includes the parade helmets on the Cuirassiers. These highly adorned helmets were never worn into battle. *MAJ (Ret.) John L. Harrell Collection. Photo by LTC (Ret.) Thomas M. Johnson.*

Prince Wilhelm wearing a child's model *Garde du Corps* helmet and holding a "*Kinder*" size *Kürassier Pallasch*. Children helmets and swords from the *Garde du Corps* are rare and highly sought after by collectors. *LTC (Ret.) Thomas M. Johnson Photo Collection.*

The mounted Crown Prince in *Kürassier* uniform. Affixed to his saddle is his *Pallasch*. This much sought-after broadsword is based on the French pattern of 1802. The *Kürassier Pallasch* is one of the longest German edged weapons with a blade that can exceed 32 inches. *LTC (Ret.) Thomas M. Johnson Photo Collection.*

277

Imperial German Edged Weaponry

The *Kaiser* dressed as a *Kürassier* complete with broadsword, plumed *Pickelhaube*, and Field Marshal's baton. The extreme length of the *Pallasch* is readily observed. *LTC (Ret.) Thomas M. Johnson Photo Collection.*

The Edged Weapons of the German Cavalry

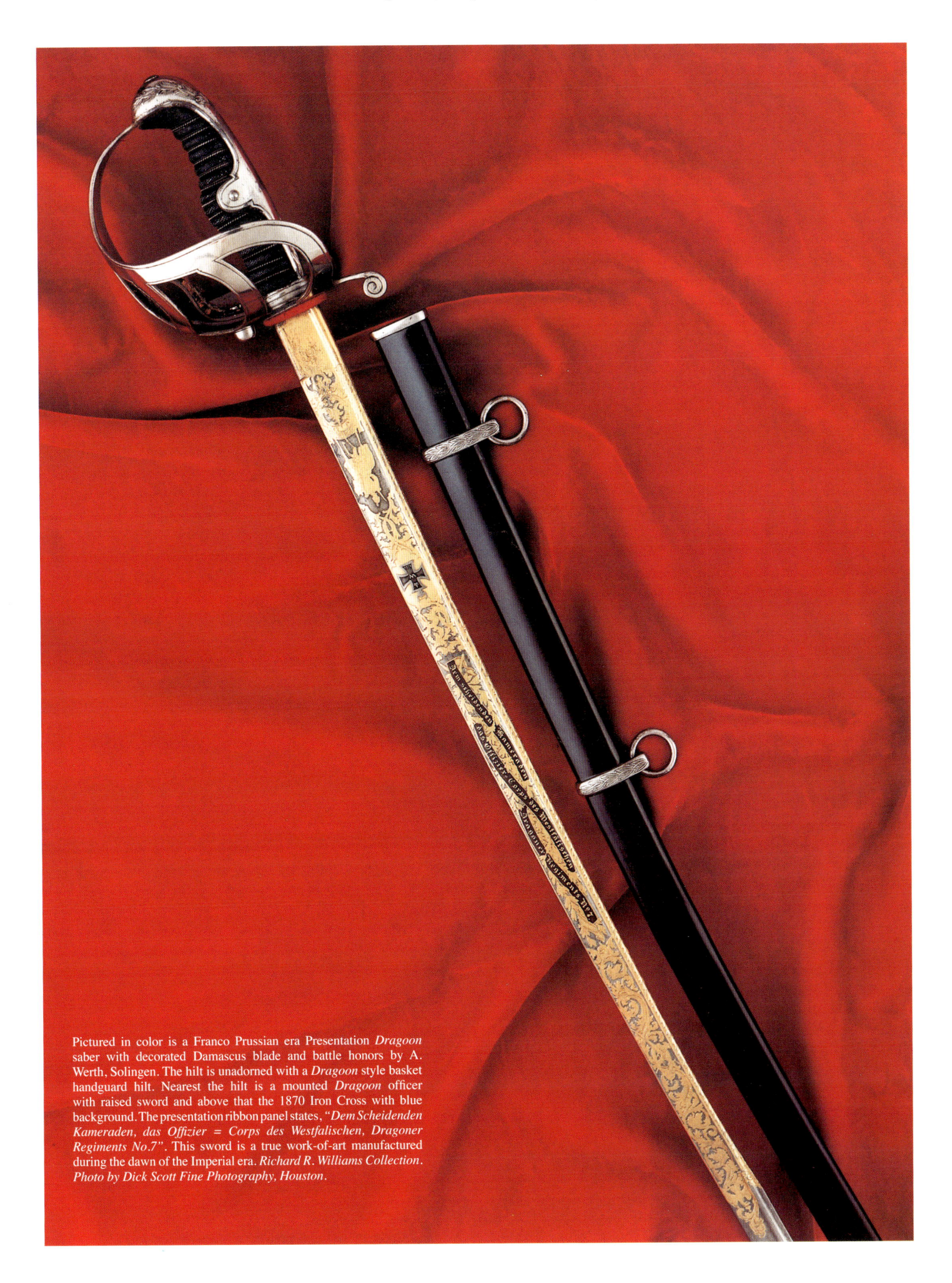

Pictured in color is a Franco Prussian era Presentation *Dragoon* saber with decorated Damascus blade and battle honors by A. Werth, Solingen. The hilt is unadorned with a *Dragoon* style basket handguard hilt. Nearest the hilt is a mounted *Dragoon* officer with raised sword and above that the 1870 Iron Cross with blue background. The presentation ribbon panel states, "*Dem Scheidenden Kameraden, das Offizier = Corps des Westfalischen, Dragoner Regiments No.7*". This sword is a true work-of-art manufactured during the dawn of the Imperial era. *Richard R. Williams Collection. Photo by Dick Scott Fine Photography, Houston.*

Reverse view of the Franco Prussian era Presentation *Dragoon* style saber by A. Werth, Solingen. The scabbard is black enamel with two brass scabbard bands. Near the blade ricasso is a crowned Imperial eagle standing on a globe of the world followed by an angel of victory. The center panel lists in ribbon format four battles of the Franco Prussian War of 1870-1871 that the regiment participated in. Following the battle ribbons the great crowned eagle is posed followed by Germania holding a crown above her head. *Richard R. Williams Collection. Photo by Dick Scott Fine Photography, Houston.*

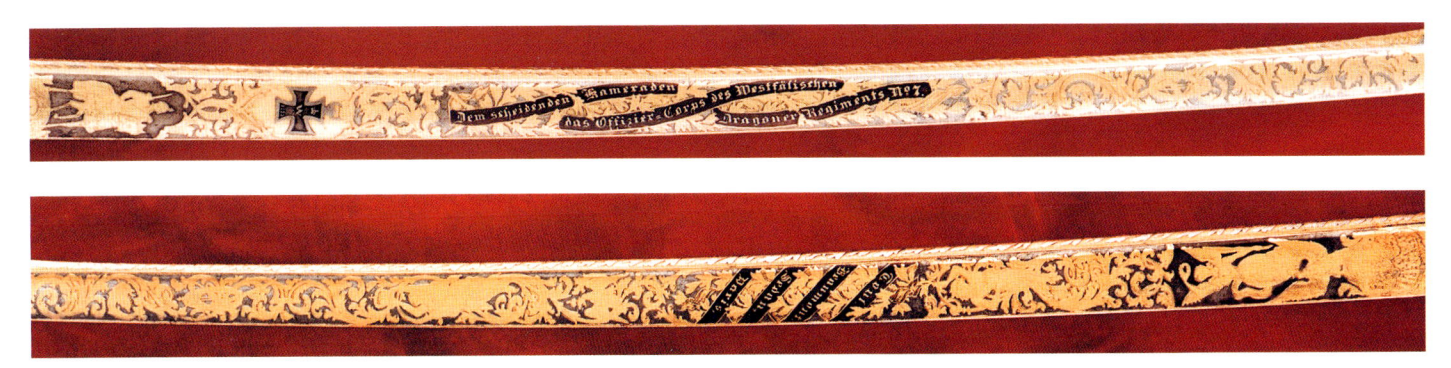

TOP: Close-up color view of the obverse Damascus steel blade of the Franco Prussian era *Dragoon* saber by A. Werth, Solingen. *Richard R. Williams Collection. Photo by Dick Scott Fine Photography, Houston.*

ABOVE: Close-up color view of the reverse Damascus steel blade of the Franco Prussian era *Dragoon* saber by A. Werth, Solingen. *Richard R. Williams Collection. Photo by Dick Scott Fine Photography, Houston.*

RIGHT: Handsome *Dragoon* enlisted man posing for his formal portrait with his nickel basket-hilt saber. Note the white leather hanging straps. *LTC (Ret.) Thomas M. Johnson Photo Collection.*

281

Imperial German Edged Weaponry

LEFT: Saber for *Mecklenburg Dragoon* Regiment Number 17 *(1 Grossherzoglich Mecklenburgisches)*. This identification is based on the Regimental cypher found on the hilt, as well as the blade etching. *Thomas T. Wittmann Collection. Photo by Charles H. Jenkins, III.*

BELOW: Ultra rare photo of an officer of the *1st Brandenburg Dragoon Regiment Nr.2*, known as the *"Schwedter Dragoons"*. The distinctive *Dragoon* eagle appears on his peaked cap. The officer is carrying the famed (and rare) Eagle head saber of his regiment. *LTC (Ret.) Thomas M. Johnson Photo Collection. Photo by Wm. Emil Tiedemann, Hannover.*

Dragoon NCO wearing the *KD89 Degen*. The folding clamshell with the *Prussian* coat-of-arms, as well as the rest of the hilt, is clearly seen. The two pins through the bakelite grip are unusual. *LTC (Ret.) Thomas M. Johnson Photo Collection.*

Member of the *2nd Baden Dragoons* 21st Regiment with *"Kavallerie Degen"* M89. The sword hanger is a variation which snaps directly to the scabbard hanger ring. *LTC (Ret.) Thomas M. Johnson Photo Collection. Copy Photo by Charles H. Jenkins, III.*

ABOVE: *Dragoon Oberleutnant* with *IOD89* with double-folding clamshells, complete with a standard sword knot in a standard "tie". Why would an officer in the *1st Brandenburg Dragoon Regiment Nr.2* be wearing an Infantry Officer *Degen*? The collector should be aware that the fortunes of war caused many unusual uniform combinations. During 1917-1918 the *Schwedter Dragoons* were transferred to the Western Front as an infantry rifle command for defense. *LTC (Ret.) Thomas M. Johnson Photo Collection.*

LEFT: NCO in the Prussian *Dragoon* Regiment "King Albert of *Saxony* (East Prussia) Nr.10", wearing his *KD89 Degen* complete with sword knot. The Prussian Eagle appears on the non-folding clamshell. *LTC (Ret.) Thomas M. Johnson Photo Collection.*

OPPOSITE
LEFT: Prussian *Dragoon* enlisted man with late pattern *M52* basket hilt saber. *LTC (Ret.) Thomas M. Johnson Photo Collection.*

RIGHT: This NCO in the *Dragoon* Regiment "Queen Olga (*1st Württemberg*) No.25" is wearing the *KD89* basket hilt sword with the *Württemberg* coat-of-arms on the non-folding clamshell. *LTC (Ret.) Thomas M. Johnson Photo Collection.*

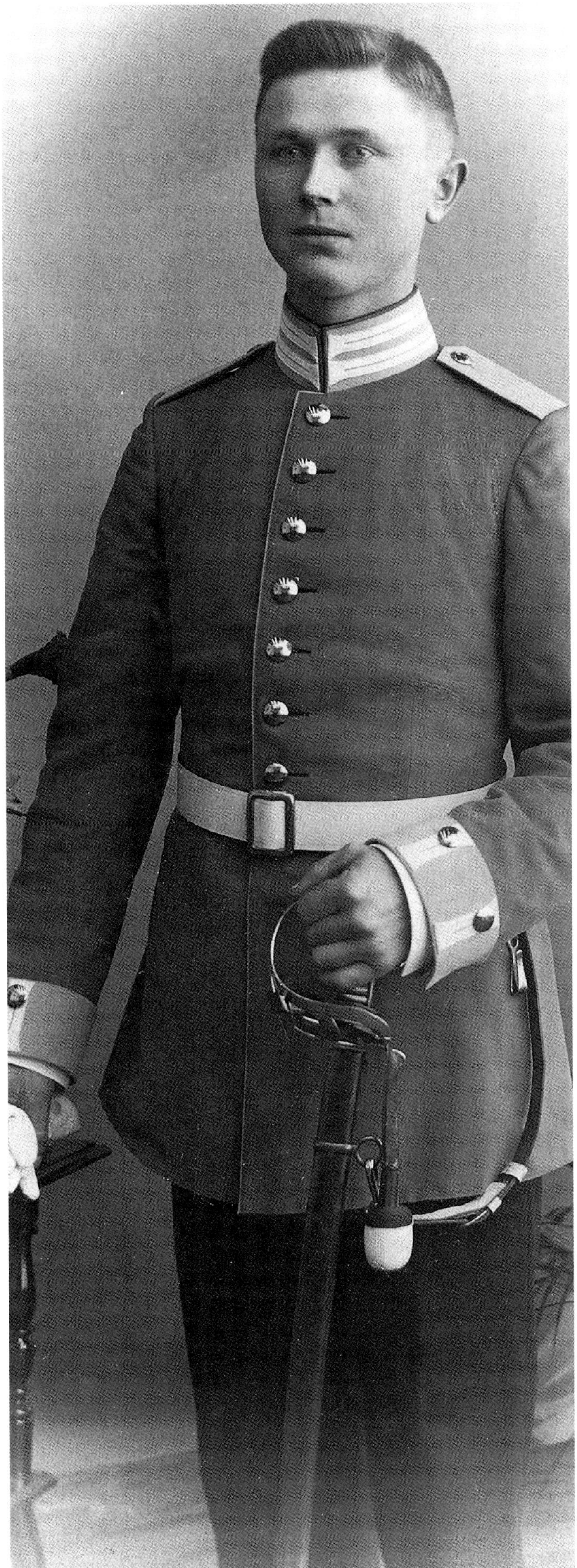

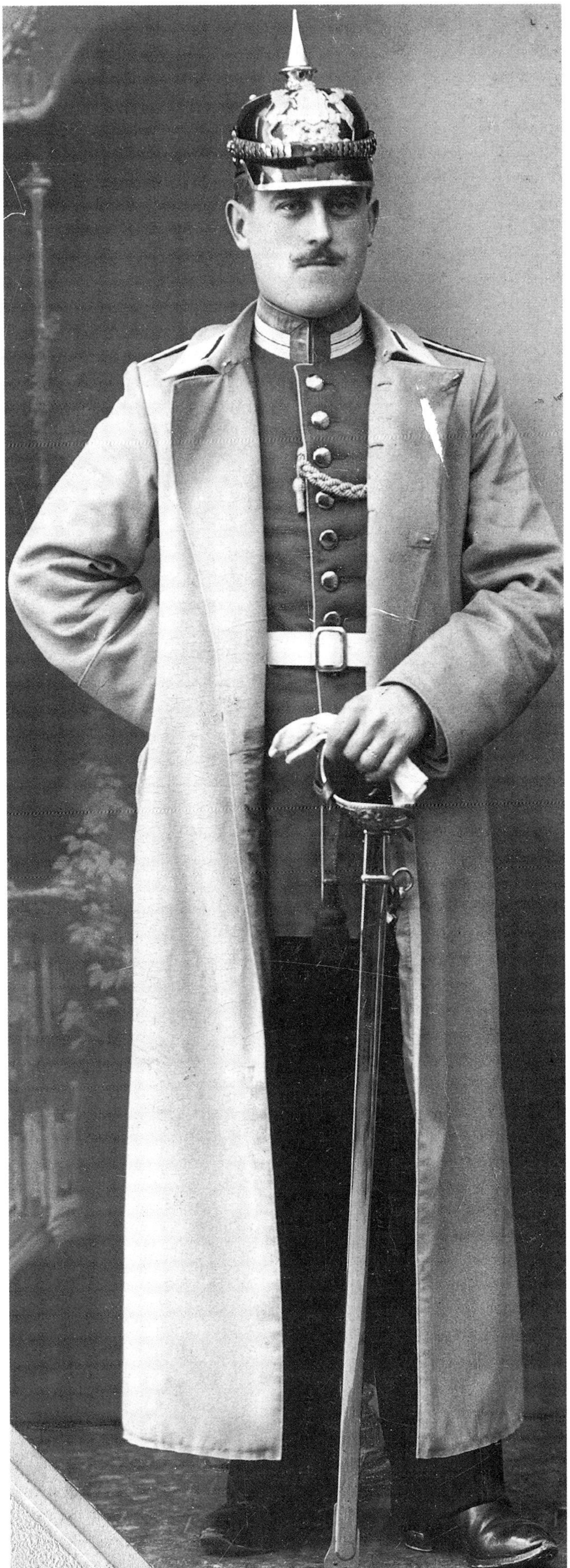

A trooper in the *Dragoon* Regiment Nr.10 wearing the *KD89 Degen* with the pierced folding clamshell without the distinctive German State coat-of-arms. *LTC (Ret.) Thomas M. Johnson Photo Collection.*

This *Dragoon* NCO is wearing a rare early pattern Lion head saber with large "P" Guard. The Lion head and backstrap are cast in high detail. Rather than being affixed to the saddle, the saber is being worn. *LTC (Ret.) Thomas M. Johnson Photo Collection.*

OPPOSITE: Prussian Army *Garde Dragoon* officer in his Field Service uniform with a mounted Lion head Saber. One can see the outline of the *Garde* Eagle under his helmet cover. *LTC (Ret.) Thomas M. Johnson Photo Collection. Copy Photo by Charles H. Jenkins, III.*

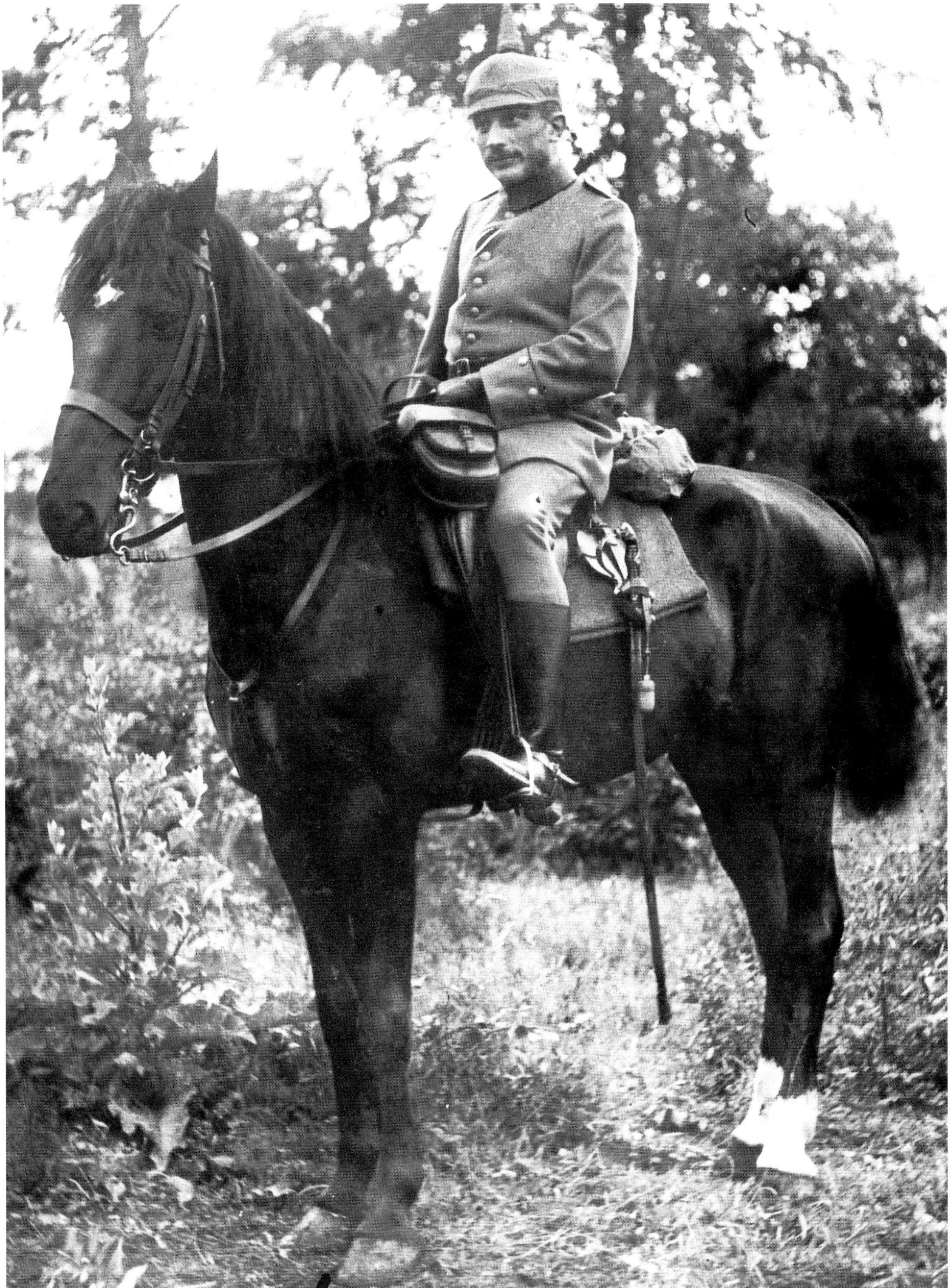

ABOVE: *Dragoon* officers enjoying the fruits of the Rhine. The uniform styles and saber scabbards help date this photograph to the period 1914. The two officers on the right are wearing "P" Guard "Dove head" sabers with officer knots. The scabbards are all post-1910 with black enamel paint and single hanger rings. The saber resting against the table displays a large dent encountered by so many present-day collectors. *SSGT (Ret.) T. Wayne Cunningham (USAF) Photo Collection. Photo Courtesy of SSGT (Ret.) T. Wayne Cunningham (USAF).*

LEFT: Prince Leopold in full dress as Colonel-in-Chief of the *Westphalia Dragoon* Regiment Number 7. The Prince carries his Field Marshal's baton and wears his Order of the Black Eagle. A standard nickel-hilted Bavarian cavalry saber completes his uniform. *Dr. David L. Valuska Collection. Copy Photo by Charles H. Jenkins, III.*

OPPOSITE: This Imperial *4th Dragoon* officer is wearing the brass mounted "P" Guard saber with a nickel, double ring scabbard. The artwork is original to the period. *Johnson Reference Books and Militaria Archives.*

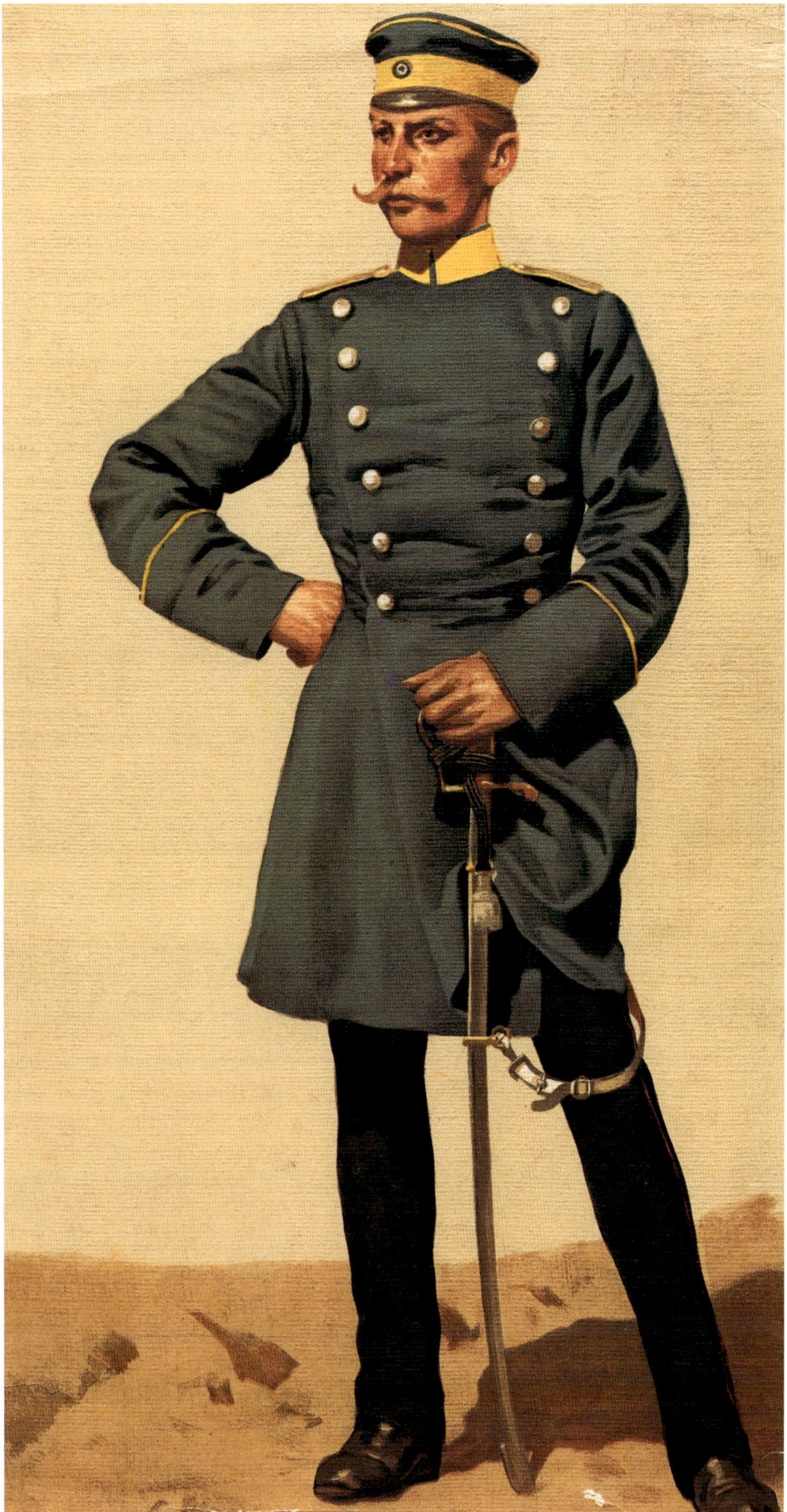

Rittmeister Leibhusaren – Regiment Number 1. This period lithograph from the 1900 book entitled, *"Deutschlands Heer und Flotte"* shows a Captain in the 1st "Death's Head" *Hüssars* (1st Royal Body Guard *Hüssars*) with drawn saber. Cavalry sabers from this Regiment and the *2nd Hüssars* (Queen Victoria of Prussia) many times contained an applied "Death's Head" on the knucklebow. *Victor Diehl Collection. Copy Photo by Victor Diehl.*

The Edged Weapons of the German Cavalry

Hüssar Lion head saber. This outstanding example has an applied "Death's Head" on the knucklebow. The detail of the gilt hilt is superior. The celluloid grip is triple wire wrapped. A Guard star is applied to the langet. The single fullered blade is double etched with antique military symbols; lances, helmets, drums, sabers, and cannon, surrounded by a floral motif. Collectors should note the correct manner for attachment of such devices as Guard Stars, Death Heads, Imperial cyphers, and other attachments as such applied emblems greatly enhance the value of swords of this period. *LTC (Ret.) Thomas M. Johnson Collection. Photo by LTC (Ret.) Thomas M. Johnson.*

A group of distinguished *Hüssars* pose for a formal studio photograph. The three in the front are carrying their Cavalry model 1889 swords with proper sword knots. *LTC (Ret.) Thomas M. Johnson Photo Collection. Photo by Cabinet Photographie.*

OPPOSITE
LEFT: A *KD89* and *IOD89 Degen* worn side-by-side for comparison. The young infantryman on the right is a member of the Infantry Regiment *"Prince Friedrich der Netherlands Nr.15"*. *LTC (Ret.) Thomas M. Johnson Photo Collection. Photo by Atelier Staude, Cassel.*

RIGHT: A *Saxon Hüssar* with his Cavalry *Degen* model 1889. This sword features a non-folding clamshell. The scabbard has been blackened according to regulations. This cavalryman is also wearing an interesting military dispatch case. *LTC (Ret.) Thomas M. Johnson Photo Collection. Photo by Rich. Brandl, Grossenhain.*

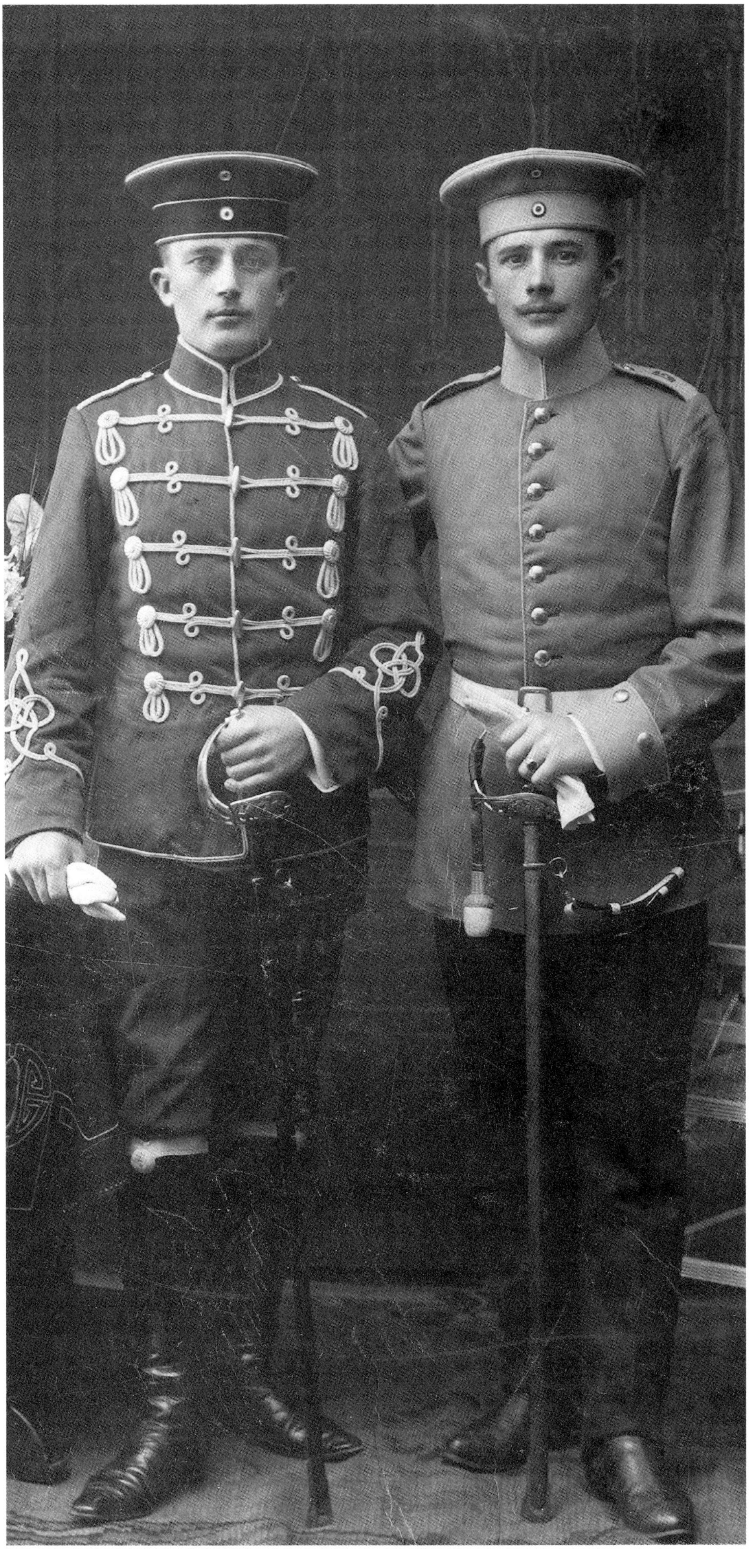

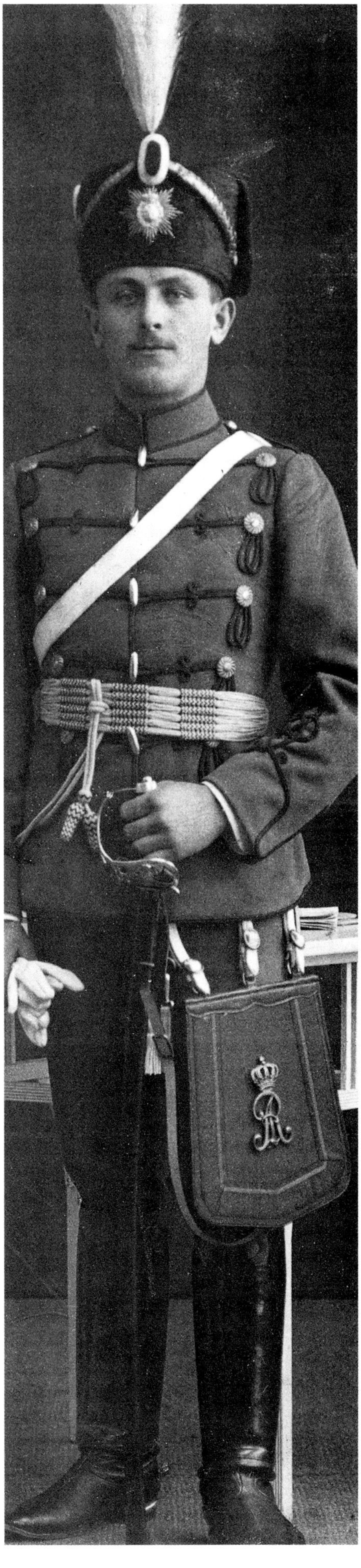

Imperial German Edged Weaponry

A magnificent *Hüssar* Lion head presentation saber with Damascus steel blade. While showing its age, this saber exhibits high quality throughout. The Damascus steel blade obverse bears a golden *Germania* outlined in blue as well as a dedication to a *Hüssar* Lieutenant named *Hardt*. LTC (Ret.) Thomas M. Johnson Collection. Photo by LTC (Ret.) Thomas M. Johnson.

The Edged Weapons of the German Cavalry

TOP: Obverse presentation panel of the *Hüssar* Lion head sword. The saber is presented to "our departing friend, Lieutenant Hardt" from the officer corps of the (*1st Hessischen*) *Hüssar* Regiment. *LTC (Ret.) Thomas M. Johnson Collection. Photo by LTC (Ret.) Thomas M. Johnson.*

ABOVE: The reverse blade of the "Hardt" Imperial saber featuring a gold, charging *Hüssar* and the names of all of the officers in the unit. A truly wonderful sword! *LTC (Ret.) Thomas M. Johnson Collection. Photo by LTC (Ret.) Thomas M. Johnson.*

RIGHT: A *Hüssar* with his trusty companion. He is carrying the Cavalry *Degen* with folding clamshell containing the Prussian eagle. This photograph provides an outstanding study of the complete *Hüssar* NCO uniform and accompanying accouterments. *LTC (Ret.) Thomas M. Johnson Photo Collection. Photo by A. Ophoven, Paderborn.*

Imperial German Edged Weaponry

LEFT: *Prussian Hüssar Leutnant* wearing the pre-1910 Lion head saber with correct sword knot properly attached. *LTC (Ret.) Thomas M. Johnson Photo Collection.*

BELOW: Elegant 1/2 Lion head saber designed for wear by the 1st and 2nd Life *Hüssar* Regiment. This piece was fitted with an "applied" Guard star on the langet, and also the addition of a silver "Death's Head" on the "D" Guard. The plain blade of this example is massive. Grip is sharkskin wrapped, and the scabbard bears a blued finish. *Robert A. Johnston Collection. Photo by Charles H. Jenkins, III.*

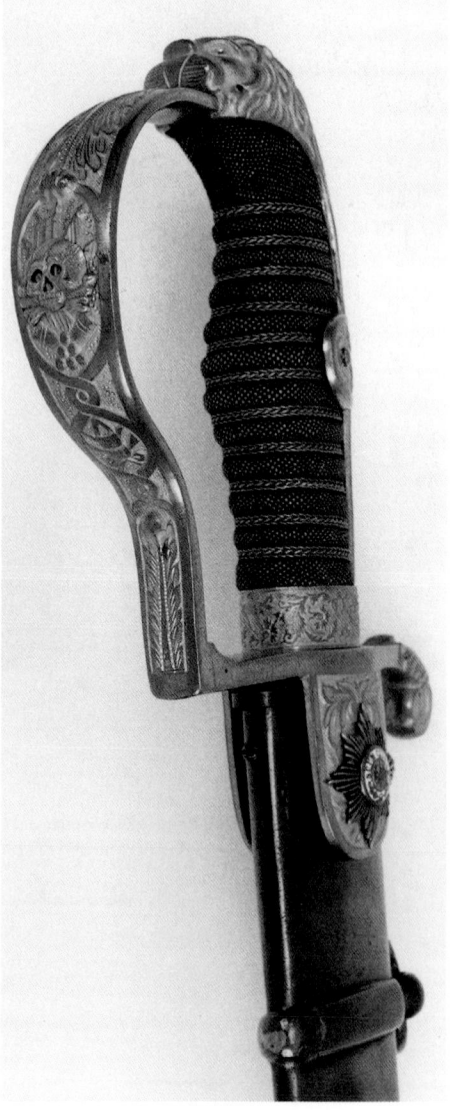

The Edged Weapons of the German Cavalry

Imperial Cavalry troopers of the *17th Braunschweig Hüssar* Regiment. The trooper in the center is carrying the standard Cavalry *Degen* 1889, while the trooper on the right is carrying a rare Lion head basket-hilt *Degen* with Prussian Eagle on the guard. *LTC (Ret.) Thomas M. Johnson Photo Collection. Photo by Max Hoffmann, Braunschweig.*

Imperial German Edged Weaponry

LEFT: Excellent original Imperial studio photograph of a *Saxon Hüssar* carrying the nickel mounted cavalry *"Extrasäbel"*. This sword was offered with both folding and non-folding clamshells. Note the accompanying "shaving brush" sword knot. *LTC (Ret.) Thomas M. Johnson Photo Collection.*

BELOW: *Hüssar* Officer's nickel-hilted Model 89 saber. Hilt is equipped with folding basket highlighting the Prussian eagle. Presentation on blade is blue panels. Its reference is to *Hüssar Regiment - Landgraf Friedrich II* of Hessen-Hamburg. Scabbard is plated nickel, matching the saber hilt. *Thomas T. Wittmann Collection. Photo by Charles H. Jenkins, III.*

OPPOSITE: *Hüssar* trooper posing with a Model 89 Cavalry *Degen* containing a folding basket-guard with Prussian eagle. The seated Infantry enlisted man is wearing an *S98* bayonet. *LTC (Ret.) Thomas M. Johnson Photo Collection. Copy Photo by Charles H. Jenkins, III.*

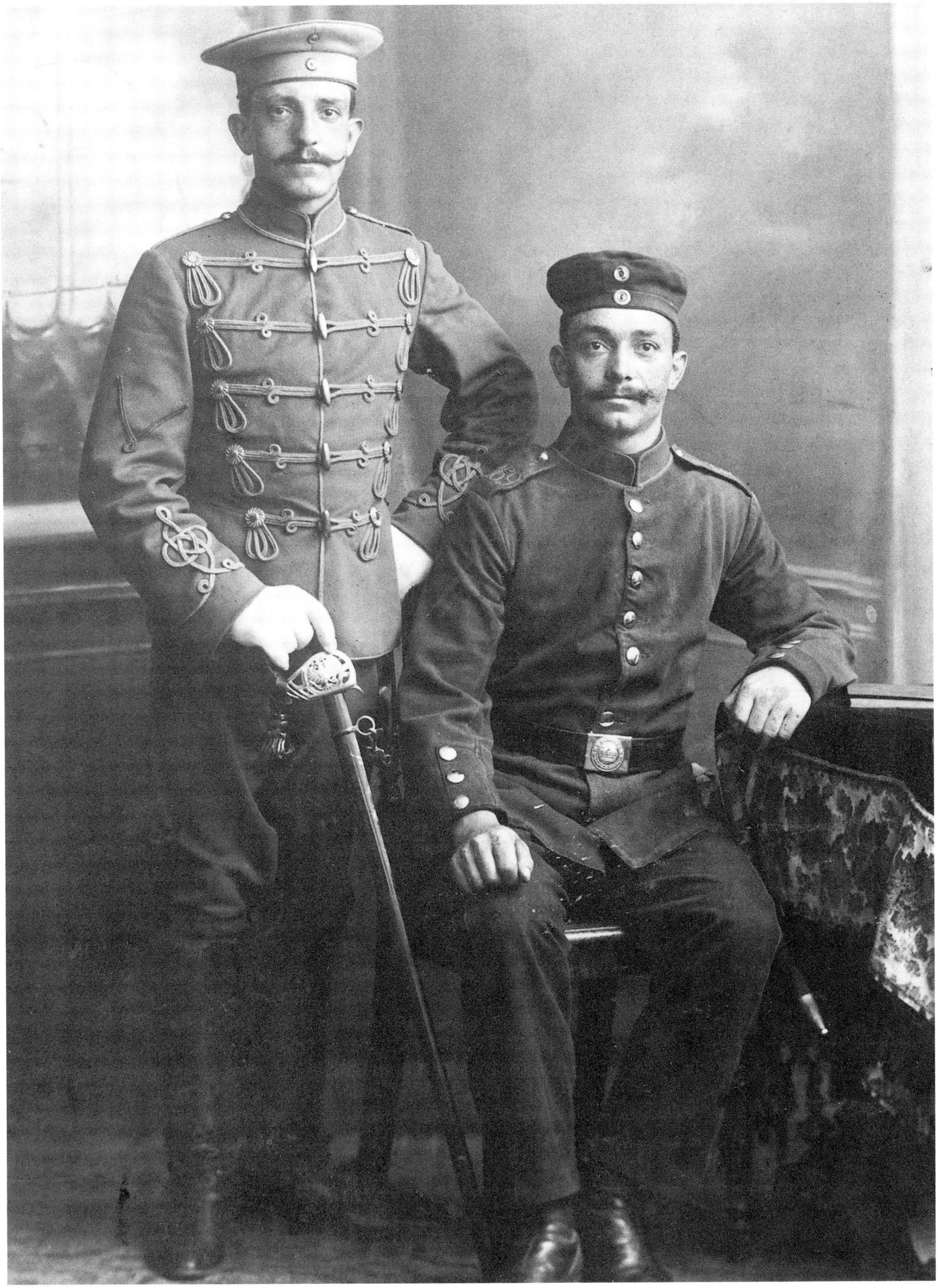

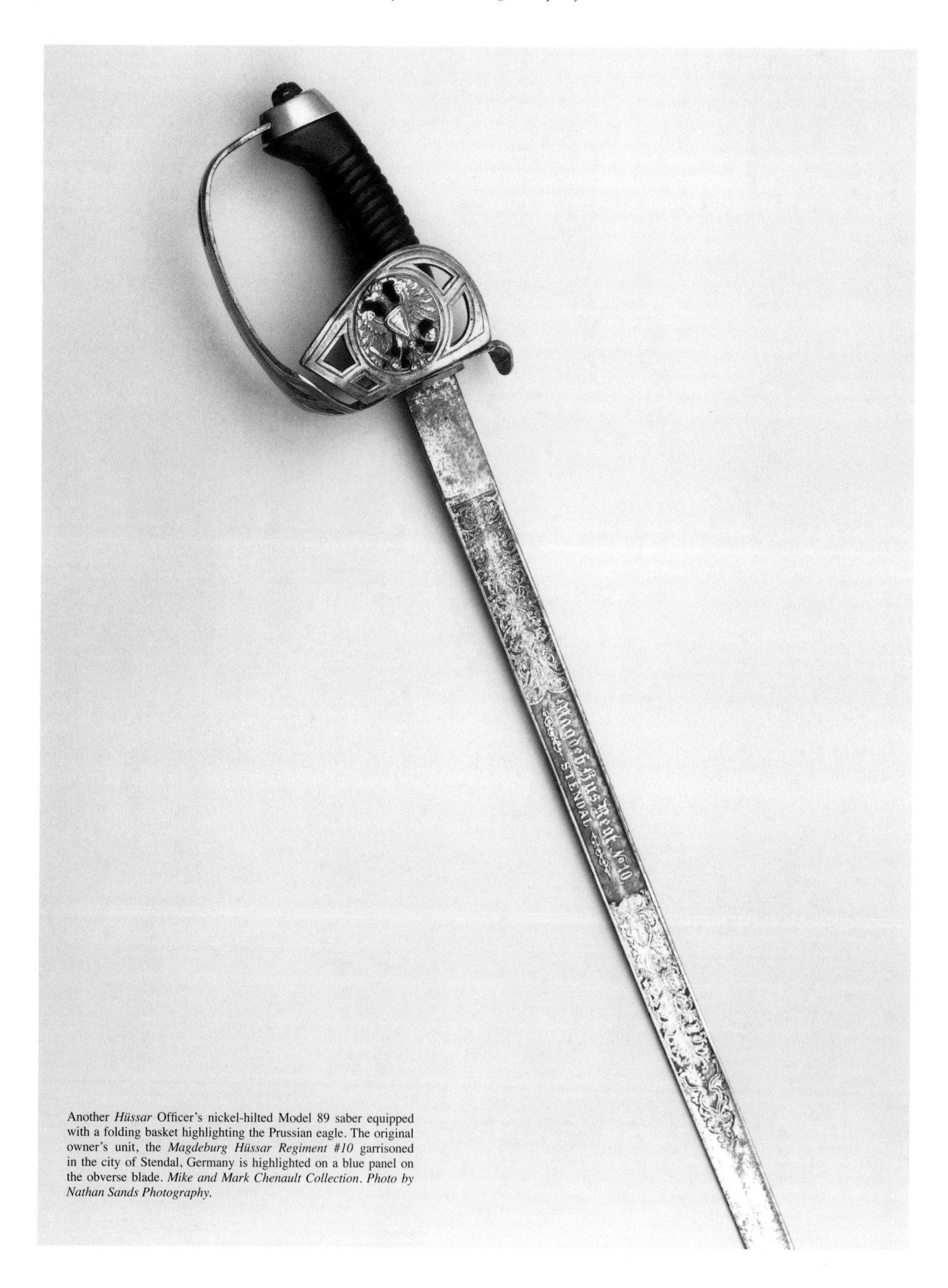

Another *Hüssar* Officer's nickel-hilted Model 89 saber equipped with a folding basket highlighting the Prussian eagle. The original owner's unit, the *Magdeburg Hüssar Regiment #10* garrisoned in the city of Stendal, Germany is highlighted on a blue panel on the obverse blade. *Mike and Mark Chenault Collection. Photo by Nathan Sands Photography.*

The Edged Weapons of the German Cavalry

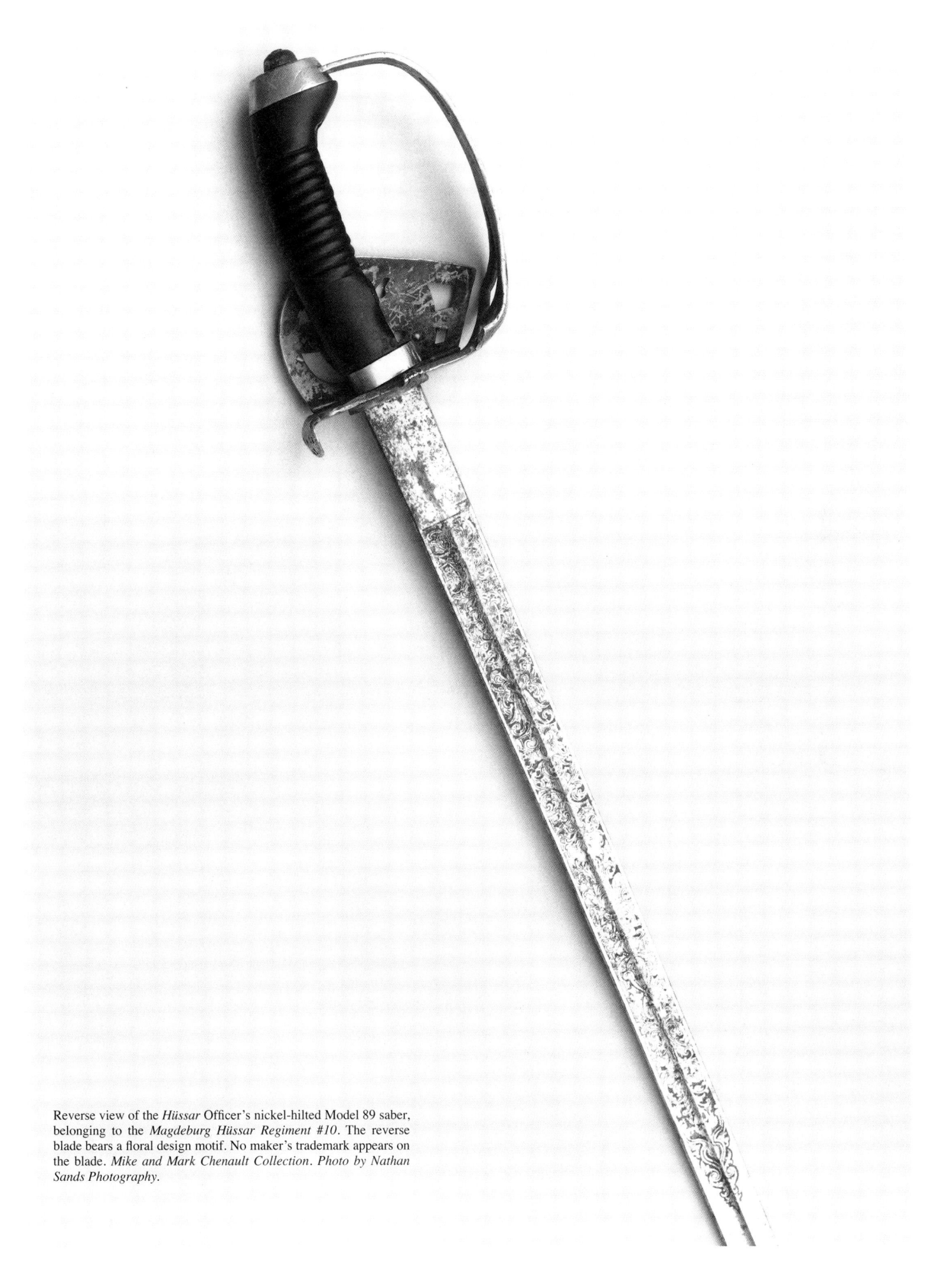

Reverse view of the *Hüssar* Officer's nickel-hilted Model 89 saber, belonging to the *Magdeburg Hüssar Regiment #10*. The reverse blade bears a floral design motif. No maker's trademark appears on the blade. *Mike and Mark Chenault Collection. Photo by Nathan Sands Photography.*

Imperial German Edged Weaponry

Hilt section of a *Cuirassier* "interim" *Degen* attributable to *Brunswick Hüssar Regiment Nr.17*. The Death's Head emblem was part of the headdress when the unit was raised in 1809 by the Duke of Brunswick during the Napoleonic Wars. *Thomas T. Wittmann Collection. Photo by Charles H. Jenkins, III.*

OPPOSITE: Two pensive *Hüssars* with cavalry swords Model 1889. Collectors should note the long hanging straps that buckle to separate straps affixed to the hanging rings. It is interesting to note that the *Hüssar* tunic is called an *"Attila"*, a name which reaches back to a most famous horseman, Attila the Hun (5th Century A.D.). Attila attacked the Roman Empire with such ferocity that he was called the "Scourge of God". *LTC (Ret.) Thomas M. Johnson Photo Collection. Copy Photo by Charles H. Jenkins, III.*

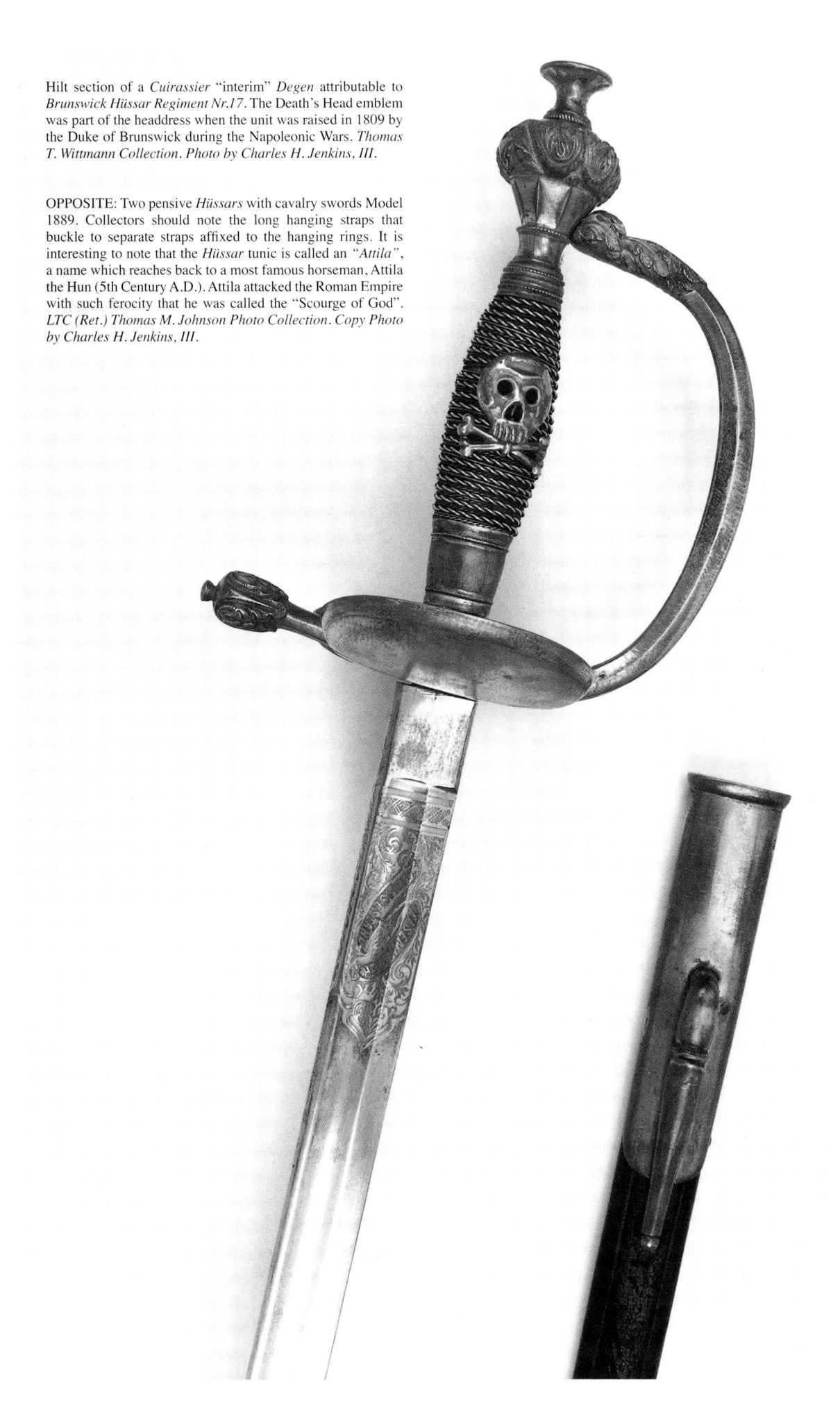

Imperial German Edged Weaponry

Pictured is a pre-war *Hüssar* in the dark green and white trimmed uniform of the 11th Regiment as signified by the dark-green *Attila* with white loops and *Pelzmutze* with red cap bag. He is wearing a dispatch bag as well as a cartridge pouch. This *Hüssar* is carrying the Model 52 saber with large basket hilt. The artwork is original to the period. *Johnson Reference Books & Militaria Archives.*

A *Hüssar* member of the Life Guard Regiment is pictured. The red *Attila* with yellow cord trim was distinctive for this unit. He is also wearing his *Pelzmutze* or "Busby" headgear. Black breeches and riding boots trimmed in gold complete the uniform. The *Hüssar* is also wearing a cartridge belt and box as well as a *Säbel Tasche* leather dispatch case. The saber being worn is the metal-mounted basket hilt Cavalry Officer saber Model 52 with knot. This saber is the private purchase model with the wide 28 mm blade. The artwork is original to the period. *Johnson Reference Books & Militaria Archives.*

A mounted *Hüssar* NCO with Cavalry *Degen* model 1889. The sword is nickel mounted with a folding clamshell featuring the Prussian Eagle. The dispatch rider is carrying the *"Säbel Tasche"*. This leather case hanging from the sword belt features the cypher of Wilhelm II and was used to carry maps and papers. *LTC (Ret.) Thomas M. Johnson Photo Collection.*

Studio portrait of "Other Ranks" *Hüssar* troops clearly shows the *M89* saber with Prussian eagle on the basket hilt. Note the beer mug in each troop's hand! *Robert A. Johnston Photo Collection. Copy Photo by Charles H. Jenkins, III.*

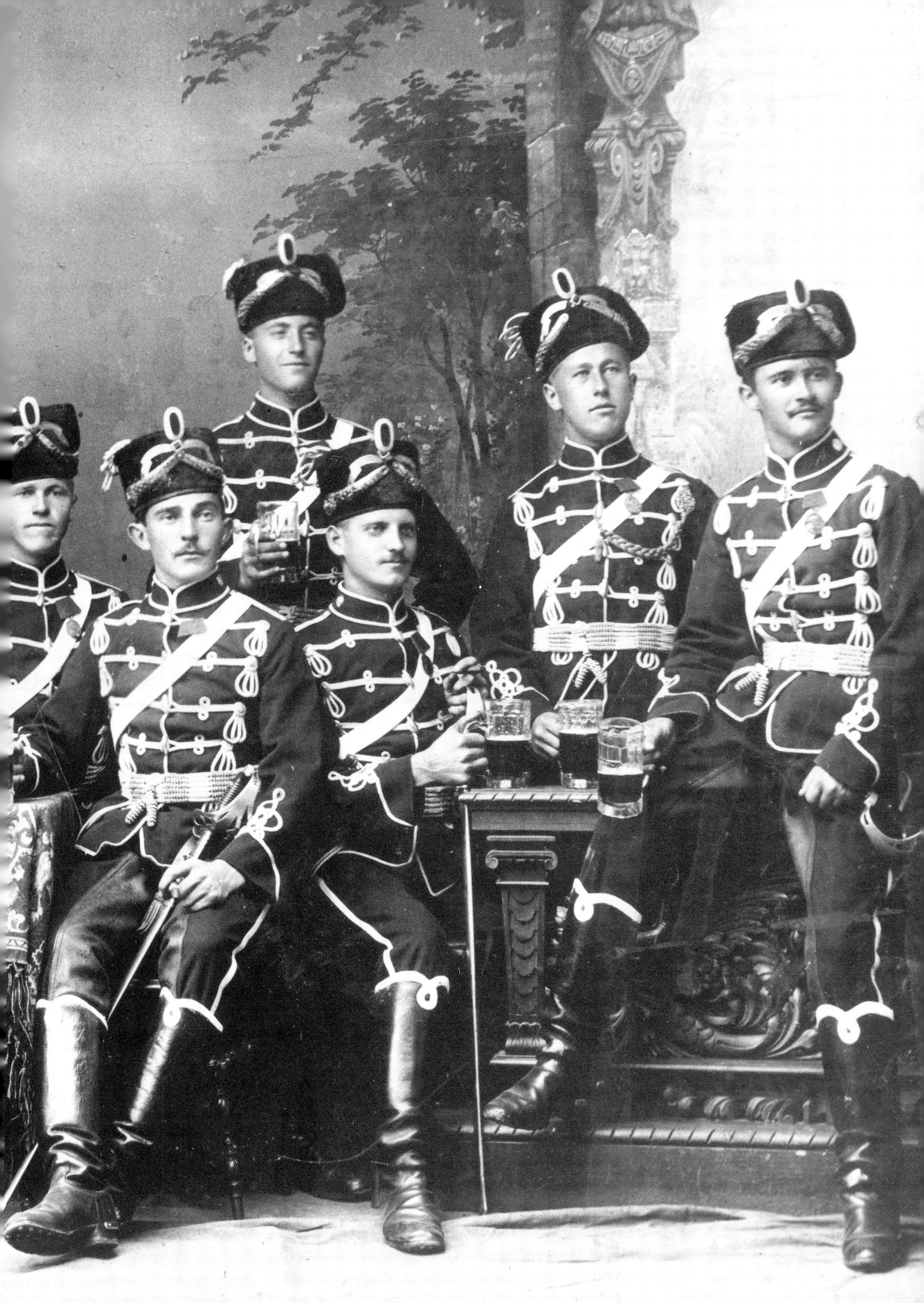

ABOVE: Officers and Non-Commissioned Officers of the famous *17th Brunswick Hüssars*, with their basket hilt officer sabers. The helmet plate consists of a silvered skull and crossbones over which a gilt metal *Bandeau* bears the legend *Peninsula – Sicilien – Waterloo – Mars La Tour*, celebrating their famous history. *LTC (Ret.) Thomas M. Johnson Photo Collection.*

LEFT: *Herzog* Ernst August of *Braunschweig* in the uniform of the *17th Hüssar* Regiment. He is carrying the gilt *Hüssar* officer saber with wide 25 mm blade and scabbard. The large basket-hilt contains the Imperial Coat-of-Arms. *LTC (Ret.) Thomas M. Johnson Photo Collection. Photo by Hoffotograf E. Bieber, Hamburg.*

OPPOSITE: A *Hüssar Obergefreiter* member of the *Hüssar Regiment Kaiser Nikolaus II v. Russland Nr.8*. He is carrying a standard *IOD89* with non-folding clamshell complete with knot attached to his saddle. *LTC (Ret.) Thomas M. Johnson Photo Collection. Photo by A. Ophoven, Paderborn.*

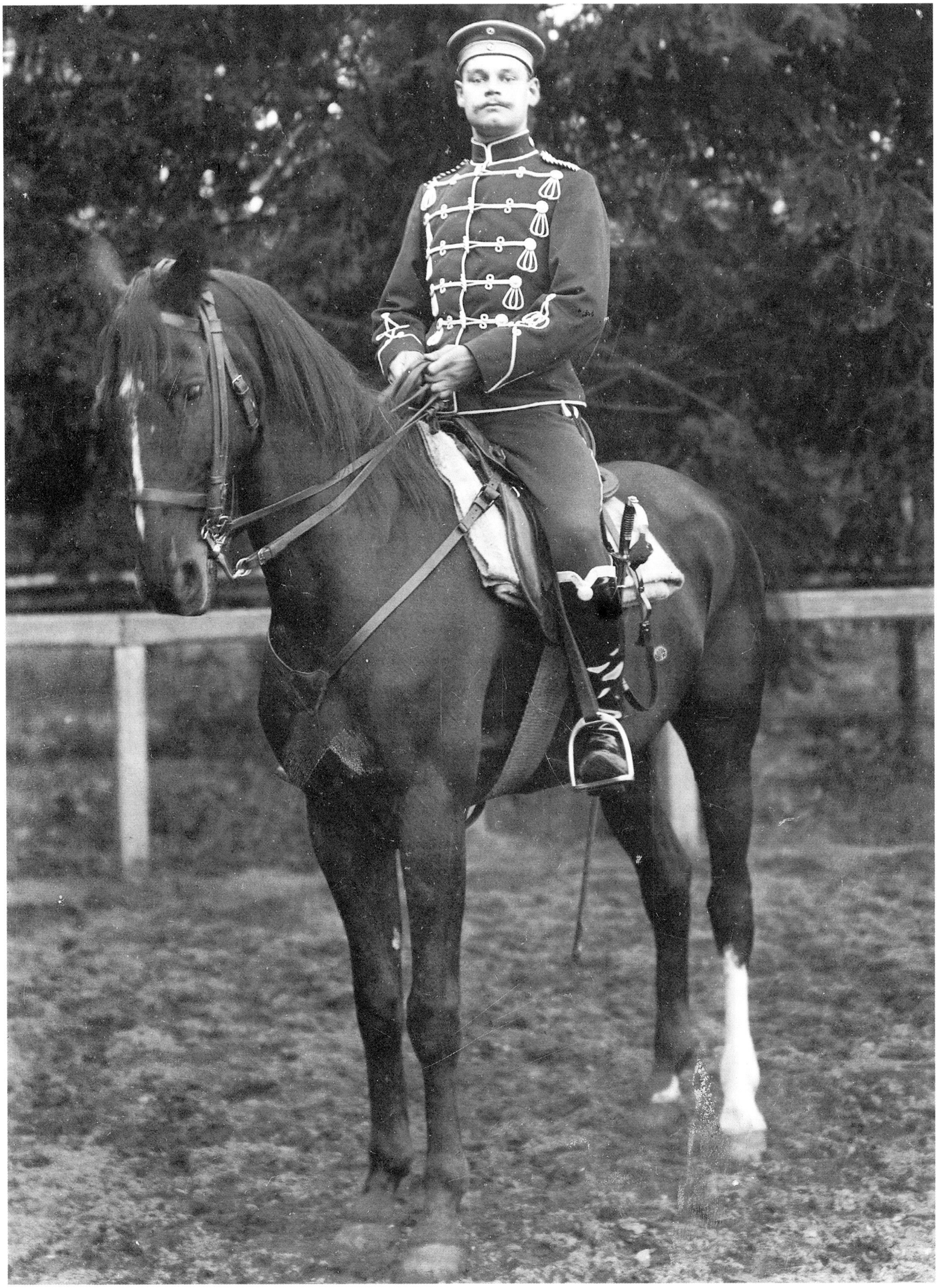

Unser Kronprinz in der Uniform des 1.engl. Husaren Regts.

OPPOSITE: The *Kronprinz* (Crown Prince) wearing a basket-hilt cavalry saber and dressed in the uniform of the I English *Hüssars*. *LTC (Ret.) Thomas M. Johnson Photo Collection.*

An 1888 photograph of Crown Prince Friedrich Wilhelm wearing the *Hüssar* uniform. The sabers worn by the children of the Royal Houses of Germany are exquisitely made and extremely rare. *LTC (Ret.) Thomas M. Johnson Photo Collection.*

The Crown Prince wears the uniform of the 1st Life *Hüssar* Regiment, No.1. His Lion head saber is complete with the applied Guard Star on the langet. Also of interest is the hanging strap, complete with Naval Lion head style buckle. *Robert A. Johnston Photo Collection. Copy Photo by Charles H. Jenkins, III.*

Pictured in color is a near mint condition *Uhlan* Presentation Lion head sword by the Alcoso firm. The Lion head pommel is complete with red glass eyes and the grip is wire wrapped celluloid over wood. *Uhlan* lances decorate the obverse langet. The scabbard is the nickel, single-ring type. *Major General (Ret.) Theodore W. Paulson Collection. Photo by Major General (Ret.) Theodore W. Paulson.*

BELOW: The obverse blade on the Alcoso *Uhlan* Presentation Lion head sword features an etched presentation panel from the original owner's *Kameraden* (Comrades) surrounded by an unusual etched pattern of flowers and vines. The reverse blade etched pattern is a continuation of the flowers and vines motif. *Major General (Ret.) Theodore W. Paulson Collection. Photo by Major General (Ret.) Theodore W. Paulson.*

Uhlan Lion head saber with crossed sabers and lances on the obverse langet. The presentation reads "Rotzler (last name) to his friend, Stein, Metz 1899". *LTC (Ret.) Thomas M. Johnson Collection. Photo by LTC (Ret.) Thomas M. Johnson.*

Pictured in color is a mint condition *Uhlan* Presentation Lion head saber by Carl Eickhorn (early C.E. trademark). The Lion head pommel is complete with the red glass eyes, and the grip is wire wrapped black celluloid over wood. *Uhlan* crossed sabers and lances decorate the attractive obverse langet. The scabbard is the black metal, single-ring variety. *Major General (Ret.) Theodore W. Paulson Collection. Photo by Major General (Ret.) Theodore W. Paulson.*

BELOW: The obverse blade on the Carl Eickhorn *Uhlan* Presentation Lion head saber features a deep blue presentation panel encouraging victory in battle from a father to his son. The reverse blade is decorated with a typical Imperial military motif. *Major General (Ret.) Theodore W. Paulson Collection. Photo by Major General (Ret.) Theodore W. Paulson.*

A 1/2 Lion head style compared to full Lion head motif. Both of these sabers are attributable to the "*Uhlans*", as exemplified by the crossed lances shown on their respective langets. Both examples have Damascus blades, the left being "band" (ribbon) Damascus, and the right being "maiden hair". Both examples have gold inlay with blue color treatment. *Thomas T. Wittmann Collection. Photo by Charles H. Jenkins, III.*

Imperial German Edged Weaponry

Reserve *Leutnant* in the *5th Uhlan Regiment*. The highly chiseled Lion head saber hilt with sword knot is clearly visible. A pointed Polish cuff with single button is distinctive to the *Uhlan* tunic. This officer is not wearing the traditional *Uhlan Ulanka* (Lancer's jacket). *LTC (Ret.) Thomas M. Johnson Photo Collection.*

Studio portrait of an *Uhlan* Officer of the 5th Regiment with Lion head saber. The name *"Uhlan"* is an ancient Tartar word meaning "of the hoof". The characteristic *Uhlan* "mortarboard" helmet originated with early Polish lancer units. *LTC (Ret.) Thomas M. Johnson Photo Collection. Photo by Charles H. Jenkins, III.*

OPPOSITE: *Uhlan* Officer in full dress uniform complete with a high quality Lion head saber. The saber has a beautiful early nickeled scabbard with two hanger rings. This photograph is dated on the reverse "1878". *LTC (Ret.) Thomas M. Johnson Photo Collection. Photo by G. Dickhaut, Düsseldorf.*

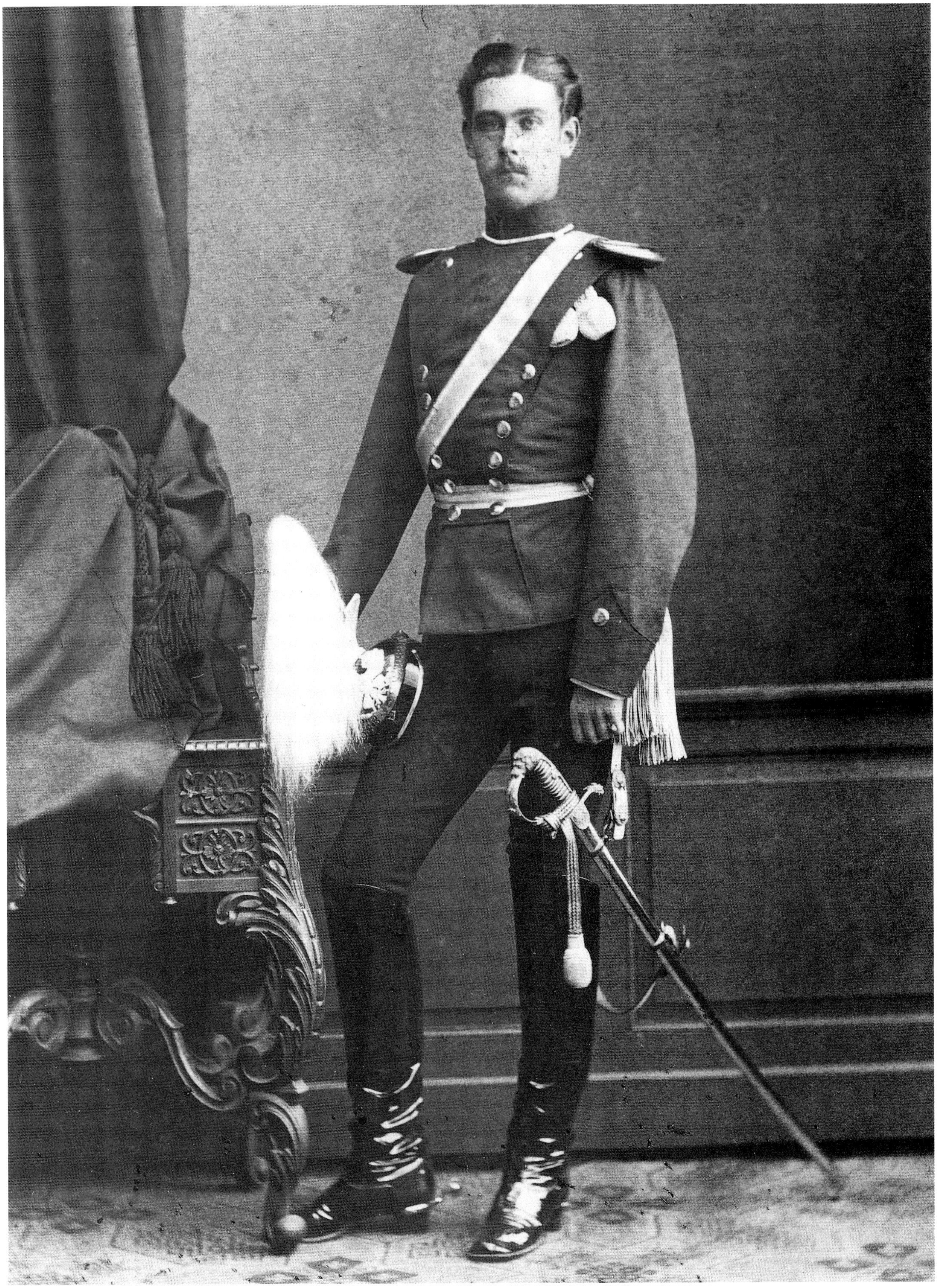

Pictured in color is the obverse hilt of a *"Grosser" Uhlan* Lion head presentation sword by WK&C in near mint condition. Note the raised *Uhlan* symbol is silver on the large obverse langet. The blade is beautifully double etched. The scabbard is nickel with two brass bands and rings. *Major General (Ret.) Theodore W. Paulson Collection. Photo by Major General (Ret.) Theodore W. Paulson.*

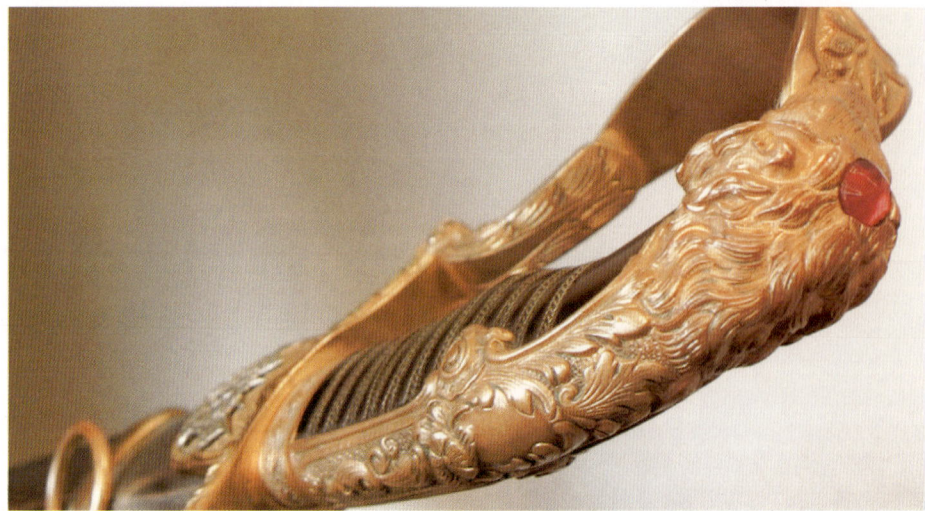

RIGHT: A red simulated ruby stone was skillfully utilized by the swordsmith to hide the top of the sword blade tang on the *"Grosser" Uhlan* Lion head Presentation sword by WK&C. Note the beautiful detailed chasing to the backstrap. *Major General (Ret.) Theodore W. Paulson Collection. Photo by Major General (Ret.) Theodore W. Paulson.*

ABOVE: The outer side of the knucklebow on the WK&C *"Grosser" Uhlan* Lion head Presentation sword features a raised profile of the *Kaiser*. Again, the red simulated ruby stone is visible on top of the Lion head pommel, and it matches the two artificial ruby (glass eyes). *Major General (Ret.) Theodore W. Paulson Collection. Photo by Major General (Ret.) Theodore W. Paulson.*

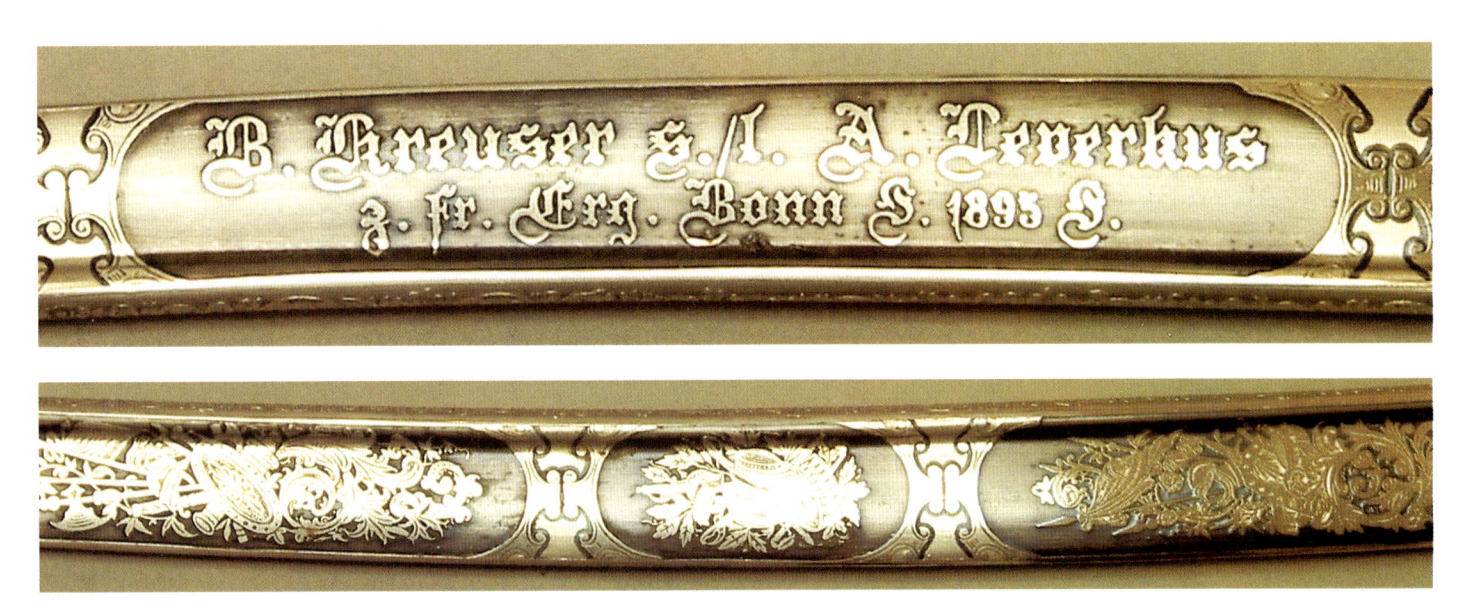

TOP: Pictured above is the presentation center panel on the obverse blade of the WK&C *"Grosser"* Presentation *Uhlan* Lion head sword. Note that the presentation is dated "1895". ABOVE: Pictured in color is the reverse blade on the *"Grosser" Uhlan* Lion head Presentation sword by WK&C. The opposite side of the blade bears not only a two-line dedication, but also the year of the presentation, "1895". *Major General (Ret.) Theodore W. Paulson Collection. Photo by Major General (Ret.) Theodore W. Paulson.*

Saxony Uhlan "Grosser" Imperial saber by the M. Neumann, Berlin firm (Purveyor to Royalty). This ornate Imperial saber features a huge Lion head hilt complete with ruby eyes. The mane of the Lion head completely camouflages the pommel nut. The grip is black sharkskin with silver triple-wire wrap. The large obverse langet features fine silver crossed flags which are peened on the obverse langet. *Max McGrath Collection, Australia. Photo by LTC (Ret.) Thomas M. Johnson.*

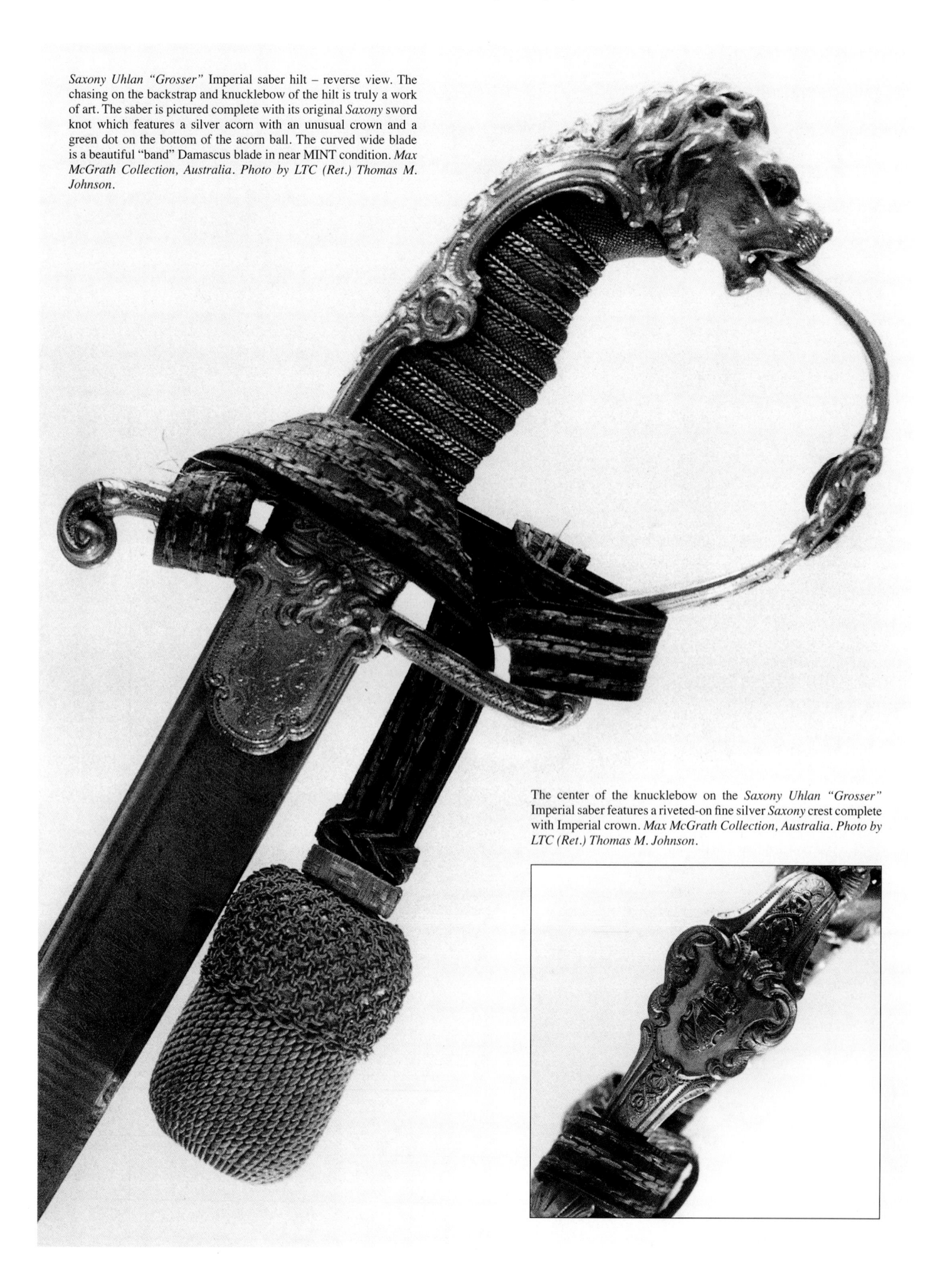

Saxony Uhlan "Grosser" Imperial saber hilt – reverse view. The chasing on the backstrap and knucklebow of the hilt is truly a work of art. The saber is pictured complete with its original *Saxony* sword knot which features a silver acorn with an unusual crown and a green dot on the bottom of the acorn ball. The curved wide blade is a beautiful "band" Damascus blade in near MINT condition. *Max McGrath Collection, Australia. Photo by LTC (Ret.) Thomas M. Johnson.*

The center of the knucklebow on the *Saxony Uhlan "Grosser"* Imperial saber features a riveted-on fine silver *Saxony* crest complete with Imperial crown. *Max McGrath Collection, Australia. Photo by LTC (Ret.) Thomas M. Johnson.*

Uhlan Officer's Lion head sword. Magnificent example featuring heavy gold-plated brass hilt. Fine chiseling gives depth to recesses, giving the sword almost a work-of-art look! Langet has an applied set of lances in silver. Grip is blue sharkskin with silver wire wrap. Blade is "maiden hair" Damascus with gold inlay presentation, having blue panel areas for highlight. Saber presentation is, "A father's gift to his loving son". Presents of this nature were popular with the aristocracy of late 19th and turn-of-the-century officers. *Robert A. Johnston Collection. Photo by Charles H. Jenkins, III.*

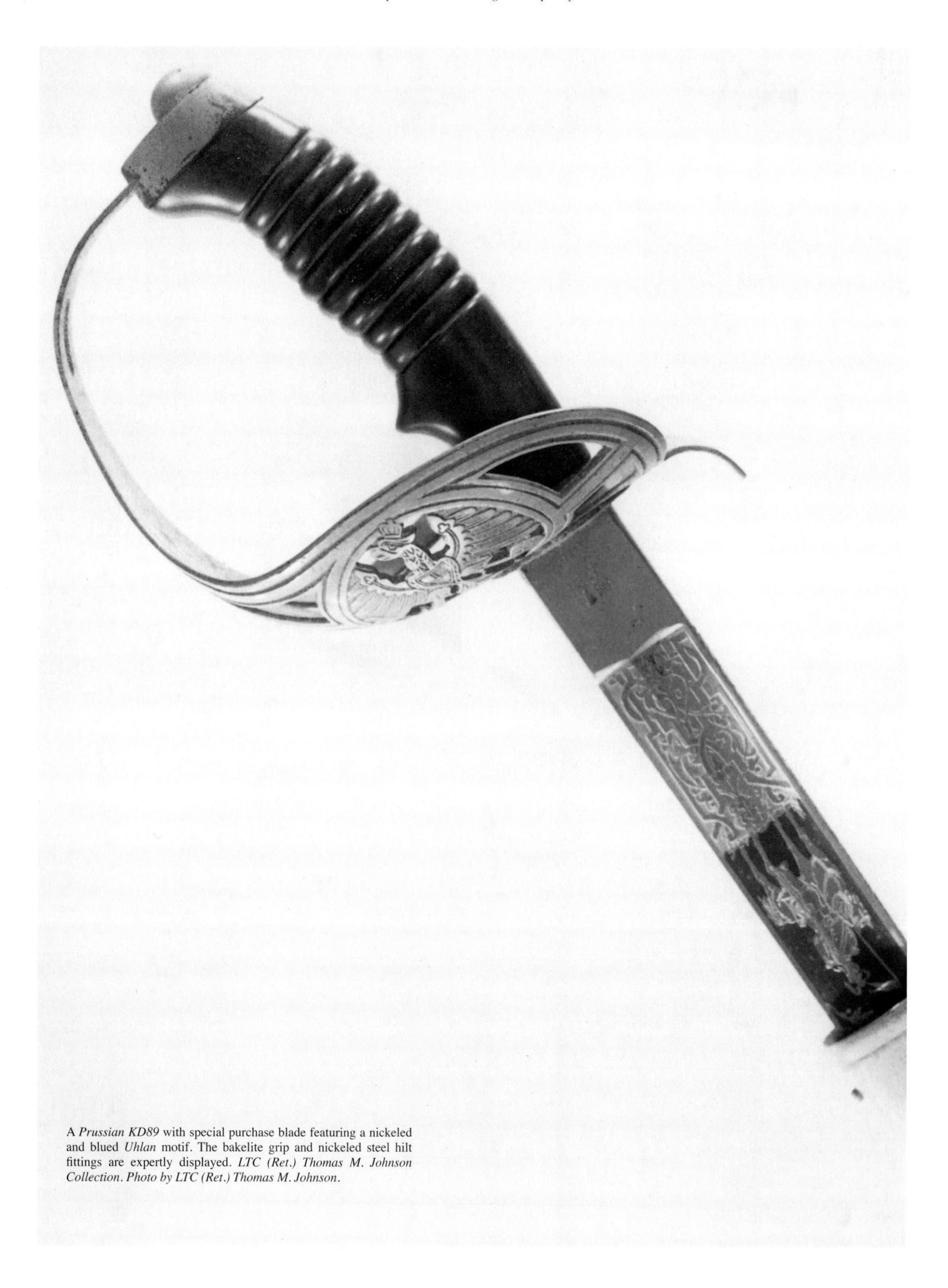

A *Prussian KD89* with special purchase blade featuring a nickeled and blued *Uhlan* motif. The bakelite grip and nickeled steel hilt fittings are expertly displayed. *LTC (Ret.) Thomas M. Johnson Collection. Photo by LTC (Ret.) Thomas M. Johnson.*

The Edged Weapons of the German Cavalry

TOP: The blade presentation of the *KD89* features a mounted *Uhlan*, his unit of service, and his steed. A large number of *Uhlan* swords contain special purchase blades of this type. ABOVE: The reverse of the *2nd Garde Uhlan* blade featuring the *Garde* Star, charging *Uhlans* on horseback, and the troopers' weapons – the lance, carbine and saber. *LTC (Ret.) Thomas M. Johnson Collection. Photo by LTC (Ret.) Thomas M. Johnson.*

RIGHT: *Uhlan* in dress uniform complete with Cavalry *Degen M89*. The NCO proudly displays his dueling scar from his university days. The edged weapon used to inflict the scar was the *"Schlager"* which was a light *Pallasch* with a 40 inch blade that was sharpened only on the sides of the rounded point. The weapon had a large basket hilt which was padded and decorated with the school colors. During the duel or *"Mensur"* the participants wore protective goggles with a steel nose guard as well as a protective neck protector. After the check cut was made, it was rejoined slightly askew in order to enhance the mark. *LTC (Ret.) Thomas M. Johnson Photo Collection. Photo by W. Höffert, Hannover.*

BELOW: An *Uhlan* cavalry trooper wearing the *KD89* sword with proper *Faustriemen*. The nickel mounted sword contains the Prussian eagle on the clamshell. *LTC (Ret.) Thomas M. Johnson Photo Collection. Photo by Josef Henne, Düsseldorf.*

Imperial German Edged Weaponry

This *Uhlan* trooper is wearing the nickel Cavalry *Degen* model 1889, with correct sword knot. The *Uhlan* leather suspension straps are also visible in the photograph. *LTC (Ret.) Thomas M. Johnson Photo Collection. Photo by Jean Feilner, Oldenburg.*

Regimental adjutant of the 1st Bavarian *Uhlan* Regiment. The officer is in parade dress, complete with Model 52 saber bearing the Bavarian coat-of-arms. *Artwork by Brian Molloy, United Kingdom.*

The Edged Weapons of the German Cavalry

An *Uhlan* trooper wearing the traditional Lancer's jacket, the *Ulanka*. In this pre-war photograph, the Lancer is wearing the cavalry *Degen* model 1889. It should also be observed that full dress epaulettes are being worn for this special photograph which will be sent to his family or lover. *LTC (Ret.) Thomas M. Johnson Photo Collection. Photo by Jul. Havemann, Hanau.*

Uhlan NCO with early pattern Dove head cavalry saber. The uniform cuffs, which rise to a single point, are referred to as "Polish" cut and reflect the heritage of the *Uhlans*. *LTC (Ret.) Thomas M. Johnson Photo Collection. Photo by Alfred Hirrlinger, Stuttgart.*

Jager zu Pferde trooper with a Cavalry *Degen M89* complete with sword knot. *Jager zu Pferde* units were the most recent branch of the Imperial German Army being formed between 1905 and 1913. *LTC (Ret.) Thomas M. Johnson Photo Collection.*

Jager zu Pferde NCO with KD 1889 bearing the *Prussian* eagle on the non-folding clamshell. The dents in the scabbard attest to much "rough-riding" by this mounted dispatch rider. Contemporary collectors and dealers are often blamed for dented sword scabbards, but many period photographs prove to the contrary. The *Jager zu Pferde* wore a steel helmet much like the *Kürassier*, but without the lobster tail rear visor. *LTC (Ret.) Thomas M. Johnson Photo Collection.*

A reluctant *Uhlan* poses with his younger sister. You can be sure the father is in the background giving stern Prussian orders. This young German cavalryman has the complete child's uniform, including *Kinder Säbel* and riding boots. The child's saber is a *KD89* of inferior quality. *LTC (Ret.) Thomas M. Johnson Photo Collection.*